LONESOME DAVE

LONESOME DAVE

THE STORY OF NEW MEXICO GOVERNOR
David Francis Cargo

David Francis Cargo

edited by
Dennis Domrzalski

SANTA FE

© 2010 by David Francis Cargo. All Rights Reserved.

No part of this book may be reproduced in any form or by any electronic or mechanical means including information storage and retrieval systems without permission in writing from the publisher, except by a reviewer who may quote brief passages in a review.

Sunstone books may be purchased for educational, business, or sales promotional use. For information please write: Special Markets Department, Sunstone Press, P.O. Box 2321, Santa Fe, New Mexico 87504-2321.

Book and Cover design • Vicki Ahl
Body typeface • Palatino Linotype and Piegnot Lt Std
Printed on acid free paper

Library of Congress Cataloging-in-Publication Data

Cargo, David Francis, 1929-
  Lonesome Dave : the story of New Mexico governor David Francis Cargo / by David Francis Cargo ; edited by Dennis Domrzalski.
    p. cm.
  Includes index.
  ISBN 978-0-86534-762-5 (softcover : alk. paper)
  ISBN 978-0-86534-753-3 (hardcover : alk. paper)
 1. Cargo, David Francis, 1929- 2. Governors--New Mexico--Biography. 3. New Mexico--Politics and government--1951- I. Domrzalski, Dennis. II. Title.
  F801.4.C37A3 2010
  978.9'053092--dc22
  [B]
                    2009053231

WWW.SUNSTONEPRESS.COM
SUNSTONE PRESS / POST OFFICE BOX 2321 / SANTA FE, NM 87504-2321 /USA
(505) 988-4418 / ORDERS ONLY (800) 243-5644 / FAX (505) 988-1025

Dedication

I dedicate this book to the members of my family:

First of all, to my daughter Elena Read, who transcribed what amounted to almost three hundred fifty pages of audio recordings. She has been a loving daughter over the years. A dental technician, Elena lives in upstate New York.

To my son Patrick, an attorney, engineer and certified public accountant (CPA) with master's degrees in both business and accountancy. Patrick attended the University of Michigan, University of Texas, and Oregon State University. He is vice president of Mary Kay Cosmetics.

Likewise to my youngest child, Eamon. He is a CPA and has also been a stockbroker and financial manager. Eamon has a master's degree in business from the University of New Mexico, as well as a master's in accounting; he holds a master's degree in finance from Notre Dame, including studies at Cambridge University and the Imperial College in London, England. He has been a great companion to me throughout the years.

To Veronica, my eldest child and a great help to me over the years.

To my son David, who is employed by a stockbroker in Arizona.

In recognition of my brother Gerald who has advised me through the years. He is a retired professor of advanced mathematics at Syracuse University, in the state of New York.

CONTENTS

A Tribute / Max Evans / 9
Introduction / 11
Prologue / 17
Growing Up / 25
The 1952 Republican Convention, Part of the Early Years / 39
Young Republicans at the University of Michigan / 45
The War Years / 47
Early New Mexico Years / 50
Election to the State Legislature in 1962 / 53
Old Age Lien and Relative Responsibility Laws / 62
A Funny Story / 63
Senator Dennis Chavez Died / 64
Reapportionment / 66
Districts for Congress / 82
1964 Election for the Legislature / 84
A Special Relationship with Labor / 91
State Senator James Patton and Capitol Furnishing Shenanigans / 102
Canones / 103
The Picnic / 109
Start of the 1966 Campaign for Governor / 110
1966 Election Continued / 112
Robert O. Anderson / 113
The 1966 Election / 115
Mack Easley / 118
Lonesome Dave / 119
Lusk Debates / 122
Election Night in 1966 / 125
Gene Lusk Wins / 127
Copper Strike and Standing up to LBJ / 128
Some Extraordinary Appointments / 131
Villanueva / 133
Hollywood on the Rio Grande / 134
Executive Orders / 148
Government Reorganization / 152

Old Time Politics / 155
Democratic County Powerhouses / 179
Party Registration and Election Results / 180
Constitutional Convention / 188
Father Roca / 190
Reies Lopez Tijerina and the Courthouse Raid / 191
Victims of the Courthouse Raid / 204
Resnick Hearings on the Effect of Federal Programs in Rural America / 206
Black Churches in New Mexico / 221
Community Meetings / 222
Governors in Support, 1968 / 223
Fabian Chavez / 224
Fabian Chavez Apology / 227
Treatment of State Employees / 228
Campaign Tactic / 230
Continuation of the Race in 1968 / 232
Labor Support / 240
Some People I got to Know / 247
Native Americans / 248
Blue Lake / 251
Potash / 264
Trouble at the University of New Mexico / 277
In the Aftermath of the University Riots / 292
State Parks / 295
Eagle Nest Lake / 298
White Cane Law / 300
The Cumbres Toltec Scenic Railroad / 303
Entertaining at the Mansion / 308
Hispanics and the Governorship of New Mexico / 309
Status of Women / 313
Prisons / 314
My Going Away Party / 315
Andy Carter / 316
Ultraconservative Wing of the Republican Party / 326
Contemporary History / 328
Chronology / 332
Index / 333

A Tribute

There is no precise way to explain the energetic life of Governor David Cargo—attorney to the downtrodden, as well as the rich and famous; a changer of legislative reapportionment, and at the same time inventing the first Governor's State Film Commission in the United States.

He was a dedicated promoter of many films shooting and spending fortunes in our state. Then the true miracle happened: a Republican became beloved by the liberal Democrats of Hollywood. It had never happened before and mostly likely never will again. He became personal friends with those behind the camera as well as the stars facing it, and consequently had acting parts in 12 of those films.

And now, while writing his priceless historical memoir, he has raised hundreds of thousands of dollars to build, and/or maintain 12 libraries in such isolated New Mexico villages and towns as Mora, Anton Chico, Villanueva and Corona. This is an unsurpassed heritage to leave for the mental and spiritual growth of the youth of New Mexico.

Viva, Lonesome Dave!
Max Evans

Max Evans is the author of *The Rounders*, *The Hi-Lo Country*, *Madam Millie*, *Bluefeather Fellini* and other novels.

Introduction

No one paid much attention to the political storm that blew into New Mexico in May of 1957 in the form of David Francis Cargo.

At the time, New Mexico was a small state that no one in the rest of the country cared much about. The local and state politicians were comfortable in knowing that the state's irrelevance meant that they could continue in their old, abusive and corrupt ways.

Corrupt they were. Governors sold liquor licenses for campaign contributions, state legislators gave themselves state contracts, county sheriffs campaigned for themselves in their squad cars; lobbyists bought lawmakers cars, trucks, liquor and everything else; political candidates bought votes with whiskey, chickens, money, threats and promises. When those incentives didn't suffice, ballot boxes were stuffed.

White conservative Southern Democrats controlled the statehouse and kept Hispanics, Blacks, Indians, women and anyone else they held in contempt and viewed as inferior down and out of government. Public schools were segregated. Government employment was based on the spoils and winner-take-all patronage system. There was no Civil Service or merit system, so every time a different faction of the Democratic Party won the governorship or a majority on school boards or county commissions or city councils, thousands upon thousands people were fired and cronies of the winners hired.

Organized labor was kept down. Legislators and local elected officials were in the pockets of corporations and mining companies. Some state employees were forced to work six days a week. Governors hired and promoted and demoted state police officers. Some governors took kickbacks from insurance company executives for making it mandatory that state employees buy insurance they didn't need. Large companies dodged taxes by making hefty contributions to governors. State government had no formal budget.

The state legislature was a joke that made people cry. Legislators were elected from counties at-large, meaning there were no districts, and meaning that, for the most part, white conservative Democrats controlled the state Capitol. They did control it. When Dave arrived, only two Republicans had been elected to statewide office since 1934. More than a dozen Democratic Party county chairmen were on the state payroll. Most never worked—they had their paychecks mailed to their homes. But they did show up—to demand five percent of employees' paychecks every payday for their infamous "Deduct Boxes."

Then there was the Republican Party—a nearly non-existent organization that was never able to muster enough guts to confront and challenge the Democrats' corruption and their lock on government.

David Francis Cargo blew into Albuquerque that May. Fresh from his home state of Michigan and armed with a masters degree in public administration, a law degree, a wicked sense of satire and irony, and an outrage at corruption and incompetence, he was a storm that lingered, built in intensity and then burst in full fury onto the corrupt system he saw.

And New Mexico was never the same.

Dave Cargo was a political junkie in Michigan—had been since age eight when he started subscribing to a host of newspapers, magazines and political tracts. In Michigan he met the heavy hitters of state and national politics and he and they became friends. He learned politics from the inside out and learned how to get votes.

There has always been more to him, however, than getting votes. Dave Cargo cared. He cared about fairness, about working people and about public service and about doing things right.

He was a moderate Republican at a time when the Democrats

were the hyper-conservatives who did all they could to defeat civil rights and any other legislation designed to give people dignity and a say in their government.

The minute he arrived in New Mexico, Cargo got involved in politics—slowly at first, and then quickly. He befriended leading Democrats like U.S. Senators Dennis Chavez and Clinton P. Anderson. He got to know former governors like Ed Mechem and John Burroughs. They liked Dave for his wit, his sincerity and his passion for good, clean government.

Within five years of his arrival in New Mexico, Dave Cargo was elected to the New Mexico House of Representatives. Within nine years, he was elected governor.

Dave Cargo was no ordinary politician. He railed loudly and publicly against corruption in a state that seemed to think that corruption was perfectly normal. He introduced bills that demanded that state legislators actually report the bribes they had taken. He threatened to pave state roads with corrupt highway commissioners. He fought for working people and minorities, and he did so with a sense of satire and humor that the state had never before seen and that left his slow-witted opponents flat-footed, frustrated and grumbling about this bellicose outsider.

When he introduced his bribe-reporting bill, one legislator stood up on the House floor and wailed, "This is going to ruin us!"

Of course it was, because Dave Cargo had every intention of destroying that old political system. And he did.

During that first term in the legislature Dave shocked the political establishment by filing a lawsuit to reapportion, or district the legislature. Until then, lawmakers were elected-at large from their counties. Because mostly white conservative Democrats voted, they controlled everything. There were no Black faces in the legislature, few Hispanics, and almost no Indian or women.

Reapportionment changed that forever. Dave won his lawsuits. The legislature was carved into districts where minorities had a chance to get elected. They got elected, and they were forever grateful to David Francis Cargo, the Republican who fought for minorities and the oppressed.

When Dave ran for governor in 1966, still a relative newcomer, he was given no chance of winning. It was impossible, the voices said, for a Republican to win a statewide office in a state that had for decades been a colony of the Democratic Party.

But they didn't know Dave Cargo. While they were predicting his defeat, Dave—a Republican—was out courting minority and Democratic voters. He went to union rallies and asked for their support. He never failed to mention all the pro-labor legislation he had introduced or supported as a lawmaker, and all that pro-labor legislation that his Democratic opponents had opposed and killed. He never failed to mention his reapportionment lawsuits that gave a place and voice in state government to minorities.

He became known as "Lonesome Dave," partly because he had little money and campaigned by himself, and mostly because he stood by himself in confronting New Mexico's corrupt political establishment. Dave might have started out alone, but he soon had a wonderfully huge following.

To the shock of many Democrats and to the horror of the state's inept Republican Party, Dave got standing ovations at those rallies. They were also shocked that this Michigan transplant—they derided him as a carpetbagger and slick opportunist—dared go out and talk with normal people, with citizens! Dave did that. He shook every hand he could, attended every funeral he could and connected with the people the Democrats had for so long ignored. He even personally delivered eyeglasses to welfare recipients after state government arrogantly decided that all those poor people needed to somehow get to Santa Fe to pick up their glasses.

Dave thrived on the criticism and the attempts to discredit him. He charged into northern New Mexico—the mostly Hispanic Democratic Party stronghold—and won the people over with his honesty, humor and empathy for their plight.

In Mora County Dave held rallies that attracted 10,000 people and more. The Albuquerque newspapers and TV stations never knew about them because they never bothered to send reporters or film crews up there.

After the votes were all counted in November 1966, Dave had been elected governor—the youngest governor in New Mexico's history.

His pair of two-year terms were a hurricane of activity as Dave worked furiously to dismantle the old, corrupt system. He passed civil rights legislation and appointed minorities to boards and commissions. He hired Blacks into state government. He treated state workers fairly. He introduced conflict-of-interest bills and he demanded hard work and honesty. For the most part, he got it.

There were other accomplishments. Dave started the first state Film Commission in the nation. It was a wild success that brought scores of films and billions of dollars of Hollywood money into the state. He saved the Cumbres & Toltec Scenic Railroad. He saved the potash industry. He created state parks. He helped give Blue Lake back to the Taos Pueblo. He tried to reform the prison system. He ended the infamous "Deduct Boxes." He demanded that people on the state payroll actually do some work. He invited Blacks and regular people to the governor's mansion in Santa Fe.

In short, Dave Cargo brought modern government to New Mexico. He was a pivotal figure in the state's political history; the bridge between the old, corrupt, spoils-based system and a modern government that treated its citizens and employees with dignity, fairness and respect instead of contempt.

Dave served only four years as governor, but those were the most important years in the state's modern history. We still feel their impact today.

State government still isn't perfect—it never will be. Lawmakers still take bribes and defraud the public. Some still can't figure out that "public service" means just that, that public officials are there to serve the public—that the public are their bosses.

State and local governments—all New Mexicans—are far

better off than they would have been if David Francis Cargo had not blown into New Mexico in May of 1957 in his beat-up 1949 Chevrolet and had not his political storm vented its full fury on that old and corrupt system.

Dave Cargo changed New Mexico for the better, and for that, he is and will always be remembered and lovingly referred to as Governor Cargo.

—Dennis Domrzalski

Prologue

They Did Things the Old Way
or
The Hell With This Modern Government

It was early in my first term as governor in 1967 when a man named Gordo Sena walked into my office in the state Capitol. He had supported me in my 1966 election campaign, and I was grateful for his support—for everybody's support that helped me win the against-the-odds election.

Gordo was blunt.

"I want a position in state government," he said.

It wasn't an unusual request. In those days—even today—campaign supporters wanted and still want government jobs. Hell, poor Abe Lincoln had to hide from mobs of job seekers after he was elected president in 1860.

"Jeezsus, Gordo," I replied. "What can you do?"

He just shrugged his shoulders and repeated his request, or should I say, his demand.

I found him a job in the state motor pool.

After a month or so, Vivian Cordova, who headed the motor pool, stopped by and asked, "What happened to Gordo? Where the hell is Gordo?"

"I don't know," I answered.

Then a guy from the Taxation and Revenue Department walked in and joined the conversation.

"I saw Gordo the other day. He said he was going to the bar to have a few drinks. He's not working as far as I can tell," he said.

"He's supposed to be working," I said rather angrily. "Vivian, are you sure you haven't seen him?"

"No," Vivian answered, "he's never been in except to pick up his paycheck."

Well, shortly afterward I picked up the phone and called Gordo.

"Jeesus, Gordo. You said you wanted a job, and I gave you a job, and dammit, you never went to work," I told him. "All you've done is picked up your paycheck."

"Listen," he barked into the phone, "I didn't tell you I wanted a job. I told you I wanted a position. I didn't think I had to work."

Well, Gordo had his "position," one that he figured required no work on his part.

"You either show up for work or you're fired," I told him.

"That's a hell of a way to treat me," Gordo answered. "I've been a loyal Republican all these years. And here's another thing. I didn't have to take a test to vote for you, and I don't know why I had to take a test for that position. I told you I wanted a position."

Gordo never did show up for work, and he did not retain his "position" in state government.

Earlier I had formed—for the first time in state government's history—a motor pool so we could keep track of state vehicles and have a centralized system of gassing them up and maintaining them. I gave the order on a Friday and said that by that Monday I wanted an accounting of every state vehicle. We had to do that, by the way, because state workers were taking state cars and trucks home. They gassed them up themselves and were reimbursed. But it was more than a little strange. We had one guy who had gassed up his car seven times in one day. I could be wrong, but I don't think he had been doing *that much* state work.

The motor pool order was not received kindly—hell, it wasn't received at all, I think. You see, those state workers used to get trading stamps every time they filled up. And—and this didn't take much investigation—they'd fill up with regular and charge the state for premium. They'd fill up their relatives' cars, and their neighbors' and probably their lawnmowers and tractors and charge the state.

I really didn't think it was asking too much to end that practice.

Well, it was, to say the least, crazy. We found a car in Mexico City, one in Juarez and one somewhere in Florida—a state worker and his wife were on their honeymoon. They were all somewhat offended when we asked for the cars back.

One guy who had a state car called me and said quite sincerely:

"Look, Governor. I've been a state worker for a number of years. Just take me off the payroll and let me keep the car. I really like this car."

"Jeesus!" I said, a bit stunned. "You can't do that. You just can't do that!"

"Why not?"

"Because it's a state car and it's not yours," I said. Then I got an answer that put everything into perspective.

"The hell with this modern government," he said with more than a little bitterness. "I don't like it."

He didn't like it, and others didn't like "modern government," and as a result, some of them didn't like me.

I came to New Mexico in 1957 to practice law. I came here from my home state of Michigan looking for adventure. I found it—a lot more than I ever bargained for, I can tell you that.

I don't want to be disrespectful and say the state was backwards or primitive when it came to politics and government, but it was. I could be kinder and say that here, they did things the old way—the real old way, I mean the really, really old way!

I had walked into something that was, well, crazy, not to mention corrupt and draconian.

The Democratic Party had controlled the state. Before I was elected governor in 1966, only two Republicans—Ed Mechem and Tom Bolack—had been elected to statewide office since 1934.

And what a state the Democrats ran.

The public schools were *still* segregated. More than a dozen Democratic Party county chairmen were on the state government payroll. All the jobs in state government were patronage positions, filled by the spoils system. Those county chairmen went around with their "deduct boxes" every payday and demanded 5 percent of the employees' checks.

Those county chairmen, by the way, never showed up for work. They had their checks mailed to their homes.

Governors hired and promoted state police officers, sending officers they didn't like to exotic beats like Pie Town. African-Americans were excluded from state government—actually they weren't. When I took office there were exactly two Blacks on the state payroll.

Conservative white Democrats controlled the state legislature and state government. That's because state senators and representatives were elected at-large from their counties. Since it was mostly Anglos who voted, and who were in the majority at the time, Hispanics, Blacks, Indians and women were virtually absent from the legislature.

And what a legislature it was. There were no lobbying or conflict-of-interest laws. Lobbyists gave legislators cars and trucks. Legislators gave themselves no-bid contracts to furnish the state Capitol. Lawmakers who were charged with building the new state Capitol went out and bought the land where the new building would be and sold it—at a profit—to the state. Governors handed out liquor licenses like candy—actually for campaign contributions. State employees were forced to buy life insurance. One of the brokers—another lawmaker—had that contract. State workers were fired en-masse every time a different faction of the Democratic Party won the governor's office. No, there was no Civil Service system in New Mexico.

Civil service, human rights, conflict-of-interest and organized labor-friendly bills were constantly killed by Democrats. The state had a mandatory straight-party ballot for elections, which meant that only Democrats got elected. Democrats did this and Democrats did that, and much of it was wrong and backwards.

There were Democratic and Republican gas stations and grocery stores. I stopped in a Democratic gas station once and was told I couldn't fill up. I did fill up, a move that left the attendant flabbergasted.

Large companies had a way of halving their tax bills. They wouldn't pay them for a few years and let them add up. Then they would walk into the governor's office, offer to pay half and offer a hefty campaign contribution. It worked—not with me, though.

I don't know that I was aghast or bemused by what I saw. I do know that I found it damn interesting, especially coming from the progressive state of Michigan.

So I got to work. I made friends and connections, railed against corruption, fraud, incompetence and injustice and made a name for myself. Oh, I talked a lot, but you would have too if you had walked into what I had.

I was a Republican in a Democratic state. And I must say that I was pretty much the lone Republican. In New Mexico, the GOP wasn't a joke. If it had been a joke that would have meant that it had at least existed. It really didn't. At my first Young Republican meeting in Albuquerque, there were exactly seven of us, me included. It wasn't exactly an energetic party.

That corrupt and old-style mindset is something I battled, whether by filing lawsuits to reapportion the state legislature, introducing conflict-of-interest bills in the legislature, appointing minorities to state jobs, fighting for civil rights legislation and working tirelessly on behalf of labor.

I'll never forget when I introduced an anti-bribery bill in the state House of Representatives. It gave people who bribed legislators 30 days to report the bribe, and gave the lawmaker 60 days to report the illicit monetary gain.

One legislator stood up on the floor of the house and said of my bill:

"This is going to ruin us!"

That was my intent; to ruin that corrupt system.

It wasn't just Democrats who played that game.

I'll never forget what happened after I appointed a certain woman—she was a Republican—to the local draft board in Mora. I started getting phone calls—dozens of them. It turned out she was drafting only Democrats! She would just draft them and they would go away just like that. It was an effective way to get rid of the opposition, but it was wrong.

I called her one day and said, "What the hell are you doing? You can't do that!"

She was defiant and said, "They're all Democrats! They should be drafted!"

Needless to say, I took her off the draft board and put her somewhere she could do less harm.

And then there was the time when, as governor, I had gotten a road paved in San Miguel County. I went up to see it with then-state Senator Junio Lopez. We looked at the road and it came smartly right along and then it stopped—meaning the pavement stopped—and then it started up again. It turns out that the pavement stopped in front of a certain house and the adjoining property. I asked Junio what it was all about, why that patch of road wasn't paved. His reply:

"That goddamned guy didn't vote for you!"

I wanted to laugh and cry. I went up to the guy's house and said:

"I just wanted to let you know that they are going to pave the road in front of your house."

"I knew you were fair," he said. "Dammit, next time I am going to vote for you!"

"You don't have to vote for me—really, you don't," I told him.

I don't know that he ever did, and I don't care. What happened there was wrong.

I tried, during my two terms as governor, and during my two

terms in the New Mexico House of Representatives, to change things for the better and to bring so-called "modern government" to the state. I think I did. It shocked many people back then. I hope my stories in this book—especially those about how New Mexico politics and government used to be—shock some of you. Things backslide, and fighting for good, honest government is a never ending job.

It has been a long time now since I served as governor. In so many ways it seems like only yesterday, and sometimes I still get the urge to sit down, get to my pen or typewriter, and work up an executive order or two. There are still so many things that need to be changed and done—so many wrongs to be righted.

I ran for other offices after my two gubernatorial terms. I mostly fell short. But, over the years I've come to realize that being governor was the job for me; the one I loved and the one that I could have done forever and ever.

Nothing does last forever, tough, except perhaps our memories and dreams. I know that in my mind, though—and I hope in yours as well—that I will always be:

—Governor Dave Cargo
Albuquerque, August, 2009

Growing Up

I feel like Winston Churchill must have when he wrote a lengthy letter to his mother during the Boer War. He said in a postscript in the letter "that I must apologize for the long letter, but I didn't have time to write a shorter one." That's the way I feel about summarizing my early life. I'll try to make it as succinct as possible.

I was born just before The Great Depression began, and I must confess that it had a great influence on my life, because not only did we have The Great Depression in Michigan, we also had labor unrest, including the founding of the Congress of Industrial Organizations (CIO) and numerous strikes throughout Michigan by early labor organizations, and, of course, the violence and turmoil that went with them. So, it was a great experience and one that made a great impression on me.

In growing up I was lucky in that my father was employed. To show you the gravity of the situation in the small town of Dowagiac, Michigan, I would point to a discovery that I made during my first year of kindergarten. The teacher one day inexplicably asked how many children in the class had parents who were gainfully employed. The response was not mixed. I was the only one who had a parent that was employed. Thirty-one others had parents who did not have jobs.

And my father, though employed, had just suffered through a sizable diminution in his compensation. He had come home the day before and advised my mother that his salary had been cut in half and that he was now making $1,900 a year and would have to teach student driving during the summers to make additional money. It was a dire situation and one that I have never been able to erase from my memory.

I am reminded of a quotation from Maxim Gorky when he stated that "life is a moral gymnasium," and that is exactly the way it appeared to me when I was growing up. Not only was everyone unemployed, but there were many, many people living in poverty. We used to get people coming to the door by the dozens every day asking for food. They would ride in on the train and get off in Dowagiac and go through town begging for food. Some of the relief programs under President Franklin Roosevelt helped, but for the most part people were living right on the edge. There was no unemployment insurance and no welfare, and these people had no money and no jobs—and no prospect of getting any—and they were terrified. I was young and impressionable, and that influenced me for the rest of my life.

Another thing that made an impression on me was the widespread conflict between an emerging organized labor movement and employers. I well remember going down as a small child and watching as strikers gathered around bonfires to keep warm in the winter while on strike. They would entertain us, but for the most part it was pretty grim business because there was a lot of strife. Prior to the time of the strikes in Dowagiac there had been only company unions. When industrial unions came to town followed by the Congress of Industrial Unions (CIO), there was a great deal of conflict. I well remember that all of the windows in the factories at Round Oak, Dowagiac Steele Furnace Company and Premier Furnace Company had been smashed out. Thousands of windows were broken. I remember company security people coming out in the dead of winter and opening up hoses on the strikers and spraying them with ice-cold water. I also remember John L. Lewis, the great labor leader, and his activity in connection with the auto strikes in Detroit and in Flint, Michigan. Lewis was a very colorful character and was a very ardent Republican. I remember listening to him as a child when he declaimed with great vigor during an appearance in

Michigan by saying, "for the record, the basic difference between the Republicans and the Democrats is that when you buy a Republican he stays bought out of intellectual conviction. But not the Democrats and you have to buy them year after year, after year, after year." He was quiet an orator and made an impression on everyone who heard him.

Later, when I was attending University of Michigan, I came to know Homer Martin, who was the first president of the United Auto Workers-Congress of Industrial Organizations. I also knew most of the leaders of the UAW, including Richard Frankenstein and Walter Reuther. It was an interesting experience, and I learned something about industrial democracy growing up, and especially growing up in Michigan.

Growing up in the Dowagiac was interesting, but not very exciting. It was a town of 5,000 people in Cass County, which survived through farming, manufacturing and the tourism industry. Cass County had scores of lakes, and people from Chicago and South Bend, Indiana, had vacation cottages at the lakes. Consequently, we always enjoyed swimming and outdoor activities, even swimming in the mill stream which ran through Dowagiac.

Dowagiac had a fairly large population of people who came from Poland to work in the furnace factories, and in the immediate area there was a large population of African-Americans. As a matter of fact, Calvin Township was a terminus for the Underground Railroad and was 100 percent African-American. I always got a kick out of it when I would go with my grandfather, John Harton, to the county seat in Cassopolis and we would drive through Calvin Township. He was an old-style Republican and took his politics fairly seriously, especially since he was Irish. However, he was a Republican, and when we passed through Calvin Township he would declaim with great pride that Calvin Township was 100 percent Black. He would say, "God bless them, they are 100 percent Republican." Indeed, in those days they were. So, my impression of politics in Dowagiac was that all of the African-Americans were indeed Republicans.

When the Second World War came everything changed and I began to find work, or to put it a little bit more accurately, my mother decided that she would locate work for me. She put me to work with local farmers weeding onions and harvesting potatoes and lettuce. She looked forward to the day when I could work at something other than in agriculture. Sure enough, as the war went on, there was a shortage of labor and my mother found plenty for me to do.

When I was 16 she had me working in the morning at the Tri-County Telephone Company as a janitor, where I would start at 5:00 in the morning. At 8:30 in the morning I left that job and went to work as a playground supervisor. I worked at that job until 5:00 in the afternoon, and then I worked in Harvey's shop on Main Street in Dowagiac where I sold tourist items and fast food until 9:30 at night. That kept me occupied. Prior to obtaining these jobs I had paper routes. I peddled the *Dowagiac Daily News* every afternoon, and *The South Bend Tribune*. On Sundays I sold the *Chicago Tribune* to tourists from Chicago. So I became familiar with newspapers.

At that time, Colonel Robert McCormick was the publisher of the *Chicago Tribune*. Without a doubt it was the most biased partisan newspaper in the country. I never really understood how cutting a journalist could be until I came across the *Chicago Tribune*.

We lived in Dowagiac until 1945, when we moved to Jackson, Michigan, where my father taught physics and chemistry in the local high school. He also taught part-time at Jackson Junior College. It was in Dowagiac that I really began to develop a lot of my aptitude and interest in political life. I first started getting the *Congressional Record* when I was 14. I got it every day from my local Congressman Clare Hoffman. I also would pick up copies of the *Congressional Directory*, which I pretty much memorized.

After we moved to Jackson I took a great interest in politics in that the Republican Party was founded in Jackson, Michigan, on July 6, 1854, to fight slavery. I became very active in the party at an early age. As a matter of fact, I started attending Republican conventions starting when I was 15. As a high school senior I was elected by the city's schools as the Youth Mayor For The Day. When I was elected by all those students from different high schools in the city, I ventured forth with great vigor as Mayor for the Day. I announced, among other things, a shutdown of gambling, which was widespread in the city. There were also pockets of prostitution that I disapproved of, and I thought that we should pass some kind of civil rights legislation. Believe me, that was long before people thought that was appropriate. I kind of saw myself as an embryonic Fiorello LaGuardia, who was the great reform Mayor of New York City.

I had long been a great admirer of literature—I started reading before I went to school. My mother spent hours teaching me to read so by the time I went to kindergarten I was well on my way to reading everything I could get my hands on. I was reading at about a fifth-grade level in kindergarten, so I really got a good start on things. I believe that there are things in this world that are worse than burning books, and that is not to read them. I read everything I could get my hands on, and I read whenever I had a minute to spare.

I began to compile a library, and that habit has stayed with me. I now have a private library in excess of 9,500 volumes, and I have read them all. I began to get political literature from all over the country, everything from the Nonpartisan League in North Dakota, to the newsletter that was regularly put out by the Republican State Central Committee in New York State. I got on every list I could. To this day I devour newspapers. I subscribe to six daily newspapers, ranging from the *New York Times* to the weekly *Rio Grande Sun*. In addition to those newspapers, I get the *Irish Independent* and the *Suddeutsch Zeitung*, although sometimes newspapers have gotten to be a little expensive. I felt that if you read enough, as H.L. Mencken once wrote, "sometimes democracy tells the truth about itself."

I also developed habits of self-study that proved to be interesting. I would not only study the text that we were given in class, but I would read all the footnotes. I explored the original sources and read history books by the hundreds. As a matter of fact, I may have gained a reputation for being a little eccentric. In any event, I managed to over-study every course that I was truly interested in, and even did fairly well in a few that I didn't have a deep curiosity about.

One interesting incident took place when I was in the 11th grade taking a history course from Ms. Ruth Ring. She was an excellent instructor who was very demanding and exacting. I used to take delight in catching her in errors, which wasn't easy. One day, in exasperation, she came in and taught me a lesson that benefited me later on in my educational pursuits. She came in and announced with some vigor to the class of 25 that I was an intellectual snob and that she was going to teach me a lesson. She said she wanted to know the textbook view of the Elkins Act, as well as the textbook explanation of the Sherman Antitrust Act. She grinned a little and said, "well Mr. Cargo let's hear your explanation."

I think I surprised her by way of comeback. I said, "well, the textbook explanation of the meaning and provisions of the Elkins Act was found on the first paragraph running through the fifth paragraph, starting on page 241 of our text, and the Sherman Antitrust Act is explained in textbook terms commencing on page 342, running from that page and continuing on with the following two pages."

I would recite the material if she so desired. She did not so desire. She said she had enough, that she wasn't going to test me on it anymore and that I had won. She asked how I knew she was going to ask those two questions. I said I didn't, but that it taught me a lesson. She asked, "what was that?" I said the lessons were watch what you say in class and be humble in how you render forth on what you think on various subjects. She taught me a good lesson indeed.

In Jackson I began to prepare for my eventual admission into the University of Michigan. I had some interesting classmates. One was Wilber Dungy, whose son became the world-famous coach of the 2007 Super Bowl winners, the Indianapolis Colts. I had a lot of other very interesting friends, but in any event I wasn't spending quite as much time working. During four years of high school I worked at the Chemist Shop in Jackson, and served my full apprenticeship in pharmacy. That taught me a little about pharmacy, and a lot about life.

Before graduating from high school I started working for the U.S. Forest Service in Idaho, Montana, Wyoming. That had a huge influence on my life. I became a dedicated conservationist and preservationist, and I learned a lot from my experiences in the Forest Service. I worked out of Coeur D'Alene, Sandpoint, and St. Mary's, Idaho. I worked in the Coeur D'Alene, Clearwater, Challis and the Kootenai National Forests.

I spent most of my time working on fire suppression, and I became a dedicated fan of the United States Forest Service. However, one summer I spent half of the summer working on the Bar B Ranch on the Big Hole Basin in Montana. I also worked out of Yellowstone National Park that same summer. It was an interesting experience, and it certainly guided me when it came to matters of conservation and forest practices. I worked on forest fires as small as five acres and on several as large as 60,000 acres. There were two summers where I went to work in early May on a single fire, and didn't finish until September. It was an interesting experience, living out of doors and away from all of the amenities for months on end, and then finally returning to the luxury of civilization.

I worked at one ranger station where we had a variety of unique experiences, ranging from seeing wolverines to feeding fish with some strange results. That ranger station was about 50 miles from Coeur D'Alene, with nothing in between by way of human habitation. We had a fairly large stream that passed close to the ranger station, and we took scraps of bacon after breakfast and fed them to the fish. The fish began to grow, and indeed, by the end of the summer they were huge. The only problem was that when we caught them they smelled strongly of bacon. In any event, it gave me a taste of the wild, and I really treasure the days that I worked for the Forest Service. At one point I even thought about staying on and making it a career.

When I graduated from Jackson High School I was voted

unanimously "the student most likely to succeed." After graduation I moved on to my career in higher education, which at the time was the University of Michigan.

I knew my parents were going to have a tough time of supporting me fully while I was at the University. I began to realize how interesting it was going to be when my father took me over to Ann Arbor and we located a place for me to stay at a rooming house. When he got ready to leave he said, "I'm going to take you down to the Old German Restaurant. I can tell you this is a great place to go, and when I was going to the University of Michigan I used to go there once in a while when I was flush with money."

He wasn't flush with money that frequently, so I don't know how many times he actually ate there. He added very quickly that, "if you earn enough from the jobs that you get here while attending the University of Michigan, you might want to go down there to eat now and again." I thought, "Uh-oh. Here we go."

So I not only started at the University of Michigan, but I also began to seek employment. Fortunately, one of the first jobs that I found was at Sigma Alpha Mu, which was the Sami House. I started out as a waiter and then worked my way up to a position as a part-time cook. Then I worked in a grocery store a couple of nights a week. I also worked as a taxi driver and managed to hang on to that position for a number of months. I also worked for the Washtenaw County Commission, as well as the Washtenaw County Road Commission. I had a job that covered many areas, but my specialty was road and street signs. I designed almost all of the road signs and street signs in Washtenaw County. It didn't include the city of Ann Arbor, but included almost everything outside of Ann Arbor. To this day you can pass by road signs that I designed and put together. The glory of that job was that I could work weekends, unsupervised, and any hours that I wanted, and that helped.

As an undergraduate I was extremely active on campus and began friendships that have lasted all through the years. It went from Roger Wilkins, a civil rights leader and editor of *The Crisis*, which is the publication of the NAACP, to David Belin who was general counsel for the Warren Commission and investigated the assassination of President John F. Kennedy. Also, Jim McDermitt, who lived across the street from me. We became close friends before and after he became an astronaut. He had lived across the street from me in Jackson, but we remained friends while he was at the university.

As an undergraduate I had to devote a considerable amount of time to my studies because the University of Michigan was highly competitive and its demands were considerable. I became very active in The Young Republicans, and became the president of the University of Michigan Young Republican Club. At one point the club had over 1,100 members. I also became chairman of the Eisenhower for President Club at an early point in the 1952 presidential election, and led the efforts on his behalf on campus. The school conducted a three-day mock election that was supervised by the *Michigan Daily*, a student newspaper at the university. When the votes were all in, Eisenhower received 51 percent of the ballots cast, while Senator Robert A. Taft of Ohio drew 19 percent. The *Michigan Daily*, which conducted the poll, had urged all students to vote and reported that a total of 5,131 ballots had been cast. Of these, Eisenhower received 2,658 and Taft 1,683. President Truman ran a poor third with 496 votes, or 9.6 percent. His only other announced Democratic opponent, Senator Estes Kefauver of Tennessee, placed fourth, with 340 votes, or 6.6 percent.

After the results were in, I told the *Michigan Daily* that it was a tremendous vote for Eisenhower and that I was pleased with it. Taft supporters said it was only a popularity contest and that it wasn't a vote of any great significance. My response was that elections *are* popularity contests, and that's what they're all about.

I also helped set up the first NAACP chapter at the University of Michigan, and was able to sit down with the presidents of The Young Democrats, The Young Progressives, and assembled a very viable club. We also lobbied for, and got a resolution passed, by the student government which euphemistically was a piece of legislation that would outlaw "discrimination forever at the University of Michigan." It's interesting that at the time, Congressman Gerald Ford of Michigan supported me in this effort. Many years later I supported him while he was trying to support affirmative action at the University of Michigan Law School.

The next event that took place when I was president of The Young Republicans was the unforeseen venture into Michigan by Senator Joseph R. McCarthy of Wisconsin. He came into the State and began to give a series of speeches telling of the problems that the country faced with Communists. He started in Battle Creek, Jackson and went to Flint, Detroit and other cities. All went fairly well for him until he decided that he was going to speak on the campus of the University of Michigan. Unfortunately for him, he had to have the approval of the university's president, The Young Republicans and their faculty advisor. The faculty advisor was a political science professor and wasn't terribly interested in having McCarthy stir up the campus.

His advice was that he would do whatever I wished, but his own personal view was that we should not have him speak on campus. He said we would probably have student demonstrations that would cause a great deal of trouble. I said I wouldn't sign the permission slip to let him speak, on campus, and that if he wanted to speak elsewhere or if he wanted to speak in Ann Arbor I would be happy to have him do so, but I did not want it to appear that I supported him. I said he was a disgrace to the Republican Party and took that position and stuck with it. Then all hell broke loose. Arthur Summerfield, who was the Republican National Committeeman from Michigan, immediately came over to Ann Arbor with the Republican State Chairman Pat Cleary and we had lunch in the Michigan Union. They both told me that they wanted him to speak at the university and that they would also appreciate it if I would accompany him to a convention of the American Legion where he was speaking in Detroit later in the week. I respectfully declined. This was an interesting venture because at the time I was seeing Pat

Cleary's daughter. We used to see each other socially now and then, and it made for a rather awkward situation.

Summerfield also advised me of the fact that Eisenhower did not stand a chance of being elected President and that he was going to support Taft and I should also review my position in that regard as well. Fortunately, I consulted with Senator Arthur Vandenberg, who told me, "son stick to your guns, support Eisenhower, he's going to be president of the United States."

Congressman Gerald Ford said essentially the same thing. He was for Eisenhower, and so was Vandenberg and Senator Vandenberg's son, Arthur Vandenberg Jr., who eventually headed the Eisenhower movement in Michigan. However, I was at odds with both Pat Cleary and Summerfield as to how they ran the GOP organization in Michigan.

In 1952, the delegates to the National Republican Convention were selected at county conventions. There were 83 county conventions, and I was the first person to announce that I was forming an organization to support Eisenhower. Therefore, I became fairly prominent in the effort to nominate him, and I commenced going from county convention to county convention urging support for Eisenhower. Amazingly enough, we commenced winning in one county after the other, until finally, out of 46 delegates we were able to get 42 of them pledged to Eisenhower.

Once the county conventions were over, the job was to select at-large delegates. I then again heard from Summerfield and Cleary that they wanted to be delegates to the national convention. They said they were going to support Eisenhower because he was most assuredly going to be president. After Eisenhower was elected, of course, Summerfield became national chairman of the Republican Party and then Postmaster General of the United States. He changed his views on Eisenhower.

Summerfield followed the advice of Bundes Chancellor Otto Von Bismark who observed "in the nineteenth century, when you hear the beats of history you grab the rider's coattail. I've got to make sure that it is the right horse." Summerfield selected the right horse and went to Washington, DC.

It was also during my time as a Young Republican that I first came into contact with Gerald Ford. He was back from service during the Second World War and practicing law in Grand Rapids, Michigan. At the urging of Senator Vandenberg he decided to contest a primary election with the incumbent from the Fifth Congressional District of Michigan: Congressman Bartel Yonkman.

Yonkman was thoroughly entrenched, and he expressed his isolationist views on foreign policy. He clashed with Senator Vandenberg. In Michigan you did not have to register by party and anyone could vote in any primary election that they so desired. All they had to do was say that they were a Republican or a Democrat and they could vote in the primary elections.

I endorsed Ford and worked strongly on his behalf. When he entered the race it was assumed that he was going to lose only because he was 32 years old and a lot of the business community was against him. His prospects did not look all that encouraging in spite of the fact that he had been an All-American football player at the University of Michigan. Oddly enough, when he was president, people used to say that he stumbled around a lot.

He didn't stumble around while playing center for the University of Michigan football team and being ranked as an All-American. He was probably the best athlete to ever occupy the presidency, and was certainly no dummy. He not only graduated from the University of Michigan, but he got his law degree from Yale University. He wasn't a half bad lawyer either.

Through my activities as a Young Republican I attracted some attention by getting out and supporting reform progressive minded individuals in their various races for state office and for Congress. For instance, I supported John Martin of Grand Rapids very strongly for the U.S. Senate even though he eventually lost. I also supported Martin again when he ran for state office, and that time he won.

However, it became very interesting as I immersed myself in

Young Republican politics. I helped form the Big 10 Young Republican Conference and we went to Wisconsin for its annual convention. When we got there, Senator Joe McCarthy was present. He cornered me immediately and asked that several of the presidents of the various university organizations convene in his hotel room. He then said that "we all needed a drink of whiskey." Most of us were really not of the age to be drinking much of anything, never mind whiskey. But then he went on and on and on on about how he was worried that we were going to present the resolution condemning him.

I had no idea of doing any such thing, and that satisfied him. We were present in his room when he received a phone call from New Bedford, Massachusetts, and held about a 10-minute conversation with a gentleman by the name of Basel Brewer, who had been the chairman of the Taft forces in Massachusetts. Brewer was backing no less than Congressman John F. Kennedy in his race against Senator Henry Cabot Lodge Jr. In addition to that, McCarthy was very close with the Kennedy family, and Joe Kennedy contributed very generously to his various Senate campaigns. And of course, Bobby Kennedy worked for McCarthy on the Senate's Government Operations Committee. He attended not only McCarthy's wedding, but also his funeral in Wisconsin when he died while in office.

It was clear that there was a great deal of friendship between McCarthy and the Kennedys. So this is a footnote in history that keeps bubbling to the surface, and more than common interest because Senator Henry Cabot Lodge Jr. had headed the national movement for Eisenhower.

Likewise, because of Young Republican politics, I had the opportunity to meet with a number of national figures in the Republican Party, one being Senator Robert A. Taft of Ohio. Although he was much more conservative than I was, I greatly admired him. He was known as Mr. Republican in those days, and I had some interesting moments with him. I once invited him to the University of Michigan to speak. He called me on the telephone. Unfortunately, I thought that it was one of my friends playing a trick on me. He said, "this is

Bob Taft," and I said, "well Bob, how are you doing?"

"David," he said, "how are you getting along?" I said, "pretty damn well. How are you?"

We talked for a couple of minutes. Then I realized that it really was Taft and I immediately switched to a more deferential moniker for him and started addressing him as "Senator." I invited him to the university to speak. He came on two different occasions. Once at a private luncheon he told me, "only unbalanced people believe in unbalanced budgets." Too bad he wasn't around when Ronald Reagan and Dick Cheney got to rendering forth that balancing the budget wasn't necessary in government anymore. Republicans in those days were an entirely different lot.

Harold Stassen came to Ann Arbor and spoke to a crowd of 5,000 and gave what I think was one of the most amazing spontaneous speeches that I had ever heard in my life, with the exception of speech that Eugene McCarthy gave in Los Angeles in 1960 when he nominated Adlai Stevenson for president. He was a great speaker, and so was McCarthy.

I eventually got to know McCarthy very well when I was governor. He was a very literate individual, and generally speaking, I rather admired him for taking the views that he did. Anyway, my adventures with the Young Republicans were interesting. Some Republicans were livid at the things I did, and the Young Democrats joined in by passing resolutions periodically supporting me in my endeavors, particularly in regards to McCarthy. It was a great adventure and a prelude of things to come.

The 1952 Republican Convention
Part of the Early Years

I was working in a factory in Jackson that made air-conditioning units for large buildings and they had a week where they let everyone take vacation. Fortuitously, it fell on the same date as the National Republican Convention in Chicago. I decided that I would take time off and go to the convention. I caught the Twilight Limited out of Jackson at 5:00 in the morning and took the train to Chicago. When I arrived I discovered that the Michigan delegation was located well back in the convention. They were really not very well-situated. I was at a loss as to what to do; I didn't want to sit up in the general audience area because I thought that would be too far away from the center of things. However, I was able to resolve the problem. I ran into John S. Fine, governor of Pennsylvania, and got into a long conversation with him. I happened to mention that I was without floor credentials. He indicated there was no problem with that. He caught U.S. Senator James Duff of Pennsylvania and explained that I needed to be a little closer to the center of the action. Senator Duff then approached the manager of the Pennsylvania delegation and secured an alternate delegate badge for me.

As a result I was inside the convention hall and on the floor right in front of the rostrum and at the center of the action. More importantly, I sat right behind the New York delegation and two seats in back of Governor Thomas E. Dewey. It was an interesting place to be because when the struggle over delegates from the contested southern states delegations started I was there. I watched the full proceedings as the Fair Play Amendment played out. The Fair Play Amendments were sponsored by Senator Henry Cabot Lodge and the Eisenhower forces to prevent Taft delegates from prevailing.

There were a lot of problems with the convention accepting only Taft delegates from contested southern states. A number of southern states were contested, including Georgia, Louisiana, Mississippi, Texas and others. In 1912 Senator Robert E. Taft's father, President William Howard Taft, had been able to take enough legitimate delegates away from Theodore Roosevelt to deprive him of any chance of securing the Republican nomination. This was kind of a replay of that event in 1912 and it looked like they might succeed once again. However, powerful arguments were made on behalf of the fair seating of the delegations, and ultimately the Eisenhower delegations for the most part were seated. However, in Mississippi the regular Republican delegation was all African-American and the national committeeman was Perry Howard. Howard was a longtime member of the Republican National Committee and a leader in the African-American Community. Oddly enough, the delegation from Mississippi was for the most part pro-Taft. The Eisenhower people switched over and supported Perry Howard, and the Mississippi delegation was duly seated.

Then the battle over the nominee of the party ensued. Senator Everett Dirksen, with one of his flamboyant speeches, nominated Bob Taft. Dirksen was a wonderful speaker, but in the middle of his presentation he pointed down at Governor Thomas E. Dewey of New York and said, "We have followed you down the path of history and you have led us to defeat. We will not follow you again in that regard."

This caused quite a stir in the convention around Dewey, who was from Michigan originally. He arose and walked out into the aisle and then turned to me for no good reason that I can think of and said "Yeah, well, that SOB is going to think so when New York casts 94 votes for Eisenhower on the first ballot." The New York delegation did precisely that. I think ultimately Taft got four votes from the state of New York. Oddly enough, Senator Dirksen and I became very well acquainted and remained friends for a number of years after the convention and I used to appear with him quite regularly at Republican events.

Dwight D. Eisenhower was nominated by Governor Theodore Roosevelt McKeldon of Maryland. McKeldon was likewise very eloquent. Then Senator Ed Thye of Minnesota nominated Harold Stassen, and Governor Earl Warren of California was also placed in nomination by William S. Knowland of California. That pretty much concluded the nominations of the serious candidates. At that point the convention was on. We knew that the vote was going to be close but we had the conviction that Eisenhower would indeed be nominated. Strangely enough, when the roll call proceeded and they came to New Mexico there was a demand by the old guard that the delegates be polled. The reason for this was that General Patrick J. Hurley was one of the delegates and was a candidate for the United States Senate against Senator Dennis Chavez, and the old guard wanted to defeat him. It wasn't that they wanted to re-elect Dennis Chavez. It was that they wanted to defeat Patrick Hurley; they expected Hurley to support Taft, but when it came down to a roll call he voted for Eisenhower which surprised everyone. Later, in the general election, Hurley lost against Chavez.

Oddly enough there was another delegation where the old guard forced a roll call, and that was in the Arizona delegation. This was an even stranger situation because the old guard again was trying to defeat the candidate for the United States Senate. Interestingly enough, the candidate was Barry Goldwater. Goldwater was bitter that he was being forced to publicly make a choice between Taft and Eisenhower and he thought that it could ultimately damage his campaign against Ernest W. McFarland, the incumbent senator from Arizona and majority leader in the Senate. Goldwater reacted somewhat differently than Hurley had in that he was vigorous in casting his ballot for Eisenhower. Goldwater went on to defeat McFarland. After that, Goldwater proceeded to fight with President Dwight Eisenhower through both of Eisenhower's terms as president. The Arizona senator was much more conservative than Eisenhower on both domestic affairs and foreign policy.

The convention came to a dramatic conclusion when, after the voting had taken place on the first ballot, the Minnesota delegation moved to change its vote. Senator Thye was chairman of the Stassen delegation from Minnesota and they switched their votes from Stassen to Eisenhower, and that put Eisenhower over the top. One of the members of the Stassen delegation from Minnesota was Warren Burger, who later was on the Supreme Court and was thought of as being rather conservative. However, this was my first national convention and it was exciting for me because my candidate had been selected as the nominee and I campaigned for him in the 1952 election.

I campaigned for Eisenhower hard during most of the fall. One event in particular proved interesting. I, of course, had been following politics very closely for several years and had been active in Republican politics since I was an early teenager, so I had a fairly good political background. But in addition to that I also read the Congressional Record every day and had spent a lot of time in politics. The event took place in Manchester, which was outside of Ann Arbor. Manchester was a small rural town where my parents had purchased a farm and were then living. My dad farmed essentially during the summer in his off time and taught physics and chemistry at the high school in Jackson, Michigan, which was not too far distant. It was an interesting community in that it was heavily populated by people of German extraction and also had a high number of active Republicans. Politically it was a very close area because Ann Arbor was becoming increasingly more Democratic and organized labor was becoming much more active in politics in the Manchester area. That tended to make for close elections.

I filed for my first political office and I was nominated for constable for the Manchester Township, and as constable for the justice of the peace district, which covered the same township. Thus, I was a candidate on the ballot and my neighbor Frank Reck was the candidate for the Democratic Party for constable on their ticket. Reck was a fairly good friend and a next-door neighbor. We talked politics with great regularity and engaged in political conversations every chance we got. He was a very intelligent man and headed the public relations department of the Ford Motor Company. He had a very responsible job and one that was very prominent in the automotive industry. He was worldly, to say the least, and very well-versed. It was amazing that he consented to run for the office of Constable, but that wasn't the end of our election contest.

The town of Manchester decided to hold a debate on the presidential race and they secured the use of a high school gymnasium to stage it. The Republican Party selected me to debate with a Democrat in connection with the presidential race. I was 22 years old and here I was, engaged in a public debate in a gymnasium packed with people listening. I wasn't sure who my debating opponent would be. The Democrats stalled for several weeks and finally made a selection for their representative in the debate about 15 minutes before the debate. I'm sure that they had planned it for a long time, but in any event it was Frank Reck who appeared as the representative to debate on behalf of the candidacy of Adlai Stevenson. I was to represent Eisenhower. It looked like I was badly overmatched, or at least the Democrats thought so because they were exuberant as they anticipated what the results would actually be.

I should also point out that another thing that I had done through the years was to sit down when I was about fourteen years old and memorize the names of all the incumbent congressmen and senators. I memorized their names, party affiliations, backgrounds and the positions that they held in Congress and the election results in the last election. I developed this into an art: I had all 435 names memorized and I had all of their backgrounds well in mind. I knew how close their elections had been and I followed their records in great detail. This background information gave me an advantage when it came to political discussions. As a matter of fact, I had one political science professor at the University of Michigan who used to open every class for one full semester by saying, "Mr. Cargo, can you describe and name the congressmen from the First Congressional District in Illinois?" Then he would switch the next day to Minnesota, New York and on and on and on. Just like a trained seal I would recite all the vital statistics and give the various backgrounds, and the other students would applaud. I had it down to a fine art when it came to voting records and all the rest, so I knew about the various representatives and senators who were at that convention. That was an interesting sidelight to my debate experience.

We started the debate off and I immediately had gone after the fact that the Democratic Party was dominated by segregationists in the Senate and the House and that most of the chairman in both the Senate and the House were from the Deep South and were segregationists. Some of them were not too bad, and actually Harry Byrd of Virginia and Richard Russell of Georgia were not people who raved on the subject of race. However, there were a number of them from the South that did, and people like Congressman John Rankin were adamant bigots. Theodore G. Bilbo was even worse, so the Democrats were saddled with the Southern wing of their party, and likewise I thought they were saddled with the nominee for vice president who was to say the least biased in his views of racial relations. Senator John Sparkman of Alabama was their candidate for vice president and he believed in absolute segregation. In addition to that, Stevenson, their candidate for president, would not commit himself on the issue of school segregation and he defended segregation in the South on many occasions and took these positions because the Southern votes were absolutely necessary for the election of Democratic majorities. They were also anti-labor and I made a point of that too. It was a very interesting debate because my opponent spent a lot of his time on the defense and very little time on the offense, and it became a debate that was almost one sided. The crowd took great delight in it because here was a 22-year-old youngster battling it out with a 55-year-old giant of the auto industry, and not only giving him a hard time, but whomping him on a good many issues by the end of the evening. When they were thanking the speakers I got a standing ovation, and in the election that followed I won the office by three-to-one majority. It was my first expedition into public debates of any size and it was my first election to public office.

Young Republicans at the University of Michigan

There were a couple of other events that drew a lot of publicity while I was chairman of the Young Republicans at the University of Michigan. One was that I appointed Horace Coleman as temporary secretary of the Young Republicans. Eventually he was selected as the secretary of the Young Republicans and he was the first African-American to hold a major position in a student organization which was dominated by Anglos. He was also very well known as a track star and was one of the outstanding track athletes in the Big Ten. It was an interesting election and it stirred up a lot of interest because we chose an African-American for our leadership team before anybody else did. It received a fair amount of attention in the *Michigan Daily*, which was the student newspaper at the university.

Likewise, I thought that I would try to expand the base of the Young Republicans and also the Republican Party by bringing in a variety of speakers to the University of Michigan. One of the people that I invited was Frank X. Martel. He was the Secretary Treasurer of the Wayne County labor central which covered the entire Detroit area. His name was suggested to me, strangely enough, by James R. Hoffa who also identified himself as Republican and suggested that Martel would be a good man to invite even though he was a Democrat. Martel spoke at a Young Republican meeting and it was widely covered by the university's student newspaper. The event degenerated into a series of arguments between a group of ultraconservatives that came to disrupt the meeting. They charged that he was against Senator Arthur Vandenberg and that he had questioned whether or not Vandenberg was physically able to continue at his job in the Senate. They likewise took off on several other positions that he took on labor law. Oddly enough, most of the positions that Martel took were in complete agreement with Senator Robert A. Taft. For instance, Taft had sponsored the Humphrey-Taft Amendment to the Railway Labor Act of 1922, which stated that 14B of Title II of the Labor-Management Relations Act of 1947 did not apply to anyone covered by the Railway Labor Act. In other words, no right to work law would apply to anyone who was covered by the Railway Labor Act. Eventually they had to concede that they were more conservative on the issue than Senator Taft. They also argued with Martel at great length over a number of other issues, but it was probably one of the most interesting speeches and sessions that we had for the Young Republicans in those years. When he concluded he thanked me for inviting him and said that if I ever ran for office he would surely be supporting me in spite of the fact that he was a diehard Democrat. Martel also said that he appreciated the people that came there to heckle him. He added, however, that he "didn't appreciate it very much." It was one of the most interesting programs that we conducted and it eventually was widely covered by newspapers in Ann Arbor, and more particularly the *Ann Arbor News*, *The Detroit Free Press* and *The Detroit News*. It gave us some visibility, but it also stirred up some controversy.

After graduating from the College of Science and Arts at the University of Michigan I then went on to get my Masters Degree in public administration. Strangely enough, my Supervising Professor was Ferrell Heady. When I graduated from the program he told me, "If you work hard and apply yourself I'm sure that you're going to be a great success." Eleven years later he came into my office when I was governor and I told him that we were going to appoint him as president of the University of New Mexico. He looked up and grinned at me, saying, "and what else do you have to say?" My reply was "If you apply yourself and work hard I'm sure you're going to be a great success." I also appointed him to serve on the Governor's Reorganization Committee and he participated vigorously in that and helped me with some of the reorganization that I was able to bring about in state government when I was in office.

The War Years

I was a student at the University of Michigan from 1949 through 1953, and at the beginning of the Korean War. When I finally decided that I was going to enroll in law school I went to my local draft board in Jackson and said "I am going to enroll in law school." The board chairman and two board members were very active in the Republican Party in Jackson County. They said they could give me a deferment for the time that it would take to finish law school.

They also had a few suggestions for me. They said they were going to groom me for public office when I finished law school and were going to try to get me elected as the prosecuting attorney in Jackson County. Then they said they'd push me for the state Senate, and then after that, they would run me for Congress. I told them I appreciated their suggestions and asked if they had any others. They did."We think that you should go into service now and establish a good war record because that will certainly help you politically," they said. I thought about it and finally I said, "Okay, I'll tell you what. I will volunteer." And I did.

I went into the Army and was assigned to Camp Atterbury and went through 16 weeks of basic training in an infantry replacement unit. When we graduated they had a ceremony and figured we were all going to Korea. A sergeant got up and said, "Do you know what a replacement unit is in the Army?" I got up and said, "Yes. That means that everybody we replace has either been wounded or killed, and it should be an interesting adventure."

However, during the course of basic training the two top officers in our unit were killed and so I took over as a supply coordinator, communications coordinator and program coordinator despite the fact that I had not graduated from basic training.

One day while I was in the unit's office it started to rain. I was sitting by myself when all of a sudden in came the most important military person that I had ever seen in my life. It was a two-star general and he sat down and started talking to me about all kinds of things. It rained almost two hours. During that time we discussed politics, world events and everything else. Finally, the general said, "I can get you assigned to a public administration unit in Korea because I just returned from Korea, and if you'd like to do that I would be happy to work it out for you." I thought that that was very nice of him, but I said, "You know, I really have a deep interest in European affairs, and to be stationed in Germany would really be my first choice."

My company was then told that we were all being sent to Seattle, Washington, and from there to Korea. However, on the day of departure an individual came in and handed me a change of assignment and I was sent to Germany.

I spent 20 months in Germany and was stationed first in Stuttgart. Then I was transferred Karlsruhe for the rest of my two-year term in the service. Ultimately, I was assigned to the Finance Corp because of my public administration background. So that's what I did during my time in the service in Germany.

When I lived in Germany I managed to travel to a number of countries. I regularly went to Berlin where I would take the Ubahn into the Soviet Zone. It was a wonderful experience, and I did it a number of times. During that time I made my first trip to Ireland.

My trip to Ireland was particularly interesting because I took the train from Dublin to Limerick, and the chairman of the Dublin Branch of the Fianna Fail political party was in the same compartment and he asked me if I would like to meet Eamon de Valera, who then was the Taoiseach of Ireland. We went into the next compartment, and sure enough, there was Dev. He invited me to sit down and we proceeded to talk for the rest of the time that it took to get to Limerick where he was scheduled to give a campaign speech. After we arrived in Limerick he gave a speech in the public square, and lo and behold, he was interrupted by a heckler. The heckler was disturbed by the fact that he had sponsored a three-pence increase in a tax on beer, and in the middle of his speech he arose and shouted at de Valera, and shouted above the rainstorm that was taking place, and said to de Valera, "What about the pint? What about the pint?" de Valera then leaned forward and said, "Good god, man, can't you think of anything in this election that's more important than the pint?" The man replied with a great deal of volume and relishes, "Name it Dev, name it!"

After the speech we adjourned to a local hotel and de Velera asked me, "How do you think the elections are going?" I said, "Sir, I think you're going to lose." Sure enough he did lose. This was the first of some 22 trips that I would take to Ireland. When I met Dev again he was President of Ireland. He had invited me and four other governors to have dinner with him, which we did. He recalled the trip from Dublin to Limerick, and he said, "You were absolutely right. I was defeated by the pint."

While in Europe I received a very liberal education in the continent's politics, especially of Germany, Spain, Ireland, Great Britain and France. I became particularly interested in the politics of Germany and Ireland and I followed it very closely. For several years I subscribed to *Suddeutche Zeitung,* the *Irish Independent* and the *Irish Times.* My service in Germany was uneventful and I subsequently was mustered out of the Army and returned to civilian life.

After I returned from service I attended the University of Michigan Law School and took an accelerated course and graduated in two years rather than the standard three years. Likewise, there was a peculiar statute in effect in Michigan which said you could take the Bar exam at any time after you had entered law school if you had served overseas during wartime. I took the Bar exam in Michigan and passed it five months before I graduated. I was then admitted to the Bar in Michigan, but I decided that I would seek my fortune elsewhere.

Early New Mexico Years

A lot of people have asked why I came to New Mexico. In my early years here in politics I was accused of having come here because it was a small state and an easy place to get started in politics. In other words, I was accused of being a cynical opportunist. Those allegations weren't true, and they hurt. In fact, nothing could be further from the truth.

I had actually wanted to get out of Michigan. I'm not sure why. I guess I was just restless. And, during college I had spent my summers out West working for the U.S. Forest Service. So I knew about the West, and I liked it.

Even before I finished law school I started writing to law firms in New Mexico, Colorado and Oregon looking for a job. It was easy to eliminate Colorado and Oregon from the list because they required a year's residence before you could take their Bar exam. The way I saw it, that left New Mexico. And, I had gotten a job offer in Albuquerque.

I'm always asked what brought me to New Mexico. I answer: "A 1949 Chevrolet that was not in very good shape because you don't get much of a car for $200."

I drove straight through from Michigan, and when I got here I went to work for the law firm of McAtee, Toulouse and Marchiondo. I took the Bar exam a few months after I got here and passed it the first time. In fact, I got the second-highest score, and was the only out-of-state attorney who passed it at the time.

I worked with Jim Toulouse and the others at the firm for six months. Then I left and took a job with the District Attorney's office under District Attorney Paul Robinson. I spent four days a week working cases in Valencia and Sandoval counties, and one day a week working in Bernalillo County.

I was a political junkie in Michigan, even as a young boy, and that didn't stop when I came to New Mexico. I got involved with politics almost immediately. Somehow I got to know Governor Ed Mechem and U.S. Senator Dennis Chavez.

I thought I might be interested in getting real involved in politics, and so I called the Young Republicans. They told me the normal process was to apply for membership. Once it was accepted I could become active in the group. Well, I had been here less than three months when I called them. My membership was accepted and I attended the Young Republicans State Convention, which was held at the Hilton Hotel in Albuquerque.

Joe Pino, who was trying to get elected as the Young Republican National Committeeman, nominated me to be the organization's president. It was seconded by Tom Clear. I campaigned vigorously and was elected State Chairman of the Young Republicans.

I have to say, though, that the campaign really wasn't that vigorous. The convention's attendance was a grand total of seven! And, they weren't that well organized.

Neither was the state's Republican Party in general. It was disorganized and dispirited. So much so that the only Republicans elected to statewide office since 1934 were U.S. Senator Bronson Cutting and Ed Mechem, who wound up serving four two-year terms as governor. Mechem and Harry Robins, who had served as the state Republican Party chairman, were my political mentors. I got a good start because Robins and I worked together in the District Attorney's office.

I spent 16 months at the DA's office before I quit to open my own law office in the Sunshine Building in Downtown Albuquerque. I shared an office with Gilberto Espinoza, who was Senator Chavez's brother-in-law. I also officed with Irving Moore, who had served as chief clerk of the U.S. Senate's Public Works Committee. Senator Chavez got him that position. That gave me the opportunity to get to know Chavez, who was a Democrat. He often came to the office to see Espinoza. When he did, we would talk—mostly about politics. Oftentimes he took me on walking tours around Downtown. We would go from restaurant to restaurant, bar to bar, shoeshine place to shoeshine place and shake hands and talk to people. Those were great times, and Chavez passed on a lot of knowledge during those walks. I also got to know Senator Clinton P. Anderson.

I must have impressed Chavez during those walks because a few months after I had opened my office, he sat down with me and said, "Young man, I think you may have a future in politics. But I would suggest that you become a Democrat." He added that he had talked to "Clint" and that the two of them thought that I could be governor within 10 years. He said the state needed some new blood and that things looked promising for me.

I had great respect for Chavez, but I had to tell him, "Unfortunately, Senator, I'm a Republican and I want to remain one." He laughed and we shook hands.

I also got to know Henry Kiker, who went on to become chairman of the Bernalillo County Democratic Party. He was a progressive political force in the county, and in the state, and he also tried to get me to switch parties.

My political acquaintances began to broaden. I met Patrick Hurley, former Secretary of War and ambassador to China, Governor A.T. Hannett and former governor Richard "Picnic Dick" Dillon, who was a small-town merchant in Encino at the time. And I came to know Seven-Foot Pickett, a member of the state Corporation Commission; and former governor John Simms and a host of other political figures.

A favorite of mine was Manuel Lujan Sr., a former Santa Fe

mayor. He once ran for governor and lost. I wished he had won. He was an incredibly capable man. I also knew people like Joe Tondre, who also ran for governor and lost.

I developed a lucrative law practice and moved along trying cases. I'll never forget a divorce that I had in Grants. I represented the husband in the bitterly contested divorce. The couple had been married eight years and had six children. The wife's basis for the divorce was that she and her husband hadn't spoken to each other for the past six years. That's right. She hadn't spoken to him, nor he to her. When I cross-examined her and asked how it was possible to have had five children during the time when they hadn't been speaking to each other, she replied, "We weren't that mad at each other."

I've had a lot of interesting cases in my career, but I think that was the best.

Election to the State Legislature in 1962

In 1962 I decided to run for the New Mexico State Legislature. In many ways it was a big decision, and in many ways it wasn't.

I had only been in the state for five years, and I know to some it seemed like a brassy, ambitious decision. It was, but I had been interested in politics all my life, and what I had seen in New Mexico cried out for reform. And, I was a reformer. I didn't think that the citizens of this state deserved the corruption and incompetence they had gotten and were getting. I knew my decision to run would be both criticized and welcomed.

Even though I was a relative newcomer, I had a lot going for me. I had gotten a lot of publicity in the year before the election by reason that I was an assistant district attorney, not only in Bernalillo and Sandoval counties, but also in Valencia County, which included Grants, which was home to the state's uranium industry.

I was assigned to Grants part time, and went there two to three days a week. I handled criminal matters as well as inquests in death cases. At the time, Valencia County extended all the way to the Arizona state line, so it was an incredibly large county.

Almost 8,000 people were involved in the uranium industry in Grants at the time. Unfortunately, the uranium companies didn't care that much about their employees' safety, and for a long time they averaged one fatal accident a month. I held inquests into some of those deaths and became very knowledgeable about uranium mining.

The mine safety issue got a lot of publicity around the state, especially in the *Albuquerque Journal* and the *Albuquerque Tribune*. I wound up fighting Governor John Burroughs over the issue. Ultimately, the state held a conference on mine safety. It became a political football. The uranium industry was vital to the state's economy, not to mention the national defense, as we were in the midst of the Cold War with the Soviet Union, and uranium was necessary to produce atom and hydrogen bombs. I went to the convention as a guest. I wasn't permitted to take part or to speak.

I had also gotten a lot of publicity because of the reapportionment lawsuit I filed in 1962. At that time there were no legislative districts. Legislators were elected from counties at-large. In Bernalillo County, that meant that nine Democrats were elected to the House, and one Democrat to the Senate. It also meant that all of the Democrats came from one neighborhood in Albuquerque, and all were Anglo. I had spent a lot of time preparing the lawsuit, and again, it gave me an advantage, especially in the area of free publicity, because the Democrats just sat by and watched me do it.

It was obviously an impossible situation for me, being that Bernalillo County voted heavily Democratic, but I decided what the hell, I'd give it a shot.

The reapportionment lawsuit I filed was one of the first of its kind in the country. It came after the U.S. Supreme Court ruled in the case of *Baker vs. Carr* that the legislatures of every state had to be districted on the basis of population and that they had to be divided countywide into districts. The old moiety system was abolished, and the court said that one-man, one-vote was the rule.

I battled the legislature, but the first reapportionment law permitted counties to maintain the old moiety system, which permitted counties to have at least one state representative and to have representatives elected at-large. It also gave each county one state senator. That's what I faced when I decided to run for the legislature as a state representative.

When I first decided to run I went and talked to the leaders of the Republican Party. They said they welcomed my candidacy, but added that I would have to run as part of a slate of candidates. I asked if they would help me with money for the campaign. They said, "no," because they were putting all their resources into the governor's and a few other races and that they hadn't set aside money for legislative races.

I didn't like the sound of that and decided that I'd run on my own rather than let them slate me, and so I decided to run against state Representative Jim Rutherford. I liked Jim, but I figured he was a good opponent because he was the most conservative of all legislators who were seeking re-election. I figured that by running against him I'd be able to pick up some Democratic votes.

We apparently worked a little too hard in the primary because Rutherford lost the Democratic primary to Henry Rodriguez, a young school teacher and a very aggressive candidate. I figured it was going to be hard to beat Henry because the Democratic Party was very well organized and the Republicans weren't going to put any money into the race. So I set out to win the election by myself—on my lonesome.

At the time I was officing in the Sunshine Building on Central Avenue in Downtown Albuquerque. My office mates were Irving Moore and Gilberto Espinoza. Moore was a former chief clerk of the U.S. Senate's Committee of Public Works. It was a patronage job he got from Senator Dennis Chavez. Espinoza was Chavez's brother-in-law.

Eventually, I also shared the office with Larry Tapia, who succeeded Moore as the chief clerk of the Public Works Committee. Thus, it turned out that I was officing with three people who were closely tied to Senator Chavez. And, I often handled cases with Henry Kiker, who eventually became a powerhouse in the Democratic Party, and who at the time was the Democratic Party chairman for Bernalillo County. He was generally associated with the Democratic Party's reform wing, and so it made an interesting situation for me.

Senator Chavez came by the office with great regularity and we would sit and talk for hours. He kept insisting that I would move on to bigger and better things if only I would switch parties and become a Democrat. Again and again he suggested I switch, and again and again I told him that I had no intention of doing so, certainly not at that point in my life.

I've always wondered, though, what would have happened if I had switched and become a Democrat. It was partially a tactical decision on my part to remain a Republican. The Democratic Party was loaded with talent, while the Republican Party had very little, with the exception of a couple of people. It appeared to me that the Republicans were in an almost hopeless situation when it came to elections, but I decided to give it a try anyway.

When I finally got around to announcing for the primary I talked with Senator Chavez about the situation. The Republicans, of course, weren't going to help me because they were all tied up with the governor's race, and they figured that a Republican running for the legislature in Bernalillo County was a hopeless cause. I thought, 'Well, okay. If that's the way they feel, I'll find help elsewhere."

And I did. I told Chavez that I really needed his help. He said he would do everything possible to get me elected. And he did. Just before the election they had a large Democratic rally in Albuquerque's old Civic Auditorium. Chavez was the master of ceremonies. He started reading off the list of endorsed candidates. He read a long string of Democrats. Then when he got to my race he said, "David Cargo." Everybody looked up and wondered what was going on. Finally, Henry Kiker took the microphone and said that Henry Rodriguez was the candidate and that I was running as a Republican. It didn't hurt too much that he did it. After all, a whole convention of Democrats knew that Senator Chavez was supporting me.

One afternoon about six weeks before the election Senator Chavez came to the office and asked how I was doing. I told him that I needed some real help—some professional help—and that I wasn't sure I would get any from the Republicans. He said, "Don't worry about it. We will go and see Luis Madrid and Cecil Garcia." They owned the Casanova Bar, which was just across the street from the Sunshine Building. We walked over and saw them and Chavez told them that I needed help with the campaign. They said they would buy $50 worth of campaign buttons.

My first real contribution came from General Patrick J. Hurley, the former Secretary of War who had also been Chief of Staff of the nation's armed forces. He had come to New Mexico a number of years before and had run for the U.S. Senate a couple of times. He first ran against Chavez, and then against Senator Anderson. He lost both times, of course, but he sent me $25, which I thought was absolutely great and incredible. I had my first and second contributions, and so I figured my campaign was off and running!

After meeting with Madrid and Garcia, Chavez and I went over to the Alvarado Hotel, which was a well known Fred Harvey Hotel and a real Albuquerque landmark. He had gathered some of his key campaign people, including Alonzo Gonzalez, Charlie Davis, his chief of staff; Steve Quintana; Lecho Martinez, who pretty much controlled Martineztown; and Manuel Sanchez, who was known as "Mr. Democrat" and who had served as a precinct chairman for 60 years.

Some others who were there included Henry Gabaldon, who

later went on to become a Bernalillo County commissioner from the North Valley. We met in a private side room and Chavez told them that he wanted them to go out and work for me right away. He started giving orders in all directions, and finally said, "From now on, I want Steve Quintana to be with you right through election day."

Quintana not only remained with me through election day, but for the rest of his life. He was a political animal and we used to see each other almost every day. Steve knew everybody and he knew exactly how to run a campaign, and so we got started in grand style.

Steve said that we needed to immediately start contacting key people in the valley, and so I put my old 1949 Chevy into action. The car couldn't have been worth more than $100, and, guess what, it ran that way! It was ragtag to say the least. One seat kept flopping over until finally Steve got some bolts and we bolted the seat down and drove off and started campaigning.

Then I set out to get money. In the end, we collected a grand total of $185, which was all the financing I had for a countywide race. Needless to say, I didn't buy any votes in that election, or any other election for that matter. People used to kid me, saying that I was the only candidate who came out of San Miguel County with more money than I went in with. I wasn't a big spender anyway, and so it worked out.

A number of issues came up in the primary. One was whether to increase the state's gross receipts tax. Governor Ed Mechem, who was running for re-election, had casually said that he wanted to increase the gross receipts tax by one percent. That surprised everyone and caught me off guard. Here's how it happened:

At the time *The Albuquerque Tribune*, Albuquerque's afternoon newspaper, had a substantial circulation, with much of it concentrated in the valley. Tony de Cola was *The Trib*'s political reporter. Actually, he was the top political reporter, and *The Trib* was way ahead of everyone else when it came to political coverage. He called me one day at five in the morning—before Mechem's announcement—and asked if I favored increasing the gross receipts tax. I said I didn't.

In doing so I had reached back into my background as a public administrator and proceed to give him the reasons why. I had gotten a Master's Degree in Public Administration from the University of Michigan, which was probably the second best school for public administration in the United States. No one in the press had ever really mentioned my degree or my expertise in public administration. I really had a good background in government.

In any event, Tony wanted to know what should be done about state government, and he thought that maybe a tax increase wasn't necessary. I told him that until very recently, state government didn't even have a formal budget. That's true. The New Mexico Taxpayer's Association, which was a private organization, used to make an estimate as to what the state's income would be in any given year. Then it would come up with an estimate as to how much the state could spend. It was a crazy and unacceptable situation.

In his last term, Mechem tried to get a formal budgeting process, but it wasn't that professional because he had started from scratch. Not only that, but I thought the state needed a merit system for employees because all state workers were political hires, and whenever there was a change in administrations, or when one faction of the Democratic Party prevailed over another, everybody in every department and institution was fired. The old Bureau of Revenue used to fire every single employee and hire all new ones. That was no way to run a government.

At the State Hospital in Las Vegas, for instance, everyone from the janitors to the superintendent would be fired. Not only that, but the state payroll, when the Democrats were in control, was loaded with county chairmen who never showed up for work and who got their paychecks in the mail because they didn't want to be bothered with picking them up. During Jack Campbell's administration, more than half of the Democratic county chairmen in the state were on the state payroll.

I told Tony that day that the entire state government needed to be reorganized, and I told him how I would do it. Tony was eager to hear it because it squared with what he believed. He was from Cleveland, Ohio, and was used to a different kind of politics and government. Likewise, I told him about the state of Michigan where a civil service program had been put in place in the 1930s, with the exception of the state highway department.

The next day Tony eagerly reported what I had told him, and the next day, Mechem announced out of the blue that he was going to ask for a one percent increase in the gross receipts tax. Naturally, that put me at odds with Mechem on that issue. It was entirely inadvertent. I really hadn't intended to take issue with him on it. I stuck to my guns, though, because I thought state government needed to be reorganized and improved, and I thought I could help accomplish it.

Almost immediately after I announced my position on the tax increase other Republican candidates began saying that they too favored a tax increase. The lone exception was Larry Prentice, who was my ideological soul mate and who, incidentally, was the only other Republican to get elected to the legislature that year from Bernalillo County.

I also campaigned heavily in the valley and before labor groups. I went to every meeting that was held on any subject anywhere and anytime, and I got some interesting support. Conservation and senior citizen groups supported me. I got endorsements from the New Mexico Federation of Labor and from the Railway Brotherhoods. At the time, the Railway Brotherhoods were very active in the state, and they had a lot of members. In addition, the Grass Root Democrats, a group of liberal Democrats, split over my race. Some supported me, and some didn't, but apparently enough of them supported me in the Northeast Heights, and that made a difference.

It was a vigorous campaign all the way around, and House Speaker Jack Campbell narrowly defeated Mechem for the governor's job. In short, the Republicans generally went down to defeat. They got trounced, not only in Bernalillo County, but statewide as well. That election, exactly four Republicans were elected to the state Senate, and we ended up with only 11 Republicans in the House. It was a lopsided and embarrassing result.

Nobody had really expected me to win, and it was only when the election returns started coming in that it became clear that I was going to win. In the valley I ran almost 2,000 votes ahead of the ticket, and I did even better in the Heights. Prentice wound up winning by 500 votes, and was the only Republican besides me to win in Bernalillo County.

I ran 5,000 votes ahead of the ticket, and, to everyone's surprise, I was elected. And it was a surprise. During a meeting after the election, Republican leaders accused me of conspiring with everyone to win. I admitted that I had indeed campaigned for Democratic votes. I had to. If I hadn't, I would not have won.

It was interesting. Senator Chavez used to slate candidates for the general elections. Normally, he slated only Democrats in the primaries and endorsed only Democrats in the general elections. I had gone to his Senate office two weeks before the election, where there was a long line of candidates waiting to see him. He came out and looked at all of them and said, "It's going to be a while and I will catch up with you." Then he looked at me and said, "You don't have to wait around because you already have my support."

I have no doubt that he was more than just a little helpful and that I picked up a number of votes because of his support. I did not conspire with him, and I didn't promise anything other than indicating where I stood on the issues. It happened that we agreed on most of them. Anyway, that was my second election to public office. I had moved from Constable to State representative, and I prepared to sally forth and go to Santa Fe.

The election had gotten me a lot more publicity and limelight, especially in view of the fact that many of the Republicans who were elected either didn't have a newspaper in their district, or at most they had one with a very small circulation—except, for course for Larry Prentice and me. Most of the other Republicans didn't even have a TV station in their district. So Prentice and I had a kind of monopoly when it came to getting press.

Anyway, I went on to Santa Fe.

Old Age Lien and Relative Responsibility Laws

When John Simms was elected governor in the mid-1950s he urged the legislature to pass two Old Age Lien and Relative Responsibility provisions that were included in a welfare bill. These two provisions created a lightning rod in politics because they meant that any person who received any kind of welfare assistance, including medical services, was subject to having a lien placed against any property they owned.

It meant that in northern New Mexico in places like Rio Arriba County, more than half the people were subject to having a lien placed on their property because they were getting welfare of some kind. The other important factor was that most of the old Spanish families in that country, of course, lived in houses which they inherited, or on land they had inherited, and therefore it meant that if the liens were ever foreclosed on, they would lose their homes and their property.

Likewise, the Relative Responsibility aspect of the law was equally punitive in that if the parents received any kind of welfare assistance, then a son or daughter who, say, left the state 20 years earlier and went to California to work and hadn't lived in New Mexico since leaving, were subject to a requirement that they compensate the state for any welfare assistance their parents may have received.

It was ridiculous and shameful. The two laws punished the people who were least able to afford it, and they caused an immediate political reaction. When Simms ran for re-election, he was defeated by former governor Ed Mechem, who based his campaign almost entirely on getting rid of those two provisions.

Those provisions stayed in place until long after Simms had left office. There was a lot of support for them from Democrats in the state legislature when I became governor. East Side Democrats were particularly strong in arguing that the provisions remain in effect and that they be enforced.

Oddly enough, the Republicans at the time had very little support on the state's East Side and followed Mechem's lead in opposing the laws. They got nowhere because Democrats controlled everything.

The provisions were finally repealed in the mid-1960s.

A Funny Story

When I first went to the legislature, the Democrats held a convention in the Capitol in Santa Fe that lasted until five in the morning. Many of the delegates had freely imbibed or indulged in the use of alcoholic beverages. Consequently, when the legislature convened three hours after the convention had adjourned, some of the lawmakers were not in the best of shape.

I was in the men's room, which was adjacent to the House chambers in the old Capitol building when a legislator whom I will not name entered. He looked around and went into one of the stalls. The janitors hadn't had an opportunity to clean up the restroom because most of them had attended the convention, and so the restroom was in complete disarray.

The legislator settled into the stall, and Will Harrison, a well-known newspaper columnist, and I were washing our hands and talking. Suddenly, out of the stall came a voice that was a little unsteady in nature. It inquired as to whether there was any toilet paper in the other stalls. We looked in the other stalls and said there wasn't.

The legislator then asked if there were any paper towels around. Again we looked around and responded that there weren't any.

He then said that he would appreciate it if we could loan him our handkerchiefs. We said that we thought we probably wouldn't do that either. Then he asked if we had any paper in our pockets that he could use. We looked in our pockets, and sure enough, we answered that we had none.

There was a long pause, and then the gentleman asked:
"Does anybody have change for a twenty?"
We didn't, and I'm not sure how he managed.

It was rather amusing. Certainly the legislator was somewhat the worse for wear, and he would have been in far better shape if the janitorial staff had been able to spruce up the bathroom after the convention.

Senator Dennis Chavez Died

Senator Dennis Chavez died in November, 1962, just after he was re-elected to his fourth term. In that year's general election, New Mexico House Speaker Jack Campbell defeated incumbent Ed Mechem for the governor's job. It was ironic in that Chavez died while a Republican—Mechem—held the governor's office. Under New Mexico law, governors get to fill vacancies in the U.S. Senate. There was no provision for a special election.

In the legislature, Representative Mack Easley, who was the Speaker of the House, had introduced a bill that would have provided for a special, statewide election to fill Senate vacancies. Fabian Chavez, who was then a state senator, worked to get the bill defeated. Joe Montoya's faction in the Democratic Party never forgave Chavez for that because it would have meant that Montoya might have gone to the Senate in such a special election.

I went to Chavez's funeral as a newly-elected state representative from Bernalillo County. I sat next to then-U.S. Senator Lyndon Johnson of Texas, who had led a delegation of senators to the funeral. During the service Johnson leaned over and asked me, "Who do you think will be elected to the Senate in the special election?"

I replied "no one" because the appointment was to be made by the governor, and Mechem was the governor until governor-elect Jack Campbell was sworn in. Therefore, he would make the appointment. Johnson said he didn't think that was the case.

But Joe Montoya had been sure, and he had wanted special election legislation passed, and he never forgot that it had gone down largely because of Chavez's efforts.

The vacancy was filled. Here's what happened:

Mechem resigned as governor and Lieutenant Governor Tom Bolack became governor. Bolack then appointed Mechem to the Senate where he served until the 1964 election.

Reapportionment

In a sense, reapportionment created the Republican Party in New Mexico. I thought at the time that the reapportionment process would also modernize the party. Unfortunately, the long-term effect of reapportionment has not been nearly as profound as I thought it would be. After reapportionment the Republican Party shifted its focus from the urban areas to the eastern portion of the state. As a result, Republicans have steadily been losing votes in the northern part of the state; the party is now almost non-existent north of Santa Fe. With the exception of San Juan County, the leadership of the party has become increasingly conservative. The most dramatic shift came in 1964 when the Republican Party in New Mexico strongly supported Senator Barry Goldwater for the nomination only to see him lose in an absolute electoral disaster in the general election against Lyndon Johnson. It should also be noted that the urban areas, particularly in Santa Fe County, Bernalillo County, Doña Ana County and in Taos County, have become even more heavily Democratic than they were immediately after reapportionment and after I left office. In fact, there are very few modern urban Republicans left. Apparently they would rather lose than accommodate to political conditions.

In a subsequent federal lawsuit involving the state Senate, I was retained to represent many Hispanic members of the legislature and some Republicans. I represented them in the federal lawsuit. As a result of the suit New Mexico was reapportioned not only for the House, but the Senate as well. There were several groups that raised money to pay the fees of the attorneys that filed the original senate suit. I was never paid by anyone for the legal work that I did. I guess that's just way things are. I filed my suit out of principle, and the attorneys that continued with the case were amply paid.

The legislature tried to put all of its resources behind an effort to defeat any reapportionment at all. They tried to fund the attorney general's office very generously to conduct the battle and they made special appropriations of $25,000 as attorneys' fees to be paid outside counsel. This was inserted in the appropriations bill, and of course, when it came before the legislature in the 1963 session printed copies of the appropriation bill were not distributed to the members and we were not advised as to what was in it. It was only when Representative John Mershon, a fiscal conservative, warned me about the appropriation. In any event, I protested and moved to strike it from the appropriations bill.

The New Mexico Legislative Council Service did a phenomenal amount of work on reapportionment and tried to do everything that they could to thwart my efforts in court. They intervened in the legislature and became active participants on behalf of Boston Witt and the attorney general's office.

The case of *Cargo vs. Campbell* was filed exactly six months and 26 days after the United States Supreme Court decided the case of *Baker vs. Carr*. It took me that long to prepare as it was complicated and I wanted to make sure that I had everything put together properly. I had been preparing for the case prior to the decision of the Supreme Court, but frankly I wasn't too sure that the courts in New Mexico would go along with me until the decision in *Baker vs. Carr*.

After I filed, the attorney general disqualified all of the First Judicial District judges. It would be up to the state Supreme Court to select a replacement. They selected Judge Caswell Neal because he was a Republican, and because his son Fincher Neal was a leader in the state senate. Interestingly enough, the House reapportionment allowed many new members to be elected. Among those newly elected members was Roberto Mondragon, who later became lieutenant governor, and David Norvell, who became attorney general. In addition, my good friend Walter Martinez from Grants was elected at that point; he would later become long-term speaker in the

House of Representatives. David Salman was elected from Union and Mora counties and he was eventually named as majority leader of the House. Had it not been for a very serious automobile accident I think that David Salman would eventually have been elected governor. Salman is a man of great integrity and intelligence; we remain friends to this day.

In my petition to the district court I sought relief for discrimination by asking for reapportionment under the terms of the 1955 plan using population as shown by the 1960 Census.

The court did not have enough time to act on the petition in a definitive matter prior to the convening of the 1963 regular session of the legislature. The legislature convened at noon on Tuesday, January 8, 1963. There were a number of other issues that were pending before the legislature, mainly because in his campaign for governor, Jack Campbell had indicated that he would not require any tax increases in order to balance the budget, and likewise that property taxes would not have to be reformed. Unfortunately, this was not the case. The legislature had to make up a substantial budget deficit during the 60-day session. Governor Campbell—although he took official notice of the pending suit along with recent trends in the federal courts—commented in a rather casual way to the problem of reapportionment. Frankly, he seemed more concerned with tax matters than he was in reapportionment. He started out his address to the joint session:

"It is my personal belief that the system in New Mexico, which is modeled after the federal system, takes the best approach to fair representation, providing the membership of the House of Representatives is in relation to population, and each county in the state regardless of its population has one member of the Senate. I believe that the people of the rapidly growing urban areas are entitled to representation in the House of Representatives commensurate with the population of these areas. I believe we can arrive at a solution to this problem by legislative actions rather than by a decision of the courts. As a lawyer, I, of course, have the greatest respect for the judges, but as governor, I am convinced that you as legislators are much better equipped to resolve this problem than are the courts."

It was obvious that he had not read the current and developing cases on reapportionment in the United States Supreme Court. The trend was toward a rule of "one man one vote." You couldn't bifurcate the problem by saying that the Senate should be based on geography and the House should be based somewhat on population. He was way off base when he said that each county should have one member in the state Senate. This did not follow decisions in reapportionment laws that were current at the time he spoke. Campbell did recognize that the House of Representatives would have to be based on population, although he did not attack the problem of having a moiety system.

I was public in voicing my doubts about his ideas. The *Albuquerque Journal* in an editorial on Saturday, December 8, 1962, following the election stated, "There will be wailing from the rural areas of New Mexico if reapportionment of the House gives Bernalillo County more than double its representation."

Then Senator Ed V. Mead of Bernalillo County introduced the joint resolution number eight which essentially provided for 75-member House composed of at least one member elected from each county. The remaining 40 members of the House were to be distributed among the counties by a method of equal proportions. Reapportioning wouldn't be made mandatory after each census and Bernalillo County was to be geographically districted. Districting in all other counties was prohibited and this was very much in accord with the position of the leadership of the state Senate, including Senators R. C. Morgan and Fabian Chavez. SJR number eight was referred to the Senate Rules Committee where it would remain until the 44th legislative day. On that day it was reported out, but with a recommendation of "Do not pass."

Counties entitled to more than one representative would be geographically divided, but districting was not included in the bill.

Those counties which had a weighted roll call vote were set forth as follows:

Catron: .20	Hidalgo: .40	Sierra: .50
DeBaca: .20	Lincoln: .50	Socorro: .70
Guadalupe: .40	Luna: .70	Torrance: .50
Harding: .10	Mora: .40	Union: .40

Other counties would be entitled to a full vote and the following number of representatives:

Bernalillo: 18	Lea: 4	Sandoval: 1
Chaves: 4	Los Alamos: 1	San Juan: 4
Colfax: 1	McKinley: 3	San Miguel: 2
Curry: 3	Otero: 3	Santa Fe: 3
Doña Ana: 4	Quay: 1	Taos: 1
Eddy: 4	Rio Arriba: 2	Valencia: 3
Grant: 4	Roosevelt: 1	

The committee substitute removed the 75 member limitation from the original proposal and provided instead that following each federal census "the legislature may, by statute, reapportion among the various counties the number of members of the House of Representatives to be elected from each county; provided that each county shall be entitled to elect at least one member of the House of Representatives, and that no member of the House of Representatives shall represent, or be elected by the voters of more than one county."

The committee substitute was obviously unconstitutional in that it continued a moiety system and provided for an election scheme that was not acceptable either to either Judge Neal or the United States Supreme Court. It also adopted Mead's proposal for geographic districting in Bernalillo County alone and that was clearly unconstitutional. Obviously the committee substitute was not relevant to the problem and it was again referred to the rules committee where it died on the 60th legislative day.

Judge Neal had obviously done his homework. I began to fully appreciate that he was a competent and credible judge. He was a legal scholar. As he told me during a court break, "I'm a judge legislating from the bench carrying out the demands of the constitution." He said, "This indeed is constitutional work and I'm going to do it." I think that that is exactly what he had intended to do and I had great admiration for him as a judge and as an attorney. However after he went through an analysis of *Baker vs. Carr* and all the other federal decisions that had been handed down he then recognized current national trends, saying:

"While I realize that the case of *Baker vs. Carr* and the decisions which follow it are the supreme law of the land, at this time, and realize that it is my duty and obligation as a judge to accept these decisions and to enforce them, I cannot do so, without expressing my own personal opinion, that these decisions are purely judicial legislation of a type which in recent years have invaded the rights of the states and the people thereof, to the extent that unless the power of the Supreme Court is in some manner curbed, as the power of the executive and legislative branches of the federal government is curbed, by the constitution, a complex centralization of all power in the federal government may come to pass and the states will be but ponds in the structure of the nation."

He then said that he had to turn from this "depressing subject to the distasteful" task of holding the existing apportionment of the House to be grossly disproportionate to population and without rational basis or justification in law. "In fact," he said, "it is invidiously discriminatory against the plaintiffs and others similarly situated and violates the 14th Amendment of the federal constitution."

The judge then proceeded to strike down unconstitutional conditions which gave each county at least one state representative. He said that this was in disregard of the population of the various counties and then he also struck down the provision that prohibited multi-county or shoestring districts and prohibited geographical districting within a district. He indicated flat out that he agreed with my contention that it was "one man one vote, one vote one man." He then declared that as plaintiff I was entitled to appropriate equitable relief both individually and as a class and that I should be given relief that would be in accordance with the provisions of the 14th amendment of the federal constitution.

However, Neal did not agree with my request that the court order the governor to convene a special session of the legislature for the purposes of reapportionment by enactment of the proposed constitutional amendment. I was not completely sold on this as a solution, and indicated to the court that I did not believe that a constitutional amendment was necessary because of the supremacy clause in both the state and the federal constitutions. I did not see that there was any real problem. However, the court did state:

"I do not feel that this court has the right or power to direct the chief executive officer of the state to call such a special session. The governor within the last few days has expressed his opinion that the House of Representatives should be reapportioned and I am confident he will take the necessary action in view of the conclusions expressed in this memorandum."

Judge Neal also indicated that it was in the inherent powers of the legislature to reapportion itself. To demonstrate, he suggested that the legislature approach the problem of the reapportionment by dividing the total membership of the House into the total population of the state as shown in the 1960 census to obtain a ratio of representation for each district. Thus he wanted to divide the population figure of 951,023 by 66. This would give each representative a district of 14,409 people.

Then he gave the legislature and the governor until the first day of November, 1963, as a deadline to act. He stressed that he hoped that "You will prepare and enact into law a reapportionment statute acceptable under the law and along the guidelines" laid out in his memorandum. He then added rather forcefully that if the legislature was inclined to shrink from this task that the court would assume responsibility for reapportionment by judicial decree.

At this point the defendants and their counsel threw in the towel. They indicated that they would comply with the court's mandate. At long last, Senator Fabian Chavez of Santa Fe County, majority floor leader, said "It is the legislature's duty to reapportion." Representative Bruce King of Santa Fe County, who was also Speaker of the House, agreed that it was the legislature's responsibility. "It is going to be an awkward position. In the end there are many members from small counties who would be voting themselves out. I think that the legislature should try to solve the problem, but I'd almost rather see the judge work on it if he has the power."

After the court's memorandum on Wednesday, September 4, 1963, Governor Jack Campbell held a meeting in his office with 13 legislative leaders for approximately two hours and 45 minutes. The legislators asked for more time in which to prepare for the special session. At that point the governor telephoned Judge Neal asking if the court could extend the deadline to December 1st. The judge agreed to this and said that the legislature had the authority to increase the size of the House in the upcoming session. I found it interesting that Governor Campbell, as an attorney, saw fit to proceed "ex parte." In other words, he approached the judge without doing it in a formal session or without my being present. I was the plaintiff in the case and also the attorney and I should have been present whenever anyone approached the court with any request on this matter.

Around the same day the court sent a letter of transmittal to the First Assistant Attorney General Boston Witt which also "disabused the legislature of the fantasy that it could delegate responsibility districting to any board or commission." The judge stated that legislative reapportionment would be a legislative function and it could not be delegated.

The reference to the delegation of responsibility was in response to a press release by Representative Simon Bustamante of

San Miguel County. Bustamante wanted the legislature to turn over the responsibility of districting to the boards of county commissioners. This was totally unacceptable to me because Senator Penrod Toles of Chavez County had already stated publicly that he was not in favor of any of districting in Chavez County that would provide for a district that was essentially Hispanic and most probably would elect a Hispanic.

Bernalillo County was the most underrepresented county having a deviation of 102.18 percent from the norm of 14,409. Harding County was the most overrepresented county because it had a -86.99% deviation from the norm. In other words, one representative from the Harding County was worth almost 16 representatives in Bernalillo County, or a Harding County representative had 15.54 times more power in his vote than did any of the nine Bernalillo County representatives.

The legislature discussed the possibility of using registered voters as a basis for apportionment. This was not a workable solution because many counties simply did not periodically purge registration lists. Therefore those records would be unreliable indicators of actual numbers of registered voters in these counties. As a matter of fact, in some counties the list showed more registered voters than there were persons eligible to vote in the entire county. On some occasions they cast more votes than there were people in the county because it was traditional in some areas for people to move out of the county and stay registered there and then return on election day to visit family and to vote.

Another problem involved the federal census and that they didn't break down the counties properly by population. This problem was eventually resolved.

Another approach was to manipulate populations so as to keep as many incumbents in office as possible. The current legislators wanted to stick around in their positions of power even if it meant diminished power for voters. They simply wanted to influence people, and that was what they attempted to do.

On the Sunday before the special session they met in the House chambers. They were not able to resolve anything in this preliminary session. The idea was to listen to the explanations of the method of equal proportions and other approaches. However, when they finally couldn't agree on exactly how they were going to proceed, Representative Fred Boone of Roosevelt County moved that a 15-man committee be appointed by the speaker to hear apportionment bills in the House. This was all done in a closed partisan session and the wheels were greased, but it didn't work out quite the way they wanted it.

The following day, on motion of majority floor leader Austin Roberts, speaker Bruce King was directed to appoint a 15-member select committee to be known as the "Special Reapportionment Committee." The committee would serve during the special session to hear all legislation introduced pertaining to apportionment. Both parties were to be represented on the special committee, so Speaker King appointed Representative Mayo T. Boucher, a Belen attorney, as chairman, and representatives Bobby Mayfield, (D) Mesilla Park; Ray Atchison, (R) Aztec; Kenneth Black, (R) Arrey; Lawrence Prentice, (R) Albuquerque; Simon Bustamante, (D) Las Vegas; Alex Martinez, (D) Santa Fe; Jeff Good, (D) Fort Sumner; Matias Chacon, (D) Espanola; and Fred Boone, (D) Portales, as committee members.

Only three Republicans were appointed to the committee, and of course, I was not one of them. I was obviously the best informed member of the House when it came to understanding the legal cases and problems facing reapportionment. Still, the process was set in motion. Unfortunately, the only thing that resulted was chaos, confusion and dodging of the issues. Likewise, they didn't know exactly how the judge was going to deal with their final product.

It was at this point the goofiest of all proposals came forth and that was a weighted vote. This made absolutely no sense. It was finally agreed that they would pass it. Senator Pim Carr indicated that even if he and Senator Gordon Melody couldn't get the Senate to go along with the leading bill, the House would pass whatever they wanted. The bill distributed voting in a very peculiar way; districting was not included, but weighted voting was.

The plan presented was as follows:

Counties entitled to more than one representative would be geographically divided, but districting was not included in the bill. Those counties which had a weighted roll call vote, as mentioned earlier, were set forth as follows:

Catron: .20	Hidalgo: .40	Sierra: .50
DeBaca: .20	Lincoln: .50	Socorro: .70
Guadalupe: .40	Luna: .70	Torrance: .50
Harding: .10	Mora: .40	Union: .40

Other counties would be entitled to a full vote and the following number of representatives:

Bernalillo: 18	Lea: 4	Sandoval: 1
Chaves: 4	Los Alamos: 1	San Juan: 4
Colfax: 1	McKinley: 3	San Miguel: 2
Curry: 3	Otero: 3	Santa Fe: 3
Doña Ana: 4	Quay: 1	Taos: 1
Eddy: 4	Rio Arriba: 2	Valencia: 3
Grant: 4	Roosevelt: 1	

Opposition to the proposal developed rather quickly in that Representative Finis Heidel of Lovington and Senator Tibo Chavez argued against the constitutionality of a weighted provision. Heidel noted "at least 12 sections which referred to votes by elected members" and doubted that this could be construed to mean weighted voters or weighted votes. Others, including Representative Jerry Brasher, indicated that this was perfectly easy to correct. Representative Joe Parsons from Catron County summarized it when he said he would agree with fractional votes on a proportionate population basis and that his main concern was to maintain physical representation for all areas.

The only other reapportionment act in the Senate during that session concerned a proposal asking Congress to call a constitutional convention for the purpose of proposing an amendment to the federal constitution to restrict judicial powers of the United States in matters of reapportionment and representation in state legislatures. This proposal was introduced by Senators Ike Smalley and R. C. Morgan, along with five other proposed amendments to the constitution which were very disturbing from the point of view of constitutional law. They were in effect taking the antiquated position that states could interfere with the supremacy of federal law merely by objecting to the action. The constitutional amendments came before the House Judiciary Committee and the Elections Committee for hearings. Representative Terry Boucher was the chair of the joint hearing and we heard from a variety of senators. The most adamant was Senator Smalley. I carried on a prolonged exchange with Senators Smalley and Morgan on the issues of constitutional law. I think that maybe my law professors at the University of Michigan had done a good job, because I prevailed in the exchanges, and was convincing enough that the measures all failed in committee and in the House.

In the House of Representatives on the first day of the session House Bill 20 was introduced by Representative Willis A. Smith, an Albuquerque Democrat. I introduced House Bill 22 myself.

On the 19th legislative day I introduced HJR2 which required all counties to be geographically districted, or counties based on votes cast for governor in the last preceding general election. This proposal was immediately postponed indefinitely and proceeded no further.

On the 34th day I introduced five more bills to reapportion the House of Representatives, and on the 38th day of the session all of those bills were reported out of committee with a "Do not pass" recommendation. That committee recommendation was upheld by voice vote, which upset me a bit. I referred to the rules of procedure and demanded a roll call vote. However, Bruce King in his inevitable way thought he would try and see how that went. I thought that the rule required he have a recorded vote, but the voice vote proceeded anyway. Again I lost in the voice vote.

Then House Bill 20 was also killed on the 52nd day by a 34 to 18 adoption of the committee's "Do not pass" recommendation. The comment on the floor was that "there's some sort of lamentation from Albuquerque." By the adjournment of the 1963 legislature there was no act of reapportionment, which they assumed would create little concern except in the district court. How wrong they were.

On July 1, 1963, Judge Neal held a pre-trial conference in Santa Fe during which he granted a motion to strike the state auditor as a defendant and to strike reference to the Organic Act of 1850 "as being irrelevant since the suit was based on constitutional grounds." I think that this was an error in that the Organic Act became a part of the constitution. The judge was wrong on that particular point. The court also permitted a substitution of current state officials for the original set of defendants. I was then permitted to amend my petition to ask that reapportionment be based on the method of equal proportion according to the 1960 census.

Judge Neal then set a court date of August 26, 1963. He added that if he ruled in favor of my reapportionment suit he would set a time by which a special session of the legislature on reapportionment must be called. Further, he said, "In my opinion if I found for the plaintiffs, I would direct the essential rules of which the legislature must follow to come up with legislation, which would meet the constitutional requirements."

He also directed the attorneys to stipulate to as many facts as possible. This included the census of the state by precincts and counties from 1940, 1950 and 1960. He noted that the amount of taxes paid by each county might be a consideration for determination of reapportionment. He also referred to giving consideration to the formation of counties since statehood in their stipulation. I had no idea where he was going in connection with the tax proviso. Would that mean that Lea County, with its oil wells and immense mineral wealth would receive more representation than Mora County, which was a poorer county? He threw it in anyway and added that we would go forward with the case.

After the hearing I advised the press that I was going to further amend my complaint and that I would seek a court judgment to cut off legislators' per diem and committee expenses and the pay of legislative employees if the legislature repeatedly refused to reapportion. This did not endear me to the legislature or the legislative employees involved in the whole process, but I can assure you that it did get their attention and it probably should have been done.

I met with First Assistant Attorney General Boston Witt in Santa Fe on August 6, 1963 and we agreed to stipulate to a massive amount of evidence, some of which was actually never prepared or submitted to the court. We tried to shorten the trial time by stipulating to as much of this as we could.

At the same meeting I indicated that I was going to call as a witness Dr. Frederick C. Irion, a political scientist at the University of New Mexico. I planned to use him as an expert witness. In the meantime the state, through the attorney general, filed its answer to my petition. This asked, in essence, that the suit be dismissed on the grounds that the present apportionment of the legislature did not violate the state or federal constitution and was not "invidiously discriminatory." The attorney general contended that Bernalillo County's population was predominately the result of the growth of federal and scientific and military installations and that this was so unstable and entirely dependent upon the whims and actions of the chief executive of the United States and the U.S. Congress, and that it was not possible to determine the true population of accounting "with any degree of accuracy."

As the trial date neared, interest in what the court would do increased. Most of the state press appeared to favor a court-ordered special session as the primary result of the trial. Governor Jack Campbell said that he would support House reapportionment if he was called as a witness and would submit reapportionment of the house only to a special session of the legislature. There was a citizens' committee in Albuquerque that finally spoke up and said that, as a result of past legislatures, the citizens of Bernalillo County had been ignored, they had been abused, and after being abused and ignored they were thoroughly insulted. Then United Press International writer Frank Morgan rhetorically asked, "Why has Bernalillo, with its nine members in the 66th member House, failed to get through the legislature that it wanted?" The only bill in the recent legislature that Albuquerque pushed and failed was a metropolitan plan. This was an amazing statement on the part of the press in that it ignored all of the tenets of democracy and was downright insulting to all the people of the state of New Mexico. I promptly got into extended arguments with Frank Morgan, and even though we were good friends we never did resolve the matter. He simply just didn't believe that reapportionment should take place.

On August 26, 1963, the district court convened in Santa Fe County in the trial of *Cargo vs. Campbell* in a matter of constitutional validity. The court examined the constitutional amendment of the House of Representatives. Three witnesses were called to testify at the August 26th trial: the first was Dr. Frederick Irion, who appeared at my request and was subjected to direct examination by myself as the only lawyer for the plaintiffs. Dr. Irion became extremely emotional and stated that the existing reapportionment scheme was "terrible and that it bore little rationality as a matter of law," and he simply couldn't understand how democracy could be insulted in such a manner. Then Dr. Spencer Hill of the Eastern New Mexico University appeared as witness and said that "the court was not the proper place for reapportionment and that this was solely a function of the legislature."

Hill also said that other factors other than population had to be considered and that the present apportionment was political and that you had to consider everything else before the court could take any action. He obviously had not read the opinion of the United States Supreme Court or any of the other court opinions that had been rendered since *Baker vs. Carr*. I then called Dr. James Edwards as a witness. He was a labor market analyst with the Economic Security Commission in Albuquerque. The substance of his testimony was that the labor force in Albuquerque was stable and not as fluid as argued by the attorney general. I think that he very neatly disposed of the arguments of Assistant Attorney General Boston Witt.

Presentation of the testimony took a little less than five hours and the court proceedings were rather informally conducted by Judge Neal; who took an active part in the discussion.

At its conclusion, Judge Neal stated, "The idea of this court redistricting of the state or legislature is repulsive, and even if it finds the section in the state constitution unconstitutional I will give the governor reasonable time to call the legislature because it is a legislative duty."

Judge Neal and ordered us to assemble the next day in court, but instead of issuing an order he issued a 33-page memorandum and it was to become a historical "first" in the jurisprudence of the state.

I was concerned about voting and representation because, it seemed to me, everything was out of whack in the state in those regards. Here's how crazy it was:

In 1963, the New Mexico Cattle Growers Association urged the state legislature to not seat two Navajos who had been elected to the legislature. The group said that representatives Monroe Jymm of McKinley County, and James Atcitty of San Juan County shouldn't be seated because they could help enact legislation that would affect everyone in the state but Indians.

A 1961 New Mexico Supreme Court ruling said that Navajos were qualified citizens and voters in New Mexico, and that should have ended the debate. But the ruling also indicated that the state had no jurisdiction on reservation lands.

At the time I said, "Perhaps the Cattle Growers Association had better take a good look at their own organization on the reporting of livestock for taxation purposes. I want to remind the people who drafted this resolution that the legislature is the sole judge of the qualifications and election of its own members."

The Cattle Growers resolution went nowhere, but it did show how backwards some of the thinking in the state was.

Districts for Congress

In the 1965 legislative session I introduced a bill to, for the first time, district New Mexico's two seats in the U.S. House of Representatives. We and Hawaii were the only two states to elect our congresspeople at-large. It was a political situation and the Democrats loved it and worked to perpetuate it because no Republican could get elected running at-large.

Up until then, Democrats in the legislature had been, as syndicated columnist Will Harrison wrote at the time, "crushing proposals for congressional districts for 25 years."

My bill was a long shot because most of the Democratic Party's leadership opposed it. Senators Clinton Anderson and Joe Montoya—both Democrats—opposed it, and so did Governor Jack Campbell.

My idea was to divide the state into two congressional districts. I put the counties of Bernalillo, Colfax, Los Alamos, Mora, Rio Arriba, Sandoval, Santa Fe, San Juan, Taos, Union and San Miguel into one district and the rest of the state into a second.

At the time, New Mexico had a ratio of 475,000 people per congressman, while the rest of the nation averaged about 400,000. The bill gave the northern counties their own district, while giving the southern and eastern counties a district. Congressman E.S.

Johnny Walker lived in one district, and Congressman Tom Morris lived in the other.

The idea and bill seemed fair to me, and who would have thought, but the House membership actually agreed with me on one vote. The bill came out of committee, and on the floor, it passed by a vote of 42 to 29. It was an amazing victory, really. As columnist Harrison wrote:

"House Demo leaders were against it, but 26 Democrats joined 16 Republicans to roll it through the chamber. Speaker Bruce King, Majority Leader Austin Roberts and Majority Whip Alex Martinez were all against it, and so were most other party regulars."

A lot of Hispanic legislators supported me on the bill because they knew that it was extremely difficult for a Hispanic to get elected to Congress in at-large elections. They knew that districting would give them an opportunity to get elected.

The victory was short-lived, though. Over night the state's congressional delegation flew into the state and went to Santa Fe. They threatened legislators, told them they needed to get in line and kill the bill, and in some cases, threatened to run candidates against them in upcoming primary elections. It was ugly and disgraceful.

The next day our two senators and both congressmen plopped themselves down in the front row in the balcony of the House chamber and oversaw the demolition of the bill and the effort to create congressional districts.

The bill was recalled and then defeated by a vote of 57 to 18.

So much for democracy.

I did have the last laugh, though. One of the first things I did in 1967 after becoming governor was to get the bill going again. It passed in the 1967 legislative session. Two congressional districts were created. Both Morris and Walker ran for re-election, and both lost.

Manuel Lujan Jr. was elected from the northern district and started a two-decade-long career in the U.S. House of Representatives.

1964 Election for the Legislature

In 1964, the state House of Representatives was districted for the first time. Albuquerque went from having nine members in the legislature who were elected at-large, to 18 members who were elected from districts. Bernalillo County went from having one member in the Senate to 10.

In its wisdom, the legislature looked at reapportionment as a way of getting rid of me. The district I was placed in was heavily Democratic, Hispanic and labor. They put the East Mountains into the district and came down into Albuquerque and took a number of areas that were heavily Democratic and put them into it, too.

I got areas like Chilili, Tijeras, Carnuel, Escobosa, San Antonio, Sedillo, Torreon, and Miera. In 1964, those areas were almost 100 percent Hispanic. And unlike today, the East Mountains were heavily Hispanic, as well. And, they were almost all Democrats.

Thus, the legislative leadership thought they had effectively gotten rid of me because they figured there was no way that I could possibly win an election in that district.

They turned out to be dead wrong. One of the biggest reasons why was that President Lyndon B. Johnson was running against Republican Barry Goldwater that year, and the Goldwater campaign in New Mexico, as it was nationally, was an absolute disaster. Ultraconservatives had almost totally taken over the Republican Party in New Mexico, and many of them were former Democrats led by Andy Carter. It was a tough situation to say the least.

During the campaign, I was told that unless I stuck to the party line and supported Goldwater without any reservation, I would lose. At the Bernalillo County Republican Convention, one woman came up to me and said, "I live in your district, and unless you have Goldwater tattooed across your forehead you are going to lose, and I mean it!"

I think she did mean it. Ultimately, she was proved wrong.

I had a contested primary election. My opponent was Frank Marlow. I won the primary, but on election night I prevailed on Marlow to become my campaign manager. He accepted and he was with me the rest of my political life. Eventually, he went to work for the Motor Vehicles Department when I became governor. He was one of my staunchest supporters.

I also got a campaign worker who lived on Sedillo Hill by the name of Anselmo Gonzalez. He was well acquainted with the mountain areas, and he knew a lot of people who belonged to the land grants within the district. The Chilili and the Carnuel Land grants were both in my district and had lots of voters.

In addition to the problems that I faced in the district as a whole, I had a very aggressive opponent in Thomas E. Davis, who won the Democratic nomination for the legislative seat. After he lost the election to me he went on to become a Metropolitan Court judge, a position he held for several decades. He was a very able man, and he made sure that I had a difficult campaign.

The first thing I did was to try and secure as much support as I could from labor, because there was a high number of union members in my district. I knew that without them I would have a very hard time in cutting into Davis' vote. In addition, I had to figure out how to cut down the overwhelming Democratic vote and convert them to my side.

One thing that helped was that I became the attorney for the Carnuel Land Grant, and remained their attorney until I was elected governor.

I went to the Republican Party of Bernalillo County and to the state Republican Party and asked them for help with the election. Their answer was a big fat "no." They said they were going to give all their funds to the governor's race and to Republican Ed Mechem's U.S. Senate campaign.

Mechem was running because of a fascinating set of circumstances. He had lost the 1962 gubernatorial race to Democrat Jack Campbell. Then, suddenly, in November of that year, U.S. Senator Dennis Chavez died—all before Mechem had left office.

After Chavez's death, as I mentioned earlier, Mechem resigned as governor. Tom Bolack, a Republican, replaced him. Then Bolack appointed Mechem to the vacant Senate seat.

Mecham's 1964 Senate campaign was a tough one. To give you an idea of how tough it was, you have to compare Mechem's vote-getting ability to the ability of Goldwater to lose votes in New Mexico and drag the ticket down.

I'll never forget an incident that happened early in the campaign when Eddie Apodaca, who had been a candidate for attorney general, assembled a group of people in Tijeras and announced that he had formed a committee of volunteers for Mechem. Once we assembled, Jesus Sanchez got up from his chair, and in a loud voice demanded to know how much the volunteers were going to be paid.

Apodaca replied by saying, "We are not going to pay anyone."

Sanchez's response was quick indeed. He said, "Then if you're not going to pay volunteers, you will have damned few volunteers!"

That was the spirit of the thing, I'm afraid.

In any event, Mechem was not terribly well organized in my legislative district, and he lost by a very sizable margin to his opponent, Representative Joseph M. Montoya.

My situation called for a really old-fashioned campaign, and I did exactly that. I began to attend every wedding and funeral and to be present at every public gathering that took place in the district. In addition to that, I regularly attended church and as many masses as I could. I also went door-to-door in the district. I covered every single residence, not once, but twice. I used to walk hour after hour, day after day, throughout the district to try to turn the election around.

I also began to represent people and families in court without charging them. It wasn't unusual for me to appear in Municipal Court in Albuquerque with eight to 10 people almost every morning. They, fortunately, came from large families, and I registered as many of the young people as I could as Republicans. Then I appealed to their families, who were overwhelmingly Democratic.

Davis raised very few issues during the campaign—he really didn't have any issues with me except that he was my opponent—but he did touch on a couple that proved to be very interesting.

One was that he took a very firm stance against veterans when applied to the taxation of real estate. At the time, veterans were allowed an exemption off the taxable value of their homes—I think it was $3,000. It obviously served to dramatically lower their property taxes. So the veterans watched that very closely.

Well, Davis—he wasn't a veteran—came out and said that the veterans ought to pay full property taxes. That didn't make the veterans very happy. In fact, the Democratic chair in Chilili was Ben Mora who ran the only gas station in Chilili. He put up a big sign in front of his station saying, "That SOB Davis is against veterans." It wasn't a good move on Davis' part. He ended up getting one vote in Chilili.

I went out and attended land grant meetings, and I canvassed very extensively in the mountains. I quickly won over a number of Democratic Party officials who began to invite me to all the Democratic rallies they held. They never bothered to invite Davis. That was a bit of an advantage. I also went around and got to know each and every one of the Democratic Party officials in the district, as well as what few Republican Party officials there were.

I worked them all very hard. I visited with them. I cajoled them. I talked to them, and I did everything I could to persuade them to vote for me. In the end, most of them did.

Davis became very concerned about the Democratic Party officials who were supporting me. Finally, Henry Kiker, who was the Democratic Party County chairman, and who had an office next to mine in the Sunshine Building, called a meeting of Democratic officials. It was held in the Carnuel Land Grant office. Thirty-two people showed up. Henry gave them his best pitch, saying that no matter how much they liked me, they needed to stick to the party line and vote for Davis.

Henry then left and went out and took a look at the vehicles that were parked outside. Most were trucks. There were 32 vehicles, and 31 of them had my bumper stickers. The only one without my sticker was Henry's. Henry talked to me about it the next morning. He said, "It's going to be a Goldwater sweep, and I don't think that you will be able to win, although I think you might make it close."

I said, "Henry, don't visit the mountains anymore, and let them alone up there. Maybe they just won't vote."

Henry laughed and said, "I think they are going to vote, and I think you know how they are going to vote."

Another problem I faced was that a number of the polling places were in private homes. One was in a home belonging to a relative of my wife Ida Jo. He was a persuasive individual, but a hard-line Democrat. I think he ultimately persuaded people to vote for me because on election night Bob Beier, political editor for the *Albuquerque Journal*, called me and said, "You lost." I said, "How's that?" He said that in a couple of polling places in the mountains he had asked how the vote had gone, and their reply was that Lyndon Johnson was sweeping the vote. He cited precinct 34, and said that Johnson had carried it by 33 votes to 14 for Goldwater, and that, therefore, I had lost.

I said, "No. I don't think so. Maybe you should best check back and see how I did." Beier called back 10 minutes later and said, "Well, maybe you're not to lose after all because Davis got eight votes and you got 78." He added that in precinct 41 it was a fairly close vote and that Johnson had gotten 148 votes and Goldwater 143. That was one of the few precincts in which Goldwater came close.

I immediately asked Bob, "How many votes did I get?" He

said, "Well, Tom Davis got 148, and I'm not sure how this is possible, but you got 229, and it's like that throughout most of the precincts."

In the mountains we had to organize it in the old way. That was that on election day we were expected to provide beer to voters. We put a pickup truck at almost every polling place, usually 100 yards away, or to put it more precisely, a legal distance from it. We had kegs of beer, and people would stop by and get a beer and then go vote, and then come back out for another beer.

We also visited the heads of each large family and made sure that they were properly stocked with a small bottle of bourbon. The bourbon was an expensive type that was known as Straight American, which came right out of Juarez, Mexico. We also provided liquid refreshments by way of bottles of Red Rocket wine, a nondescript variety, and hardly a vintage in that it cost 75-cents a bottle. I'm not sure how many of those were passed out, but apparently enough to move me up in the polls.

My total expenditure for the campaign came to $540, so we were obviously not loaded with money. However, the precincts that came in were lopsided in my favor. In precinct 7 it was 120 votes for me and 44 for Davis; in precinct 10, I got 64 votes, and Davis 18; in precinct 16, I got 97, and Davis 24; in precinct 34 it was 78 for me, and eight for Davis; in precinct 46 I got 353, while Davis got 141.

The voting patterns were obvious in the Hispanic precincts, which I carried heavily, and in the labor precincts, which were in the city. I ran extremely well and well ahead of the ticket. In the city, the Communications Workers of America had phone banks which were directed at Democrats. They rounded up votes for me in areas that were heavily Democratic and labor.

The end result was that I carried 14 precincts and narrowly lost three. To give you an idea of how the rest of the races went, Johnson carried 12 precincts, while Goldwater carried five. The final vote in my race was 2,967 for me, and 2,142 for Davis. I would also note that I carried the Hispanic precincts by lopsided margins. In many cases I carried them by three to four times the vote that Davis got. In many of the larger precincts I beat him almost two-to-one. But there were a lot of Democrats in the district, and so I had expected that the race would be a lot closer.

Davis was a good man and a tough candidate. I prevailed because of the help of Democrats. I had to lean heavily on them for support, and had depended on people who were very active in the Democratic Party. It made the difference, and my margin was mostly in the East Mountains.

In addition to winning, I was the only Republican legislator to be re-elected in Bernalillo County, and one of the few statewide. Almost all of the new Republicans had never been in the legislature. They were there, quite largely, by reason of the effect of reapportionment. For instance, in the Heights, where Goldwater did get a pretty fair number of votes, there were a number of Republicans who won House and Senate seats. In fact, the Republican gains in 1964 were the largest they had made in any election since statehood. Reapportionment did a number of things; it elected Hispanics, Native Americans and Republicans.

I have to credit Frank Marlow and Anselmo Gonzalez for having spearheaded my re-election effort. They both worked hard and accompanied me all over the district. And believe me, Anselmo knew everyone. He was able to turn some precincts around decisively. Most of our campaign money went towards gasoline. We traveled all over the district, a great deal of which was rural. Anselmo had lived there all his life, and he did a wonderful job of assisting me. We went weekends, evenings and everything in between. It was a highly personal campaign, and one that I learned a great deal from. It moved me to the point where I realized that if I was going to win against all odds in New Mexico, I had to campaign heavily in Democratic districts.

I did that when I ran for governor two years later. I went to the northern counties and campaigned door-to-door. I also learned that if you didn't insult Democrats, as a matter of fact, didn't even mention their party affiliation, the chances were good that you would get their votes. I also learned that when you went to union halls and attended meetings and shook hands and said a few words you could get their votes as well. Because I did that, labor worked very hard for me in future elections.

The Goldwater disaster was one that I prevailed against all the odds. We ran a very efficient campaign, used voter lists, kept tabs on those who had voted and not voted, and hauled people to the polls in droves. We had to because otherwise we would have lost. It was a good victory and one that boded well for the future.

A Special Relationship With Labor

In 1962, I ran for the New Mexico state legislature from Bernalillo County. At that time all of the nine members of the house were elected at large; in 1960 all of the members elected at large had been Democrats. Bernalillo County at that time had one state senator representing all the county's residents. The Republican Party in District 9 nominated me in 1962 as their candidate for the legislature and I actively sought the endorsement of organized labor. As a matter of fact, I was the only legislator to assiduously court the AFL-CIO's New Mexico Committee on Political Education, or COPE, for an endorsement.

I attended the COPE meeting in the Alvarado Hotel and spoke to the convention which consisted of about 300 individuals, and so did my opponent, Henry Rodriguez. At that time, Tom Robles was the organization's executive secretary treasurer. He was a close personal friend of mine, as was Jim Price who was the president of the state AFL-CIO, and was very active in the building trades. With the two of them on my side I thought that I stood a fairly good chance.

However, Henry Rodriguez made the pitch that labor should only endorse a Democrat.

Rodriguez indicated that I was a heretic of sorts and solely because of my party affiliation should not be endorsed. The convention proceeded to debate the issue at some length and the discussion became acrimonious. However, immediately prior to the vote the representatives—in particular Jack Redding of the national AFL-CIO COPE—took the floor and indicated that they wanted a dual endorsement. They wanted me to be endorsed, and if the convention were to decide otherwise, Redding indicated that they would act on behalf of the national organization and override the state organization's endorsement. As a result they endorsed me, and labor proceeded to support me heavily. In the subsequent election Lawrence Prentice and I were elected as the only Republicans in the House of Representatives from Bernalillo County. Larry won by a very narrow margin, while my margin was substantial, but the two of us were the only GOP representatives to be elected in Bernalillo County.

Subsequently, the scorecard of votes in the New Mexico State Legislature in 1965 during the 27th legislative assembly gave me a perfect voting record of voting with labor, with the exception of a vote on Fair Trade for liquor. I voted to abolish fair trade on liquor and contended that labor was wrong on the issue. However, at that time I established a close relationship with organized labor and from that time forward they determined that they were going to support me. In 1962 I had filed a reapportionment suit, and in 1964 the legislature was elected by district. That year I represented District 18, which consisted essentially of the mountain areas and a small block of votes in the city of Albuquerque. The district was overwhelmingly Democratic and very heavily Hispanic. However, in that election I was the only Republican to be re-elected to office in that county despite the overwhelming defeat of Barry Goldwater by Lyndon B. Johnson in the district. It was a difficult situation for me; obviously I had to pick up a large segment of the "vote-splitting" electorate, as we called those who voted for one party in national races and the other for other offices, in order to make it. However, I managed to split enough votes to be elected.

During the 27th legislative assembly I again continued my good relationship with organized labor. They ranked me on legislation as having voted correct almost 100 percent of the time. The exception was a bill (HR181) on collective bargaining by public employees. The measure proposed authorizing employees of state or local entities to mutually organize and engage in public bargaining agreements with public officials. It was introduced by Arsenio A. Gonzalez and defeated 42 to 24. I voted against it so that the bill could be reconsidered. The political reality was that, having voted against it, I would have the opportunity to be in a pivotal position if we did decide to reconsider the matter. Labor rated me well on a number of issues: The Fair Housing Act (HR150) prohibited discrimination in housing because of race, color, religion, national origin or ancestry; for an increase in the minimum wage (HB157); for the public works minimum wage (HB206); as well as the Occupational Disease Disablement Act (HB240), Agricultural Labor Act (HB242), Municipal Employees Collective Bargaining (HB439), Occupational Disease Benefits Increase (CS-HB502), Right To Work (HJR14), Workers Compensation (CS-HB267) and Teachers' Activities (CS191). Thus I stood in high regard with labor. I had a good enough voting record that the AFL-CIO would later co-endorse me in the Republican primary for governor.

I supported several pieces of legislation that were introduced in the 27th legislature in 1965. One bill was HB141 which permitted the late filing for unemployment compensation, and a motion on HJR14 which was a Right to Work law. I voted to table the Right to Work laws indefinitely and I cast the deciding vote on that issue. I also sponsored HB 35 FEPC, a $25,000 appropriation which would have raised the appropriation for all of the agencies from $5,000 to $25,000. That motion was defeated rather decisively, but I was the main sponsor of it, and I took a strong position on it.

At the AFL-CIO endorsing convention held in the La Fonda

Hotel in Santa Fe I was unanimously endorsed in the Republican primary and John Burroughs was endorsed in the Democratic primary. After the primary election another convention was held in the La Fonda Hotel where they proposed that organized labor endorse a single candidate in the 1966 governor's election. An initial vote was taken and surprisingly enough the delegates endorsed me over Gene Lusk. At that point Senator Penrod Toles took the floor and once again made the argument that labor should not endorse a Republican. Paul Cruz, who was in the back of the room and who represented the Sandia employees' union, shouted out "We already have!" As the afternoon was drawing to a close a couple of Democratic campaign workers supporting Gene Lusk arrived at the convention and began to argue with the delegates. By that time probably half of them had already left, thinking the decision was made. The earlier vote was reversed and Gene Lusk received a halfhearted endorsement. It was surprising in that I had been endorsed initially, and even more surprising that it was reversed late in the day by a greatly reduced number of delegates. However, it did set the stage for the election and that helped me a great deal.

Gene Lusk's voting record on labor issues was absolutely terrible; it was one of the poorest in the state legislature and I exploited that fact all during the campaign. As the campaign progressed, most of the labor organizations reversed the decision of the state convention and began to endorse me with great regularity. As a matter of fact, the individual organizations were almost unanimous in doing so. I had a lot of support from organized labor, and especially from my good friends Tom Robles and Jim Price. They worked hard to convince members of organized labor to support me, and that support came in overwhelming numbers which, seeing that I was and still am a Republican, was probably a first for organized labor.

After the election I didn't have any offices initially and Jim Green of the teachers' union offered to give me space in the New Mexico Education Association building. At that point Governor Jack Campbell had intervened to allow me office space next to the governor's office. I was able to begin putting together my administration a week after the election.

The first thing that I did was to put all of the unions in the state on notice that I wanted to give them representation in my administration. They responded very quickly, and we set up a meeting. A contingent of 60 union leaders assembled in the state capital and I decided on a little surprise for them. I opened the meeting stating that labor had not had many appointments through the years and that I intended to appoint them to various boards and commissions and jobs of high visibility within the administration. I then proceeded to ask them to make recommendations to me for boards and commissions that had little or nothing to do with organized labor. I placed a number of them in high-ranking positions that I felt should be headed by labor people. The appointments ranged all the way from appointing Chano Merino to the New Mexico Parks Commission to putting labor leaders other positions in the state government. As a matter of fact, during my time as governor I appointed more people from organized labor to state boards and commissions and other positions than any other governor in the history of New Mexico. Needless to say they were surprised, although in my case I did not receive any large contributions from labor when I was running. I did it out of conviction and conviction alone.

On December 22, 1966, I received the recommendations made by organized labor for various appointments, submitted by Al Rodriguez, who was the executive secretary and treasurer of the state AFL-CIO. I named Ricardo M. Montoya to head the Labor Industrial Commission which was probably one of the most important jobs in state government. I appointed Paul J. Cruz as administrator chairman of the Employment Security Commission. Paul, as I said, had been president of Sandia Employees' Union, one of the largest unions in the state. I might also add that there was a controversy among some of the labor people as to whether Cruz should head that commission. Some requested that I appoint Ricardo Montoya. I went ahead and put Montoya in charge of the Labor & Industry

Commission, and then I appointed Cruz to the best job.

I also appointed R. C. Brooks, Lawrence Wilkinson, Tim Robbin, Henry Rodriquez, Leon Dobson, Jim Price, Brother August Raymond, John B. Carrillo, Neal Gonzalez, F.W. Sanders, John Miksovic, Luther Sizemore, Bert Trantham, Henry Longacre, and Duven Lujan to various state boards and commissions.

Another practice that I initiated and which found great favor with organized labor was that I entertained officials from the various unions at the governor's mansion at least once every six months. In between I would sometimes host open dinners at the mansion for the whole membership of a particular union. Nacho Morales and Chano Merino arranged a dinner for all the members of Local 890 in Grant County. They showed up in droves and they greatly enjoyed themselves. One of the union members was called by a relative from California and I overheard part of the conversation. It went as follows "Well hell, dinner at the governor's mansion and I don't care if he is a Republican; he supports us and we are going to support him. If you lived in New Mexico you would do the same."

I had social gatherings for them quite often and I entertained them quite frequently at the mansion. On one occasion the United Steelworkers sent a group from Washington, DC, and they walked into the governor's office without an appointment. Fortunately they had Chano Merino with them. Chano said that he was going to introduce them to the governor and they said they couldn't believe it. There were five of them. I told them that if they could hang on I would take them all out to the mansion and feed them a steak dinner, which I did. Subsequently, Chano was hired by the steelworkers as one of their top political people. I tried to keep the relationship open with all of the union people during my time in office.

In 1967 legislative session I sponsored a number of bills that were to the benefit of working people as listed below:

1967 Legislative Measures

HB 93 Prohibits open lights in coal mines

HB 76 Increased membership on the Mining Safety Advisory Board to include two representatives of coal mining

HB 148 Provides for payments by employers in certain cases for failure to supply of reasonable safety devices

HB 254 Worker's Compensation benefits increase

SB 251 Provide safety standards, administrated by State Corporations Commission, for railroad employees

SB 402 Prohibits employee-employer agreements stating that prospective employees shall not join a union

1968 Legislative Measures

Amendments of 1967 Workmen's Compensation measure to correct language

HB 241 Late filing, unemployment compensation

HJR 14 On motion to table indefinitely "right to work"

HB 167 Minimum Wage Act

I also increased the minimum wage every year that I was governor with the exception of one, and on that occasion it was defeated by the Democratic members of the legislature. They thought that you should not be increasing wages every year so they omitted it that year. Then some of them took exception to the fact that I said I wanted people to raise the minimum wage because I wanted people to earn enough money so that they could felt like they were Republicans whether they voted that way or not. Some of them took exception to that remark and didn't do a thing on wages that year. They did raise it during every other year that I was in office.

We also had a Capitol Building Commission which controlled the hiring and firing and conditions of employment for the people who worked in the Capitol and in state buildings in Santa

Fe. The secretary of state was on the commission as well as the attorney general and myself. However, the Attorney General Boston Witt would regularly try to curb any efforts to improve the conditions of employment for the people who worked in the Capitol and he was supported most of the time by Secretary of State Ernestine Evans. At that time the maintenance employees were almost totally political and virtually all of them were very active in the Santa Fe County Democratic organization. This took a strange turn when I wanted to reduce their work week from six days to five days and I was outvoted two-to-one. I then proceeded by executive order to reduce their work week to five days.

Then I decided I was going to raise their wages. They were all very poorly paid, so I gave them a 40 percent increase in salaries by executive order. This increase had previously been defeated by a two to one vote, but the legislators finally acquiesced and it went into effect. The strange part of all this was that I established extremely close relationship with the employees. They used to invite me down to have lunch with them in the basement. We would periodically have chile and tortillas and enjoy ourselves while getting to know each other. It proved to be a very interesting situation in that Johnny Vigil was the Democratic county chairman and George González, who is related to Johnny Vigil, was the mayor of Santa Fe. When I came up for re-election in 1968 against Fabian Chavez, the Capitol building employees voted unanimously to support me in the election and proceeded it to do so with a great deal of vigor. In addition to that, Mayor George González became a very close friend of mine and likewise supported me. Johnny Vigil would come into the Capitol and wander around and make sure that the workers were well organized and prepared for the 1968 election. All this support proved to be an asset indeed. In 1968 I ran the best race for governor as a Republican in the city of Santa Fe in many years. As a matter of fact, I came very, very close to carrying the entire city in the election.

I undertook a number of actions to improve working conditions in New Mexico. I took the following actions:

In 1967, raised minimum salaries from $180 to $220, with steps up to more than $250 a month as quickly as possible.

Proposed creation of a State Labor Department in the 1967 and 1968 legislatures. It called for bringing together into a single department the Employment Security Commission, the Labor and Industrial Commission, the Fair Employment Practices Commission and the Apprenticeship Council.

Proposed enactment of Administrative Procedures Act to standardize appeals procedures for administrative decisions, to the 1968 legislature.

I also changed the practice whereby employees of the state prison were partially paid in food rather than wages. This was a strange situation in that they raised food at the penitentiary and then they gave a lot of the food to the employees instead of paying them a salary. I went ahead and increased their salaries at their recommendation, and I believe that they probably continued to eat as well as they had before.

Proposed to the 1967 session legislation raising the minimum wage and increasing unemployment compensation payments. The Minimum Wage Act provides the following: (A) for employees other than service employees: $1.25 an hour beginning July 1, 1967; $1.40 an hour beginning February 1, 1968; $1.60 an hour beginning February 1, 1969; (B) for service or other employees except agriculture: $1.00 an hour beginning July 1, 1967; $1.15 an hour beginning February 1, 1968; $1.30 an hour beginning February 1, 1969. (C) for agricultural workers: $1.00 an hour beginning July 1, 1967; $1.15 an hour beginning February 1, 1968; and $1.30 an hour beginning February 1, 1969.

And then I proposed that a number of other proposals be enacted into law and sought the support of organized labor to enact them:

Improvements in Worker's Compensation Act and occupational disablement law to provide more protection

Comprehensive industrial safety law and mine safety improvements

Hearing date for injunction against labor

State restrictions not only against labor, but management

The contract right of labor and the management to enter into an agreement regulating union security should not be abridged by statute

The law should provide that it shall be a felony to transport strikebreakers into the state

The law should specifically set forth the right to employees to form, join or assist labor organizations and to bargain over wages, hours and conditions of employment

State law to provide a procedure for determining representation, supervised by State Labor Commissioner

Injunctive relief against not only workers, but employers

I likewise initiated a program whereby state employees would be permitted by law to engage in collective bargaining. I set out a procedure whereby they could seek recognition and laid the foundation for State Collective Bargaining Act. Oddly enough I had increased salaries so rapidly and generously for state employees that there were not many of them organized as a result of this action.

The position of the state employees was that what I was doing was extremely beneficial and in their interest and they did not think that the union could do any better for them. I kept warning them that subsequent governors might take a different view of it. As a matter of fact, the state employees eventually were covered by state law and a State Employee Collective Bargaining Act was passed. It stayed in existence pretty much until Governor Gary Johnson came along. Then in his infinite wisdom he decided that he didn't want to renew it and didn't. The state employee bargaining was reinstated by Governor Bill Richardson, but it was accompanied by massive infusion of political contributions into his campaigns. It was kind of a quid pro quo. I don't think that state employees should have to contribute to a political campaign in order to secure what should be a basic right to collective bargaining. Anyway, that's what happened, and that's how it was eventually resolved.

When I ran for re-election in 1968, labor decided that they were going to let individual unions endorse in elections rather than endorsing at a state convention of the AFL-CIO COPE Committee. This helped me, of course, because the various unions in the state proceeded to endorse me one by one. They endorsed me separately and in my re-election campaign and probably made a difference in the outcome. So my relationship with labor was one that I enjoyed, and I must say that they seemed to enjoy it as well. Since that time I have been elected to serve on the Albuquerque City Labor Board on several occasions and also I was selected unanimously by city employees to serve on the Albuquerque Bernalillo County Water Authority Board. I guess they never forgot my support for them. I have received labor support in almost every election, which is highly unusual for a Republican, and something that is not likely to be duplicated in any time in the future. Members of the current Republican Party don't seek the support of organized labor and probably won't get it in the foreseeable future. My relationship with labor was good and it remains so to this day. I still address labor conventions and I am received very well. That gives me a lot of satisfaction because I really appreciated the relationship that I had with them.

State Senator James Patton
and Capitol Furniture Shenanigans

Corruption in Santa Fe and the legislature was out of control when I was first elected, and it continued to be that way, despite my best efforts to publicize and embarrass lawmakers into some semblance of honesty.

A prime example of this was state Senator James Patton, a Democrat from Doña Ana County. Not only did Patton vote to build the new Capitol building, but he then got contracts to furnish the place! Patton sold $500,000 worth of furniture to the state for the Capitol.

The insulting thing is that Attorney General Boston Witt issued an opinion that said it was perfectly okay for Patton to get contracts to furnish the Capitol that he voted to build. I thought it was disgusting.

In December of 1965 I called for a full-scale investigation into Patton's dealings. Here's what I told the *Albuquerque Tribune* about the matter:

"He (Patton) was paid as a consultant, appropriated the money (as a legislator), and now has drawn the specifications in such a manner as to eliminate all competition. He was paid $2,000 as a consultant and will be paid in excess of $25,000 as a commission for being the low and only bidder on the furnishings."

Patton didn't like what I had to say. He told the *Tribune*: "Cargo, as usual, is not informed. He likes to grab an issue and holler long and loud about it. I'd like to know where he gets his authority. It's obvious he hasn't read the specifications."

I responded: "This situation is shocking enough, but when you consider that Senator Patton will not only be the sole businessman to bid, but also that as a member of the legislature he helped appropriate the money and then went on to serve as a consultant to the architect who designed the building makes it even more repulsive."

The building of the Capitol was a disgrace in itself. The entire project was supposed to cost $7 million. At one point we had already spent $8 million, and it was estimated that an additional $7 million would be needed to finish the job.

I told the *Tribune* at the time: "I have talked to a number of legislators, most of them Democrats, who have been unable to find out from anyone how much this building project eventually is going to cost the people of New Mexico. A number of us in the legislature now are convinced that the only way in which to keep a check on the spending is to insert line items in the bill instead of pushing through a bulk appropriation with no check at all. I also plan to insert in any appropriation bill for this complex a prohibition against any member of the state legislature doing any business with the state on this project and I make no bones about it."

Here's the irony of Witt's opinions that Patton's contracts were legal. Not too long before Witt's office issued the opinion, Patton's Las Cruces furniture firm got a contract to provide $9,000 worth of furnishings to the Attorney General's office.

It seemed like they were all on the take.

Canones

The Village of Canones in northern New Mexico became a campaign issue in 1966, although I didn't deliberately make it so. It became an important factor because it showed that I was listening to rural Hispanics in the northern part of the state.

I am reminded that Napoleon once advised rather graphically, "Never interrupt your enemy while he is making a mistake."

Gene Lusk not only didn't do anything in connection with

the problems that arose in Canones, but he sat by and watched it happen without making much of a comment except to say, "There's not much I can do about it." As Rudyard Kipling wrote in his famous book, Kim, "I shut my eyes in the sentry box so I didn't see anything wrong." That indeed was the problem, because Lusk never saw anything wrong.

Canones illustrated very well what happened in the 1966 election. The village had a lot of problems that no one wanted to address. The villagers would gather the night before an election in the old schoolhouse where they would debate issues and candidates and determine how they were going to vote. They were pretty much all Democrats, and they usually decided to vote that way.

But in this election the situation was reversed. I got 44 votes while Lusk got four. Other Republicans on the ticket got a grand total of two votes!

The situation in Canones was similar to all the other villages in the area. First of all, the people were poor. Secondly, there had been steady moves to close their schools and churches. There was a move to consolidate the schools, and in some cases, churches were shuttered because there were too few parishioners. Thirdly, they lacked roads, or at least good roads, and they had problems with deteriorating water and sewer systems.

In 1965 Canones had 175 people, including children. The state Department of Education had threatened to close their public school. In fact, consolidation of facilities had taken place rather rapidly.

The big problem was that the road from Canones to Coyote, which was 15 miles away, was in a deplorable state. Not only that, but it was a toll road that was controlled by a private individual. In the winter, the road was impassable. The parents of younger children simply refused to send their children to the school in Coyote on the school bus that was provided by the school district.

To make matters worse, the district attorney brought criminal charges against the 12 families that refused to put their children in harm's way by putting them on the bus in winter over that terrible road. The entire village united to defend the families. They hired a lawyer and went to court. They lost, and the lawyer's fee was promptly paid with contributions from almost every family in the village.

The story was covered by the *Albuquerque Journal*, *The Albuquerque Tribune*, *The Santa Fe New Mexican* and the weekly *Rio Grande Sun*, which was published in Española. The wire services finally picked up the story and it was picked up by the *Denver Post* and many other papers across the country. Likewise, Tom Weicker of *The New York Times* called me and followed with a feature story in the *Times*. Then radio stations picked it up, and it became national news.

The locals had sought and received support from Emilo Naranjo, who was the political leader of the Democratic Party in Rio Arriba County, and from Albert Amador, who was a candidate for the State Board of Education. Amador had taught at and had been principal of the school. The villages hired attorney Edwin Felter, who later became a judge and who was close friends with Amador.

The villagers went even further in that they wanted to interview me and Lusk about the situation, and they scheduled a time for the interviews. I showed up and immediately gave loud and enthusiastic support for Canones and similarly situated villages. At first, Lusk didn't respond. Later he said he didn't have any particular interest in the problem and that it should be handled by school officials without much input from anyone in public office.

I think that sealed his fate because he was simply indifferent. I had a vision for the community and Lusk didn't. Jonathan Swift once said, "Vision is the art of seeing the invisible." Well, I saw the invisible. It also occurred to me that the situation resembled Oscar Wilde's observation, "the greatest sin that one can commit against another is the sin of indifference."

For Lusk, indifference was the pervasive mood of the day.

The toll road was the next problem. Not only did the road lead off the public state highway, but it was unusually bad, even by New Mexico standards. Many of the small school children had to walk home in the winter from the stalled school buses, and in doing so, they often got frostbite. In a Navajo community not too far away, one child froze to death after being forced to walk from a muddy road to her home.

That girl was Helen Ignacio, an eight-year-old who lived near Torreon. Helen and her sister Rose, 15, left a school bus one March afternoon after it got stalled in a snowbank near their home in western Sandoval County. The two girls were found the next day about three-tenths-of-a-mile from the Hogan they lived in with their aunt and uncle. Helen was dead, and Rose suffered severe frostbite. It was a disgrace. I was a state representative at the time and the girl's family hired me as their attorney. I investigated and found that there was little concern among state Department of Education officials for Indian children.

What was even more outrageous was that the school bus driver was under indictment at the time for murder. The driver, Mark Castillo, then 34, had been charged with murdering one Joseph Otero by beating him with a jack handle and burying him.

The *Albuquerque Journal* quoted me at the time:

"I don't think anyone charged with murder should be hired by a school system to haul children around."

I also said that the State School Board had "officially whitewashed" the death and that the attorney general's office "expressed no interest in it at all. They're too busy with politics."

The attitude seemed to be that they were Indians and that no one cared what happened to them. A report by the state Department of Education said, "The driver, Mark Castillo, is driving his sixth year as a regular driver and has not been charged with a preventable accident. Every reasonable safeguard and precaution was taken."

My investigation found otherwise, though. The driver said he had tried to prevent the girls from leaving and that he chased and tried to catch them. Other children on the bus, though, said that Castillo did not try to stop them. And some children told me that Castillo ordered the girls off the bus.

The bus was supposed to have been equipped for snow with tire chains and a shovel, but I was told that those chains and shovels had been previously "taken, borrowed or sold" from the bus.

I got into it with Thelma Inman, a member of the state Board of Education, who basically said "so what" to the deaths. She also said that the deaths were the family's fault. At that point I told her she was disgrace to the state.

The girl's family didn't want to sue, but the Education Department's insurance company eventually settled with them.

Newspaper editorials across the state were overwhelmingly in favor of the village in its battle against the Education Department. Things became a little more difficult, though, as the judge in the case threatened to throw the parents who kept their children out of school in jail. I told everyone that I would do several things about the situation. The first was that if the parents were convicted and jailed, if elected, I would pardon them. Second, I said I would create a state park in the area in order to improve the roads leading from Interstate 25 up to Canones.

The state park never materialized because the legislature was slow in acting on it. But I did get the road completed. We made it a state road all the way to Canones. I also did away with the toll road. It became part of the state highway system and people no longer had to pay to travel over it.

I had visited Canones a number of times before the election to visit and to hold campaign rallies. One rally attracted almost 3,000 people. It was typical of many of the rallies we had in those northern villages. It wasn't unusual for us to get between 3,000 and 12,000 people at those things. After the election I continued to go to Canones, both in announced and unannounced ways. I used to go to the Morada and meet with the Penitentes, often attending mass before meeting with them. A lot of times I just went up there by myself and simply walked around and talked to people. They would tell me about the local situation and I would try to respond by making improvements.

In June of 1967 we had another large public meeting and reception in Canones. I bought a number of state officials along so they could become familiar with the area's conditions and problems. I often invited village leaders to the governor's office where we would talk at length. Afterwards, we'd have dinner in the mansion.

One meeting in my office included Tony Gallegos, Medardo Lovato, Elipio Garcia, Orlinda Gallegos and Preciliana Salazar from Canones. We spent several hours together and they briefed me on the area's problems. I managed to resolve some of the school problems, although the school was eventually abandoned, much to my disappointment. My relationship with the village was one of Misericordia, which is Spanish for "You are speaking from the heart." I tried to do that with the people of Canones, and I think I did it with empathy and compassion. They returned the feeling.

Amador was really the brains behind the Democratic organization in Rio Arriba County. He became a state senator and was a good friend and supporter of mine. He helped, not just in Rio Arriba County, but all throughout the northern counties. He had extensive contacts within the Democratic organization, and he used them to good advantage for me.

Former governor Jack Campbell and I had a friendly difference of opinion over what was happening in northern New Mexico, particularly in the field of education. Campbell once said in a public meeting, "Do you want to preserve the villages and be romantic, or do you want to get them out of the villages?" Frankly, my idea was that the people should stay in their villages and be able to preserve their culture with a maximum amount of help.

The Canones post office was another problem. On June 8, 1968, it was moved out of the home of Jacob Salazar—the man who ran the toll road—into Canones. Once it was moved, Postmaster Marvin Watson wanted to close it. I worked with Senators Clint Anderson and Joseph Montoya to keep it open.

Author Paul Kutsche, in his book, *Canones Values: Crisis and Survival in a Northern New Mexico Village*, wrote that I had never failed the people of Canones and that I should be saluted for having done what I did for them, all under difficult circumstances. I was sincere in my efforts, and former governor Bruce King said that it was also extremely good politics for me to have aided Canones in the way that I did.

The Picnic

On Sunday, March 21, 1966, my wife Ida Jo went down to Belen for a family picnic for her 25th birthday. However, the picnic was held, not in Belen, but almost 20 miles away along the Rio Grande.

It was during the Republican primary and I had gone campaigning in Española, Los Alamos and Taos that Sunday and returned at about 10 o'clock at night, and lo and behold, there was no Ida Jo nor my two children, Veronica and David. I had no idea where they were, so I called her parents in Belen and spoke to Ida Jo's father, Trinidad Anaya.

He said he didn't have the faintest idea where she was or what had happened to her. He did say that she had never shown up for the picnic. He was surprised that she didn't show up because they had prepared a rather elaborate party. He then contacted the sheriff's office, and I contacted the Belen police and we tried to figure out where she was.

I went down to Belen and we went along the road to the picnic area. We actually found the family vehicle with a broken axle, but no one nearby. We then searched further and finally located Ida Jo and the two children. She had become bogged down with the car and walked 17 miles to try to get back to Belen. Apparently she had started walking about noon on Sunday and continued on with the two children. It was a trying episode to say the least. The next day *The Albuquerque Tribune* had a headline that said, "Mrs. Cargo, Children Safe after 17 Mile Hike."

I wasn't exactly happy with her, but there wasn't much I could do about it. Some speculated that it might have been planned in order to get publicity and sympathy, I can assure you that it wasn't. It was not only unplanned, but it wasn't a desirable thing either.

Start of the 1966 Campaign for Governor

I wasn't expecting the phone call I got the night I beat Cliff Hawley for the Republican Party's nomination for governor, but I'm glad I got it.

It was around 11 at night and we were at the old Alvarado Hotel in Downtown Albuquerque celebrating my primary win over Hawley. That was a sweet victory because Hawley had actually beaten me in the Republican Party's pre-primary convention earlier that year. Since there weren't a lot of Republicans in the state, not a lot of people voted, but it was a victory nonetheless. I was going to on to face former state senator Gene Lusk, who had beaten former governor John Burroughs in the Democratic primary.

The phone call both stunned and excited me. It was from Burroughs, who, again, had just lost to Lusk.

"Can you meet with me and my people tomorrow morning at seven?" Burroughs asked. "We're going to beat this SOB, and that's it. I have a bunch of people and they're going to help you in the general election."

That was a little more than interesting. Here was a top Democrat, and a former governor, calling me and offering to support my candidacy. Even today I'm still a little surprised by it.

Burroughs had a suite of rooms in a building near Downtown. I arrived at seven sharp the next morning.

When I walked into the first room I stunned again. Burroughs was there. So was Victor Salazar, a big Democratic Party money man. So was Alonzo Gonzalez, who had once been the chief of staff for Senator Clinton Anderson. Charlie Davis was there. So was Filo Sedillo, party chairman in Valencia County and another Democratic Party powerhouse. There were about 35 people in all, money men and organizers, pretty much the infrastructure of the Democratic Party. It was, to put it mildly, a potent group.

Burroughs started off the meeting by saying they were going to help me beat Lusk. It seemed that almost no one in the Democratic Party liked Lusk. Burroughs disliked him for obvious reasons. People close to U.S. Senator Joseph Montoya were there. Montoya despised Lusk because Lusk had run against him for Congress a few years earlier.

I looked at that crowd and thought, "Holy Christmas, I actually stand a chance."

Filo Sedillo, for instance, controlled votes in Valencia County, and I mean controlled votes. He would slate candidates and then go around and tell people who they would be voting for. Usually they listened. Filo would tell candidates how many votes they would get in a particular race, and he was often off by only one or two votes.

Victor Salazar had a list of all the precinct chairs in the state, and he also talked about money.

"On election day I'll be passing out money," he said, explaining that he would give money to drivers whose job it would be to drive people to the polls so they could vote for me.

They hatched plans and Burroughs gave directions and orders. Everyone had something to do. They all had to explain to voters how to split their tickets, which was not an easy thing to do in those days, what with the mechanical voting machines.

The meeting lasted two-and-a-half hours. After it was over, I felt I might be on my way to winning the governor's race.

Burroughs helped me in other ways. At the time he owned, I think, nine radio stations around the state. Those stations helped me immensely. When I'd go to Farmington or Roswell or Las Cruces the stations would invite me on the air. They played a little dirty. They'd also invite Lusk, but he'd usually never show up. So the announcer would say something like, "We invited Gene Lusk here to debate, but he didn't want to show up because he doesn't want to talk about the issues. So we're just going to talk to Dave Cargo."

It all helped, especially that initial meeting with Burroughs and his people. I wound up carrying the valley in Bernalillo County decisively. In fact, I carried every precinct but one in the valley.

What was really happening is that I was peeling off segments of the Democratic vote. I was getting Hispanics to support me, which was huge, and I was getting the more liberal wing of the party as well. It turned out to be a good strategy.

1966 Election Continued

I knew that I had to carry Albuquerque by a huge margin in 1966 because I didn't have any money. In fact, fact I had spent only $16,000 on my campaign. My opponent reportedly spent $350,000, which gave him a huge advantage. I knew that I had to dominate in Albuquerque in order to win. In that election I lost 19 of the state's 32 counties, and 37 percent of my vote came from Bernalillo County. By way of contrast, 23 percent of Gene Lusk's votes came from Bernalillo County. Putting it differently, I won Bernalillo County by nearly 20,000 votes, and lost the remainder of the state by 12,000 votes. Bernalillo County was critical to my election.

The reapportionment lawsuit that I had filed gave considerably more power to urban Republicans. For instance, 10 of the 25 Republican members of the House came from Bernalillo County, and 6 of the party's 17 state senators also came from Bernalillo County. By contrast, of 70 Democrats in the 1967 legislature, only 12 came from Bernalillo County. It should also be noted that Bernalillo County's portion of the total state vote went from 14 percent in 1940 to 31 percent in 1966. The limited finances that I had required me to hunt where the ducks were. I got 63 percent of Albuquerque's votes and that was enough to put me over.

Robert O. Anderson

On a Sunday afternoon shortly after the primary election we had a meeting at Sonny Johns' house in Santa Fe with a number of very active Republicans who were supporting my candidacy in the general election. Willie Ortiz was there, so was Tom Bolack, Robert O. Anderson, Albert Mitchell, Ed Mechem, and, of course, Sonny Johns. They all began to give me advice on how to run my campaign. Finally, Mechem and Bolack pulled me aside and said, "You need to hit up Robert O. because Robert O., as president of Atlantic Richfield, could put some real money into your campaign." They suggested that I talk to him confidentially, which I did by pulling him aside.

Anderson and I went outside and started discussing the campaign. He said, "I think you're going to win the election. I've done some background work on it and I think you can do it."

I told him that I thought I could, too, but I added that what

I really needed was some campaign money, a contribution. At that point, Anderson reached into his pocket and pulled out a piece of paper which he said was a poll that he had hired a pollster to conduct. He went through it carefully with me. It showed me running behind at the time, but it also showed that I was within striking distance and that I could indeed win the election.

Anderson said he agreed with the numbers. He also said that as time went on he believed that I would pick up additional support and that I would ultimately win.

"I know that," I told him, "but you know, I could use some gas money."

He wasn't pleased, and replied: "Well, I understand that when you go out campaigning by yourself, and maybe with one or two other people, most of the gas stations you stop at give you free gas and you don't need to pay for it."

He also said that he understood that I never stayed in hotels or motels because I usually stayed with friends or supporters.

I told him that that was true and that people often fed me and that I rarely paid for meals as well.

"That's the key to your election," he said.

"Yeah," I responded, "but I do need a little something to get by on some of the other expenses."

"I don't doubt that," he said, "but you are doing awfully well, and you are going to win."

Then he put the piece of paper back in his pocket and said, "Well, I'll give you a thousand dollars."

That's what he did. He wrote out a check for $1,000 and we adjourned and I at least had a thousand dollars for my campaign.

Three weeks before the election we met again with the same group at Sonny John's home and went through pretty much the same stuff. Bolack pulled me aside again and said he wanted me and Anderson to go outside and talk about the campaign. We did. This time, Anderson pulled out another piece of paper with another poll and said, "By god, you're going to win the election, and here it is!"

He handed me the paper. I read it, and sure enough, it showed I was ahead. I was sure that a lot of it had to do with the way I was campaigning. I once again suggested to Anderson that I would need a little money to finish up the campaign. Again, he wasn't moved.

"Heck, you don't need any money, and that's why you're winning," he told me. "You don't have any money, you're running by the seat of your pants and everyone knows you're broke and they also know that you're going to win the election."

"Bob," I pleaded, "could you make a little contribution?"

"Well, yeah," he said as he reached into pocket. He pulled out a $100 bill, gave it to me and added:

"You're going to win because you're poor. I don't want to spoil your whole campaign."

I thanked him, and as I left the gathering a short time later, Anderson patted me on the shoulder and said, "Just bear in mind that you're going to win."

It turned out that Anderson, other than Albert Mitchell, who was our national committeeman and who had given me $1,000 the day after the primary, was one of my largest contributors.

The 1966 Election

On June 18, 1966, Robert McKinney, owner and publisher of *The Santa Fe New Mexican*, addressed the New Mexico Press Association in Red River. He gave a rather insightful speech, although he was a committed Democrat and normally only endorsed Democrats editorially. Gene Lusk and I were present during his presentation.

He pointed out that since 1920, New Mexico's population had gone from 82 percent rural in character to being 75 percent urban in

1965. He also said that organization politics was fading rapidly. He noted that in the Republican pre-primary convention, the old GOP organization won the top positions on the primary ballot because Clifford Hawley controlled 65 percent of the convention votes. He also said that the "Democratic party was deeply split." At that time we had a pre-primary state convention, and you had to have 20 percent of the vote to get on the ballot. Of course, I had pledged get rid of the pre-primary convention and go to a straight primary.

McKinney pointed out that there had been a quantum leap in votes cast in the Democratic primary in 1966, and compared it to the primary election in 1960. In 1966, a record-breaking 142,350 votes were cast for governor. The previous primary record had been set during the presidential election in 1964 when 123,795 Democrats voted in a three-way race between John Burroughs, Joseph A. Bursey and Tom Holand.

He said that Burroughs managed to carry only seven counties with mostly small populations. State Senator Ike Morgan of Portales led Burroughs' campaign in his home of Roosevelt County. In Rio Arriba County, Emilio Naranjo's forces managed to gather a 518 vote lead, and state Senator George Baca gained a slim 125-vote-margin for Burroughs in Socorro County.

Tom Montoya, brother of Senator Joe Montoya, got Burroughs an 8,697-vote-margin in Sandoval County. Burroughs, he added, also carried Guadalupe, Mora and Sierra counties by even slimmer margins.

In populist Bernalillo County, Lusk won over such well established political personalities as Victor Salazar and Charlie Davis.

In his home Eddy County, Lusk overcame the opposition of County Chairman Lon Watkins and several strong union leaders by nearly 2,800 votes. In Grant County, the mine union endorsed Burroughs, but Lusk won by a 60-vote-margin.

Lea County was another real surprise in that Burroughs was supported by the Democratic Party hierarchy. But he lost by a two-to-one margin.

In Santa Fe County, veteran political leader, Judge Samuel Z. Montoya, and former attorney general Fred Stanley, failed by over 1,100 votes in their effort to carry the capital city for Burroughs.

Possibly the hardest hit was old time politico Filo Sedillo of Valencia County, a staunch Burroughs supporter who failed to carry his own bailiwick by nearly 400 votes.

In another upset, Frank Zinn, Ernie Garcia and state Senator George Amaya failed by nearly 1,100 votes to carry McKinney County for Burroughs.

McKinney then concurred with my opinion about the pre-primary convention and said that "the legislature in the next session should repeal it," which they did.

McKinney also said that "the state Senate in New Mexico should be apportioned on a geographic basis." He took some issue with me in that I had taken a position in the reapportionment lawsuits that it should be reapportioned along the lines of populations only.

McKinney went on to say that "so radically has the Republican Party changed since 1964 that it's hard to believe what we see. That a party can go from Barry Goldwater's conservatism in 1964 to David Cargo's liberalism in 1966, borders on the incredible. With the Republican Party back in the hands of the Progressives, it could be once more a serious challenge to the Democrats, and this competition should be good for New Mexico." He thought that the competition between me and Lusk was welcomed, and he didn't endorse either of us at that time. However, editorially, he later endorsed Lusk fairly strongly and supported him in the election. He was also a delegate to the Democratic National Convention in 1968.

Mack Easley

In 1966, then incumbent Lieutenant Governor Mack Easley spoke to a group of African-American ministers in Hobbs. It was a traditional talk for Democrats in that he was there to tell them who they were supposed to work for in the election. A large group of them gathered and he started off by saying that he was supporting Gene Lusk for governor and he was sure that Lusk could get elected. He then went on to what proved to be an unwise series of remarks in regards to me. He said that "you don't want to cast your vote for David Cargo because he's from Albuquerque, he's liberal, he's a Republican, he's Catholic, and he's married to a Hispanic." Then he realized what he had said and stopped. At that point, Reverend Frank Wells rose and looked at him straight in the eye and said, "Mister Lieutenant Governor, what would you say if he was married to a Negro lady?"

That set the meeting back. There was a long period of silence, and then Reverend Wells added, "Well Mr. Lieutenant Governor, we made up our minds and were going to support Dave Cargo for governor."

It indicated in a way the way the election was being conducted on the East Side. They were leaning heavily on the fact Gene Lusk came from the area. They reflected a lot of the views that people held on the East Side. The result, of course, was that not only in Hobbs, but throughout New Mexico, I got more than 90 percent of the African-American vote.

Lonesome Dave

Sometimes in life you just plain get lucky.

I could have hired an advertising firm and paid them hundreds of thousands of dollars—I didn't have that kind of money, and even if I did I wouldn't have spent it on that!—and they never would have come up with a name as catchy and as dignified as Lonesome Dave.

I got the name in the summer of 1966, and it stuck. It defined what I was doing at time and how the campaign was going. I didn't have a lot of money. Gene Lusk was tooling around the state in a caravan of Cadillacs with dozens of aides and spending hundreds of thousands of dollars. The Republican Party had disowned me. Nobody thought I could win, and I was reduced, as some saw it, to talking to people one-on-one and shaking their hands.

I knocked on doors, rang doorbells, rapped on windows, stopped in gas stations, grocery stores, taverns, bowling alleys, beauty parlors, restaurants, union halls, went to funerals, church services, you name it. If there was someone breathing somewhere I was bound to find them, introduce myself and ask for their vote.

It was the old-fashioned way of campaigning, and I think it offended people in the media because they saw me as a candidate without a lot of money. And back then, as it does today, in politics, money talked. I think they saw me as this crazy, sort of clownish guy who made fun of things. To them, humor didn't belong in politics. Humor to them—at least in politics—was undignified.

Well one day about seven weeks before the election, John McMillion, the editor of the *Albuquerque Journal*, called me and asked if he could spend a few days with me campaigning. Reporters always do that. They spend a few hours with you and then go back and write something and pretend they know you deeply. It's a fraud, but they manage to pull it off. To a reporter, talking to someone for an hour is "deep."

McMillion had already spent a week with Gene Lusk, and he wanted to see how I campaigned. I welcomed his call because I was way behind in the polls and needed all the—free—publicity I could get.

"Sure," I told John when he asked if he could tag along. "I don't think you'll get much of a story out of it, but you're welcome to come along."

"Good," he said. "When will your driver pick me up?"

I laughed to myself. Gene had drivers, Cadillacs, money and dozens of aides, but me, well, I had myself. I told John he'd be picked up at eight in the morning at his office.

You can imagine the look on McMillion's face the next morning when a battered, 1959 blue Chevy pulled up with me behind the wheel and no one else in the car. The Chevy was worth about $200, and that was mainly the tires.

"Where's your entourage? Your aides?" he stammered.

"John," I said. "This is it. I'm the driver and entourage all in one."

He grumbled something to himself in obvious disappointment. I'm sure he was expecting the royal treatment of Cadillacs, leather seats and a big lunch, complete with plenty of alcohol. He got into the passenger seat, I got behind the wheel and off we went.

I was off to the small village of San Ysidro south of Santa Rosa in Guadalupe County. To get there you had to get off the main highway and take an unpaved county road for several miles.

I pulled off the highway and onto the county road. On the map it was a road, but in reality it was a rutted cow path. I was surprised. I think McMillion was shocked. We bumped along. John didn't say much or ask many questions. I think he just wanted to get out of there. I think he wished he was back in one of Gene Lusk's Cadillacs.

We bumped along and then, in the early afternoon, it started to rain. Actually, it started pouring. I drove on, but it became obvious that my $200 Chevy wasn't going to be able to negotiate the cow path that was quickly turning into mud. I stopped the car at the bottom of a small rise to wait out the storm. We were in the middle of nowhere out on the open range. The thunder boomed and the lightning flashed and the rain poured down and the two of us just sat there in the car.

After about 30 minutes it all stopped, as it always does in New Mexico, and the clouds moved on and the sun came out. The cow path had indeed turned to mud and I was going to continue on.

Then, off to my right, coming over the hill, was a huge herd of sheep. They came on slowly. Then, in the middle of all those sheep came a horse with a man on it. A human being! There was an opportunity and maybe a vote, I thought. I got out of the car and slopped and slipped around in the mud and made my way through the sheep to the man on horseback. McMillion followed. I got up to the guy—he was obviously startled. He was a sheep herder and he wore a black cowboy hat and had on leather chaps and he was all wet and soggy. I had on black slacks and a white shirt and tie and was dry. He was *really* surprised. I started to introduce myself. He leaned forward in his saddle and interrupted me.

"I know who you are," he said. "I don't know what the hell you're doing out here, but Lonesome Dave, you've got my vote. Hell, I've never seen anyone out here before. No one ever comes out here. And no one's ever come out here to ask me for my vote. Lonesome Dave, you got my vote."

We talked some more. McMillion scribbled it all down. We bid the sheep herder farewell and drove down to Roswell.

A few days later McMillion's story came out with the headline "Lonesome Dave." He accurately told the story of the sheep herder, the 1959 Chevy, the lack of an entourage and the cow path. The name Lonesome Dave stuck.

Actually, McMillion was a big Lusk supporter, and by labeling me Lonesome Dave he was trying to show how pathetic and unsuccessful he thought my campaign was. I had no money, no supporters and had to resort to asking a solitary sheep herder in the middle of nowhere for his vote. His article tried to belittle me and my campaign.

Well, it backfired on him. People started seeing me as a guy who was battling business-as-usual and the special interests all by himself. Although I had always been the underdog, the name Lonesome Dave crystallized that in peoples' minds. That story and the name showed them that I was just like them, an outsider when it came to politics and government. It showed them, I think, that my "special interests" were individual voters—themselves. If I cared enough to slop through the mud in the middle of nowhere to ask a solitary sheep herder for his vote, well, I was okay.

The name stuck. It defined me and my campaign, and I was on my way to the governor's office.

Lusk Debates

Gene Lusk and his supporters actually gave me my biggest help in the 1966 campaign. *Albuquerque Journal* editor John McMillion, a Lusk supporter, got the name Lonesome Dave going in an effort to discredit me and my campaign.

Lusk himself helped by agreeing to debate me. It was his mistake.

Gene was a nice guy, but he was rigid, not very creative and slow on his feet. If his numerous aides didn't give him an answer to a question or a position on an issue, he generally didn't have one.

Our first debate was in Santa Fe before the Junior Chamber

of Commerce. Gene had once headed the organization and so most of the thousand or so people who showed up were on his side. That changed quickly, though, when a man in the audience stood up and asked this question:

"Mr. Cargo, I know a woman, a neighbor of mine who is on welfare and keeps having children without the benefit of marriage. I think she's got five by now. You claim to care about the little people and the downtrodden. Let me ask you this: What are you going to do for this woman?"

I was in a good mood and didn't even think about it and I just blurted out:

"Let me tell you, the first thing I'm going to do for her is get her back on her feet!"

It took a few moments for the remark to sink in, and when it did, the audience howled. I was blessed with a quick wit and sense of humor, and it served me well in that campaign. Gene couldn't match me in that area. Laughter is one of life's greatest blessings.

Our second debate was about five weeks before the election in Albuquerque at the Hilton Hotel. It was to be an hour-and-a-half long, and was to be broadcast live by Albuquerque's TV stations.

By then I had already gotten the name Lonesome Dave. It had stuck and I was beginning to pick up steam, although I was at least 25 points behind Lusk in the polls. Gene helped me immensely. He showed up with a half-dozen aides and stacks of briefing books and other materials. The aides sat at a table behind him for all of the hotel and TV audience to see. I was by myself with no one behind me and just a few sheets of paper—Gene's legislative voting record—in my hands.

We got started and Gene lumbered on. I made a few jokes and got a few laughs. Then Gene gave me an opening. At one point he looked at the audience, and in his stern and somber voice asked:

"From whence comes this man of mystery who says he was born and raised in Dowagiac, Michigan?"

The question went on, but I had my opening. When Gene

finished, I answered: "For the edification of those in the audience, Dowagiac is equidistant between Cassapolis and Pokagon."

The audience was stunned. They just sat there. They had to be wondering what I was talking about and where on earth Cassapolis and Pokagan were. Then they laughed. My response had the effect of making them forget what Gene had asked and what he had been talking about.

The debate went and the TV audience was able to see Gene with is aides and briefing books and me by myself and a few sheets of paper. I was quicker than he was and I didn't need aides to give me answers or positions on issues. The audience saw that.

At one point I started criticizing Gene for his voting record in the state legislature. He answered me by saying that when he had cast those votes he had been "politically immature."

That gave me another opening.

"Political immaturity," I said. "When you were casting those votes you were older than I am now!"

The audience laughed and I scored more points.

Then Gene blundered again. He started talking about his mother, who had been in the U.S. House of Representatives.

"In 1953 when I was a leading figure in the state legislature and my mother Georgia was in the U.S. Congress, what were you doing? Where were you, Mr. Cargo," he said in attempt to hit at me.

I replied: "I was in the U.S. Army during the Korean War serving my country. What we want to know, Mr. Lusk, is where were you?"

It went over well. The audience laughed and I was cruising to a debate victory. That's not just my opinion. A few days later, McMillion wrote in the Albuquerque Journal:

"LUSK VULNERABLE: Lusk was trapped into a debate with Cargo and this was a tactical blunder.

"Debating Cargo is like tangling with a keen-witted octopus. Cargo thinks fast, moves fast and can fire from the hip with ease.

"Lusk is a little more rigid and in addition has to be more

careful of what he is saying. (He's been trying to choke down the words 'political immaturity' ever since he uttered them in a foolhardy moment of candor.)

"Cargo has the whole Democratic organization to snipe at and Lusk is in the unenviable position of having to defend another man's activities.

"And when it comes to shotgunning generalities, Dave Cargo is a past master."

That second debate turned the election around for me. Before it I was 25 points behind Lusk. Just a few weeks later I had beaten him decisively for the governorship.

Election Night in 1966

It was 11:30 at night on election day in 1966 when I stood on top of a table in the Alvarado Hotel and told everyone at my election night party to hang on and not be discouraged. It was easy for them to be discouraged and disappointed. The returns had come in slowly, and as we sat and stood listening to them the message was clear: Gene Lusk was leading—had been leading all night—by an average of 5,000 to 7,000 votes.

I knew something, though, that no one else seemed to be paying attention to: all of the returns up to that point had been from outside Bernalillo County. I knew I would run strong in Bernalillo County.

"Look," I said, "The Bernalillo County vote hasn't come in yet, and we're going to do well here."

I don't know that many people believed me. I don't know that I believed it myself. After all, 7,000 votes was a lot to make up.

And, history was against me. The only two Republicans to have won statewide elections in the 35 years prior to that were Ed Mechem and Tom Bolack. Mechem had been elected governor, and Bolack lieutenant governor. It had been a stunning dry spell for Republicans.

Even worse was that the election results were being channeled through Los Angeles and the TV networks. Several networks had called me, saying that I had lost and wanted to know if I wanted to make a concession. I didn't, and I told them, "I don't know how I could have been defeated because I'm carrying every precinct in Bernalillo County except one."

Based on our poll watcher reports I knew that I had a substantial lead in Martineztown and that I was leading by an average of five points throughout the valley and Bernalillo County. Those results hadn't officially come in yet, and so, officially, I was losing.

Well, while I was up on that table and giving that talk, someone handed me the telephone. On the line was Bill Feather of the Associated Press. He said rather abruptly, "Governor, you've just been elected." I asked, "just been elected?" He said, "You're carrying Bernalillo County by more than 22,000 votes, and it's elected you are."

Within 30 seconds I had gone from being well behind to being well ahead. Feather told me I had won Bernalillo County 50,149 votes to 29,563 for Lusk. It was amazing and wonderful. I had gotten more votes than did president Dwight D. Eisenhower, who, in 1956 got 41,839 votes in the county. I had gotten 9,000 more than he did!

The ballroom exploded, and within 20 minutes there were more than 5,000 people in the hotel. It was bedlam. All I can say is that they celebrated loudly. I thanked everyone. And even before I got through thanking them, people were asking me for jobs.

To say that I was pleasantly surprised is an understatement. I was thrilled and overwhelmed. Part of me really couldn't believe it.

The bedlam eventually subsided, and I realized that I would be governor. I started to prepare mentally for the inauguration and the beginning of my first term as governor of the state of New Mexico.

The political situation in New Mexico was about to change for some time to come.

Gene Lusk Wins

On Wednesday, November 9, 1966, the headline in the *El Paso Times* read, "Gene Lusk elected New Mexico Governor." Below, it said, "Democrats Win Easily Among New Mexico Voters."

The paper then went on to expand upon the story: "Gene Lusk held a substantial lead in the race for governor against David Cargo."

Despite the fact that I was running strong in Bernalillo County, and also ran strong in some unexpected areas, "a strong outpouring of votes from heavily Democratic southeast New Mexico kept Lusk on top." They then added, "The governor's race between Cargo and Lusk had been expected to be a close one at the top of the ticket."

It was definitely a Harry Truman kind of headline. Of course it brought to mind the headline in the Chicago Tribune in 1948 which said "Dewey Wins," meaning the presidential election. I still have a framed copy of the Lusk headline even though it really wasn't too factual.

Copper Strike and Standing up to LBJ

I don't know how many people—if any—stood up to President Lyndon B. Johnson, but for some reason I did, and by doing so I helped end a national copper strike.

The copper strike hit the country in July of 1967, and it wasn't settled until April 2, 1968. It cost the nation and New Mexico a lot of money.

In New Mexico we lost 30,000 tons of production, $2.7 million in wages and $720,000 in Severance Tax income. When it was all over, after nine months, New Mexico was out $4.9 million.

On a national basis the issues for the strike were significant, but in New Mexico they were minor.

I called the union and company people up to Santa Fe one day near the strike's end and asked them what they were arguing about. The answer I got was ridiculous.

Work gloves, I was told, and who would furnish them, the workers or the companies.

"Can't you guys get onto something bigger than that?" I asked them. "There are 1,200 people out of work because of work gloves?"

It made me feel bad because I had been personally paying the utility bills of some of the union members during the strike. They were without heat or electricity and I couldn't let that stand.

Early on in the strike I went to Bayard, New Mexico, to talk with the miners, who were members of Local 890. There had been a strike in 1950 or 1951 when Ed Mechem was governor, and there had been a lot of violence. Two people were killed and a lot of property had been damaged. The National Guard had been called in and I didn't want a repeat.

So I went there and told the union members what I would do and what I expected in return. There were two state police officers in the district, and I said I'd transfer one to Santa Fe, which meant there'd be one left. I said I didn't want to have to call out the National Guard. Then I told them:

"I don't want any violence. If there is, you all will be personally responsible. If you hear of anybody planning any violence, you need to stop it."

The strike wore on and 1,200 New Mexicans were out of work. It was awful.

Well, one day I got a call from the White House saying that the president wanted the governors and the senators from the copper mining states in his office. We assembled on a Friday afternoon.

There were several governors, including Tim Babcock of Montana, Jack Williams of Arizona, Don Samuelson of Idaho, Cal Rampton of Utah and me. Both of the senators from those states were there as well.

We were in the White House and President Johnson addressed us:

"Your president is goin' to find a friendly judge in Wyomin' and I'm going to get an injunction and force these miners back to work. We can't have this strike goin' anymore and that's what your president is goin' to do. Now how many of you are goin' to support your president?"

Then Johnson looked around the room for answers from everyone.

All the governors and the congresspeople answered the same:

"Yes sir, Mr. President."

No one dared cross him. Then it was my turn.

"No sir, Mr. President," I said. "No sir!"

"Goddammit. You're the only person here who's got

any guts," Johnson said. "Now why don't you want me to get an injunction?"

I explained the best I could: "I'm tired of paying the utility bills for many of these people, and I have been. And in New Mexico they don't have anything left to argue about except work gloves, and who's going to supply them. I'm fed up with it. I think the families are fed up with it and you and the industry people need to sit down and settle it."

Johnson was a funny guy, and he said, "Your president is proud of the governor of New Mexico who had the guts to speak up. I'm gonna settle this strike."

That was a Friday. He apparently made calls all weekend and got everybody in Washington on Monday. Shortly afterwards he announced that the strike had been settled.

Sometime after that, Senator Joe Montoya went down and spoke to union members in Bayard, and one guy got up and asked how the strike had been settled. Montoya told them what had happened and gave them an explanation according to the facts.

"Governor Cargo did it," he said that day. "The rest of them just sat there and agreed with Johnson, and the governor disagreed and the strike was settled.

"I might disagree with Governor Cargo from time to time, but I take my hat off to him. He settled the strike."

I hadn't gone to Washington intending to challenge LBJ and settle the copper strike, but that's what happened, and I'm glad it did.

Some Extraordinary Appointments

I had the good fortune to have hired some outstanding people onto my staff during my two terms as governor.

One was Maralyn Budke. She had been employed by the legislature since she had graduated from college, and she had worked for the legislature for a long time in various capacities. Essentially though, she worked for the Legislative Finance Committee and was an expert on state finances and budgeting. She came into my office with me because she had gotten into a fight with a Representative Bobby Mayfield who was the committee's chairman. Consequently, Maralyn was a little uneasy about her job.

At that point, Representative John Mershon, who headed the House Appropriations Committee, and Senator Harold Runnels came into my office and said she might be available and might work for me. I immediately contacted Maralyn and she came to work for me and was an extraordinary individual. She was bright and had a firm grasp of policy and legislative matters. She was one of my key employees.

Another was Ed Hartman, who took over as head of the Department of Finance and Administration. He had served in that same capacity during the terms of Governor Ed Mechem. He was bright and an expert in his field. I was lucky to have him on board.

I hired Franklin Jones, who was a longtime operative in the legislature and who was the leading expert on taxation, not only in the legal profession, but in state government as well. He was a Democrat and had actively supported my opponent during the 1966 election. But when he came in one day I asked him if he would like to take over the old Bureau of Revenue and if he would like to develop it into a viable Department of Taxation and Finance. To my amazement, he said he would. But he added that he had not supported me in the election.

"I know you worked against me," I told him, "but I'd like to put you on board because I want to straighten out the department."

At that time, all of the department's employees would be fired after every election, and the bureau was inefficient to say the least. Franklin got busy and cleaned out the department, and we went from being ranked 49th by the Council of State Governments to being ranked third in the country. He was able to modernize the department and had a great influence on tax matters. Collections increased to the point where we had a sizeable budget surplus every year I was in office. During my last year we were able to give a tax credit on the next year's taxes to all state taxpayers in the amount of 25 percent of what they owed in taxes.

I also hired Walter Kerr. He had been the Associated Press bureau chief in Germany during the time of Hitler's rise to power. He then he transferred to the Soviet Union and headed the AP there during the war and during the years of domination by Joseph Stalin. He had also been the editor of the Paris edition of the *Herald Tribune*. After he left the *Herald Tribune* he became editor of the *Santa Fe New Mexican* and I hired him in my press office. The people in the governor's office used to get a real kick out of it because there were a number of times that Walter and I would converse in German. The staffers didn't have the slightest idea of what we were talking about. But he was a brilliant man and he wrote several books and was just outstanding.

Don Perkins was an athlete who was extraordinary. He had strongly supported me for election and was paying football for the Dallas Cowboys. I was very fond of Don and I hired him as the first Afro-American department head. He became head of the newly-created Transportation Department. He is an outstanding actor and can perform in theatrical plays with a great deal of skill. He's a good and decent individual and a person I have a great deal of affection for. There were some complaints when I hired him, but he proved that they were wrong. He did an excellent job.

Villanueva

It was the last week of November in 1966 when I got my first real taste of politics at a higher level. The Republican governors—newly elected and those holding over for re-election—met in Colorado Springs. For the first time I met Nelson Rockefeller, Winthrop Rockefeller and John Love. We spent three days in Colorado and it was an interesting experience. I learned a lot and also learned that the governors were far more moderate in their outlook than the congressional Republicans. This was perplexing in that the Republicans in Congress were extremely conservative. I also was faced with my first real problem, one that gave me a preview of what to expect when I took office.

Upon returning to New Mexico I made arrangements to fulfill my promise to visit Villanueva and to do so right after the election. I pledged to do my best to get the road paved to Villanueva and also to create a state park in Villanueva. When I went up there, John McMillion, the editor of the *Albuquerque Journal*, went with me. He wrote a delightful article describing the beauty of Villanueva and how spectacular it was in that area of San Miguel County.

When we arrived at the turn off to Villanueva from Interstate 25, we had to take a route that was inappropriately named Highway 3 to Villanueva. It didn't really warrant the title of highway at that point. When we got to Villanueva there were 1,500 people waiting for us and they had probably 200 people on horseback. It was a colorful scene to say the least. I was impressed that so many people would gather to take me out to the village. People were thrilled: for the first time a governor was going up to the village. They showed it by turning out in droves.

McMillion accurately described it in that he stated that "the road up to Villanueva rammed through the town of Ribera and the villages of San Miguel, Pueblo and Sena. At Sena the pavement ends and the remaining few miles into Villanueva are over a narrow, twisting, boulder-studded road which defies the best efforts beyond repair." And then he said, "While he had promised to pave the road, it was something which Cargo and his conscience would have to wrestle with." He then continued, "It may be a shame to pave the road to Villanueva as thus far the area has been comparatively unsullied by tourists and commercialism." It was his position that the road not be built and he admitted that "the final few miles of the road—the unpaved portion—are choked with dust continually."

Eventually I paved the road and built a magnificent state park up there. People have been duly appreciative. As a matter of fact when I initiated a project to build a library in Villanueva they named it after me. I don't regret building the road, building a park, and certainly not working towards building a library.

Hollywood on the Rio Grande

Churchill, in his seminal work on his ancestor, the Duke of Marlborough, told of a time in 1820 when the great English statesman Canning resigned as Prime Minister and a Tory Lord declared with great relish, "Now we have got rid of those confounded men of genius."

I'm sure there are some people who wish that we hadn't had the people of genius that we ultimately had on the New Mexico Film Commission.

It was in 1967 that I set up the nation's first official film commission. The idea was to spur economic development by attracting filmmakers to the state. I was helped in that effort by a Film Commission that was exemplary indeed. We were a great success, and the credit must go to the commission's members. They were:

Chuck Middlestadt, Lou Gasparini, artist Fred Harman, writer Jack Schaefer, two-time Academy Award winner Charles LeMaire, Jack Stamm, former Albuquerque Tribune editor Ralph Looney, Dick Skrondahl, writer Max Evans, writer Don Hamilton and representatives of Albuquerque's three TV stations, Jerry Danziger (KOB), Max Sklower (KOAT) and Stretch Scherer (KGGM).

They were ably assisted by my press secretary Bill Previtti. Bill was one of the driving forces behind the commission. He had lots of contacts and was invaluable when it came to setting the thing up.

It all started informally. One night I was seeing a movie in Albuquerque. The theater's manager, Lou Gasparini caught me after the film and said, "We need to set up a film commission."

We talked for 15 minutes, and I thought to myself, "Well, that's an interesting idea indeed." Shortly afterward, Middlestadt, who was a newspaper columnist, called me and made the same suggestion. Not long after that we set up a meeting through Previtti and talked. Bill was very excited about the prospect. I came up with the names of a number of people who eventually wound up on the commission.

One problem we had was that Looney was the *Tribune*'s editor. The *Albuquerque Journal*'s editor, John McMillion, didn't like that. He said the deal would give Looney the inside track when it came to stories and that the Journal would be rather selective and restrictive in its coverage of the Film Commission. That proved to be true. I offered to put McMillion on the commission, but he rejected the offer.

The commission was a well-balanced, but unpaid board. Each member had his own field of expertise. Middlestadt and Skrondahl were both writers and photographers and immediately went to work writing press releases for the *Hollywood Reporter* and *Variety*. They proved to be absolutely invaluable because we attracted a lot of attention in both publications. Likewise, Looney began touting in his paper the possibilities for making movies in New Mexico. Harman was a nationally known and renowned artist. Evans, though, was the real leader of the pack. Without his efforts we would have gone absolutely nowhere. Schaefer had been involved in a number of films, including *Shane*, and LeMaire was a two-time Academy Award winner. That gave us an entrée into Hollywood's prestigious inner circle.

Many people have the impression that New Mexico's film history goes back only three or four years. In fact, the state has had a long and glorious film history. The first film to be shot in New Mexico came in 1898. It was a documentary by the Edison company called *Indian Day School*. In 1911, *The Dude*, a western, was produced by the Powers Company. That was followed in 1912 by *A Pueblo Legend* and *The Tourist*. Then Tom Mix came here and made a number of films. Over the years, many films were shot here. From 1898 through 1999, 337 feature films were shot in the state. Most of them came after we started the Film Commission. In the three years before I became governor, there had been only four movies made in the state. In 1967 there was one, *The Covenant With Death*. I watched them film most of that movie and took a lot of interest in the film industry and in moviemaking.

Since 1999, New Mexico state government has loaned millions of dollars to movie companies to shoot films here. The number of productions made here has grown dramatically. Since 1999, 251 films have been made here. Some were short, and some have been TV series. The film industry has been an absolute gold mine for the state.

The Film Commission was a history-making project. Some

succeeding governors have had a great deal of interest in films, and some have not been interested at all. When Governor Bill Richardson came into office he immediately saw the advantages of having the state be a center for the industry, and he has pushed the film effort here with vigor. The news media has also been generous in its coverage of the state's efforts to attract the film industry.

Actually, Tom Mix was the most prolific of all film people to have come here. He was a worldwide western star and made his earliest films in Las Vegas beginning in 1915.

Director and producer Burt Kennedy was another one who was interested in New Mexico. He was of great assistance in bringing films to the state. He took a special interest in Evans, and especially his contemporary cowboy novel *The Rounders*. The book was a classic, and Kennedy and producer Richard Lyons decided to do make a film out of the book. Originally it was scheduled to be filmed south of Santa Fe on a ranch owned by Alva Simpson. Eventually, though, they were forced to go to Sedona, Arizona, for locations. Evans' book *The Hi-Lo Country* was filmed in New Mexico.

We eventually persuaded David Dortort, the producer of the long-running, top-rated TV shows *Bonanza* and *High Chaparral*, to make a quick trip to the state. He was impressed and eventually shot several films here.

We were seven months into the film project when LeMaire and Evans started making phone calls to prominent producers and directors. Their plan was to set up a meeting with me, Film Commission members and producers and directors at the Beverly Hills Hotel. Early in February 1968, Evans went to Hollywood and began phoning, cajoling and asking everyone he knew what we could do to get a meeting. Finally he called Gasparini and set a date for a large breakfast meeting at the Beverly Hills Hotel. It meant that Evans had really stuck his neck out in connection with the thing, and we just had to be successful.

I went to the hotel with Ida Jo, Gasparini, Looney, Middlestadt, Steve Kopac, Charles Cullen, Previtti and LeMaire. The night before we got together with actors Robert Montgomery and Chill Wills. Burl Ives, whom I knew, and a few others pitched in as well.

The next morning at 10 o'clock the breakfast room was loaded with the heads of two studios and 35 major producers. There were also another 35 or so production managers, screenwriters and others connected with the movie industry.

We had made a short film to promote ourselves. I've got to say that it was probably the worst promo film ever made by anyone, anywhere. That august group received it with uproarious laughter and lots of applause. They couldn't believe what they had seen. It was an incredibly primitive piece. They all knew it, but they appreciated what we were doing, and they knew that we were sincere and that we were trying to do the best by the movie industry that we could.

It quickly became apparent that those present liked New Mexico. They also liked the Film Commission, and they firmly came to believe that we had the ability to make filming more accessible and easier for them.

I gave a short speech that I had carefully prepared, and fortunately, it came across as genuine, sincere and to the point. I explained why we had set up the Film Commission and what we hoped we could do for New Mexico. Evans said the speech was, "magic." Well, magic or not, it was probably one of the better speeches I had ever given.

The meeting was a combination of things. First, they were interested because it was the first film commission that had been established anywhere. Secondly, I think they were rather interested in me and Ida Jo because we were a very young couple. I was the youngest governor in the U.S., and she was by far the youngest first lady in that she was 25 years old at the time. It was a nice combination. Looking back on it, we seem to have struck the right note, and things looked promising for the venture.

By lunchtime we had three commitments to do films in New

Mexico. Kennedy said he was going to shoot *The Good Guys and the Bad Guys* here. Mark Hanna had brought his producer for *King Gun*. Oscar Nichols and Clair Huffaker brought in producer Jerry Adler and indicated they would shoot *Nobody Loves a Drunken Indian* here. All three lived up to their promises. Kennedy and I became close friends. He introduced me to Bill Castle, and we became friends. Castle dominated Paramount Pictures because he had produced a number of successful films and because he had pioneered the horror film genre.

We visited both Universal and Paramount studios and met with Hoss Cartwright (Dan Blocker), Little Joe (Michael Landon) and the whole Cartwright bunch when they were filming *Bonanza*. We were escorted by producer David Dortort, who also became a good friend and who frequently visited me in the mansion in Santa Fe. Blocker had come from Carlsbad where he had been a school teacher. I knew him when he was in Carlsbad, and he was also a close friend.

The irony of it was that Blocker had done a campaign ad for Gene Lusk during the governor's race, and when I came in he put his hands over his eyes and said, "Well, Gene was a damn good man, but you're a damn, damn, damn good man. And if I'd lived in New Mexico on election day I might have voted for you. In any event, even if I hadn't voted for you, I'd vote for you next time."

The following day Max and I went by ourselves to Warner Brothers to meet with Kenneth Hyman. He said he would do several films in New Mexico, including *The Wild Bunch*, with producer Phil Feldman and director Sam Peckinpah. I realized at this point that we were on the road to success.

After we finished with that conversation, I then met with the heads of the various unions in Hollywood. They were especially excited because I was a Republican and they were Republicans as well. It was interesting because just about everyone else in Hollywood were Democrats. In the ensuing years the unions purposely sent films to New Mexico whenever they could.

Hollywood stringers Middlestadt and Skrondahl were able to get a number of stories in the *Hollywood Reporter*, *Variety* and the *Box Office* in New York. California Governor Ronald Reagan took note of it. He called me a number of times to ask what we were doing. I don't know if he was just interested in the fact that we were there or if he was trying to pick up inside information. In any event, the Film Commission was in full gear and we were starting to pick things up considerably.

Evans, Ida Jo and I made several trips to Hollywood after that by ourselves. We did it by appointment because the Film Commission didn't have a budget. The legislature hadn't given them any money. Eventually, lawmakers gave the commission a $30,000 budget. During my last year in office they increased it to $100,000. Even then we faced an uphill battle because state Representative Tom Hoover of Albuquerque wanted to cut it to $40,000. Other legislators didn't want to fund it at all. Hoover said I was using the commission to further my own career in films, which was rather silly. Hoover's motion was defeated 50-10 in the House after two hours of debate. Hoover said I could have done a better job of public relations, but Representative Jamie Koch defended me and said I was doing just fine.

During one trip to Hollywood we met with Hal Wallis, who was a very famous producer. He told me that he was thinking of doing a film in New Mexico. Prior to that I had been asked by state employee Richard Bradford if he could take some time off to go to Hollywood, as he had written a book called *Red Sky at Morning*, which was about New Mexico and set in Truchas. I said he could, and he gave me an autographed copy of his book. He said he was doing a script for the movie. I read both the book and the script and encouraged him.

Wallis took a liking to New Mexico and we became fairly close friends. He also liked to stay at the governor's mansion in Santa Fe. While there, he would phone people in California and tell them that if they needed to get hold of him they could reach him at the governor's mansion in New Mexico. You have to understand that in large states like New York and California, people rarely get a chance to meet a governor, let alone stay in the governor's mansion.

Around this time I learned a nice little trick. If I really wanted to attract attention with the Hollywood crowd I would wait until they were on the set shooting in a different state. Then I would call a particular director or actor. Then everything would come to a halt because they would hear over the PA system that the governor's office was calling. They'd get on the phone, we'd talk, and the next thing you knew, they would often move the production to New Mexico.

It was also around this time that Burt Kennedy decided to give me one of my first movie roles. He said he was going to film *The Good Guys and the Bad Guys* in Chama and that he wanted me to play the part of a reporter. I did and I still get residuals in the mail every year. Robert Mitchum was in the movie, as was Bob Kennedy and Marty Balsam. They were spending $50,000 a week in Chama, which was great for the local folks. Burt Kennedy spent $150,000 to use the Cumbres Toltec Railroad for the film. Of that, $50,000 was used as a down payment to buy the railroad for the states of New Mexico and Colorado.

Shortly after our trip to Hollywood, actor Anthony Quinn decided to come to New Mexico and film Clair Huffaker's film, *Nobody Loves a Drunken Indian*. Quinn and I became friends. He delighted in staying at the mansion. We used to talk all hours into the night about politics. He came from Chihuahua City in Mexico. Once we took a trip to Chihuahua. There we had our pictures taken together with Pancho Villa's widow, or at least one of his widows. For many years that picture hung in her museum, and there we were, the three of us together.

One disturbing event occurred on June 29, 1969, when the *Albuquerque Journal* ran an article by Jim Newton that was headlined: "Vultures May Kill State Film Industry." The effort was being jeopardized by the fact that the city's hotels and restaurants were hiking up their prices for the movie crews. It was an unacceptable situation. We weren't out to gouge people. That was wrong. We held a meeting with business leaders in the old Western Skies Hotel and came up with a code of conduct that was highly publicized. I asked that they not only maintain the same rate for film industry people as they did for others, but that they also give them a reduced rate. It was an interesting twist, but one I felt was necessary if we were to maintain and build on the good will that we had created. The idea took hold and we were able to stabilize the costs to the film industry.

Another pair who came to New Mexico to film in 1969 were Peter Fonda and Dennis Hopper. They, of course, did *Easy Rider*. It was a great success. Hopper still comes to the state regularly, and every so often I see him in Taos.

Fonda was a very formidable guy. He would come to the mansion and visit. One night he got a call from his sister, Jane Fonda. He turned to me and said that Jane had volunteered to put in a word for me in a speech that she was going to give down at the University of New Mexico. I politely told him that I would take a pass on it.

Another enthusiastic supporter of the film industry was J. W. Eaves. He set up the J. W. Eaves Ranch south of Santa Fe as a movie ranch. He did a great job of making the ranch a successful movie operation. I will forever be in his debt for what he did for the movie industry. He was a very prominent politician in Lea County. He held a number of political offices down there. His son Mel was in the legislature. I became close with the whole family, and they really helped build the film business here.

I also got to know Greer Garson and her husband Buddy Fogelson. We became good friends and they contributed to my political campaigns both in money and other ways. I helped her set up a film program at the College of Santa Fe. It became an invaluable part of the state's film effort.

There were some funny and unusual things that happened with the film business. One involved Burt Kennedy. We were preparing to shoot *The Good Guys and the Bad Guys* in Chama. A couple of tough looking guys approached me and Burt one day. They said they were active in Alianza and then announced that they were going to disrupt the whole thing and that the train they were going to use for the film would be blown up and that there would be all kinds of other problems.

I said I couldn't understand what the problem was because they were going to work for the production company and be extras in the film and they'd only be endangering themselves. They stood and looked at us in kind of a blank way and then said, "Oh, when do we start?" I said, "Well, you're starting soon. Mr. Kennedy here will explain it to you." Kennedy winked at me and gave them twenty bucks and told them to report to work the next day. I'm not sure what they did on the film, but they were duly sworn in as members of the crew.

I also played the part of a lawyer in the film *Lock Down*, which was filmed at the old penitentiary in Santa Fe. One of the actors asked if there had ever been riot at the prison. I told him "No," but there most certainly would be in the future if the governor following me didn't follow my reforms. Little did I know that some years later, in 1980, that we would have the worst prison riot in the nation's history.

We also had an interesting situation when *The Cheyenne Social Club* was being filmed here. Jimmy Stewart was in the film along with Henry Fonda. Gene Kelly was also associated with it. One night we went out to dinner. When we came back to the mansion, the baby sitter was watching TV with a beer in her hand. She was obviously enjoying herself. All of a sudden she looked up and saw the three of us. She turned to me and quietly said, " Governor Cargo, I only drank one beer. But I am having problems right now." I asked, "What problems?" She said, "I'm seeing three movie actors and they look awful real to me right now, and I should probably go to bed." I said, "Do as you please, but they are for real."

We had a problem in 1970 with the filming of *Red Sky at Morning* in Truchas. One of the locals came into the meeting we were having in the town and said he thought it was going to be awfully difficult to film in Truchas because there were going to be a lot of interruptions. He looked very unfriendly, indeed. Finally I spoke up and said we didn't want too much noise because if things were interrupted it meant that we wouldn't be able to serve food to the local villagers after the crew and actors had eaten. I said if that was the case, the wives would probably have to feed the men at home. The wives immediately took an interest in the thing and said they thought there would be no problems. Sure enough, there weren't.

I also went to Las Cruces and appeared in the movie *Up in the Cellar*. I hadn't had a chance to read the script other than the part I was going to play. So I did my part and departed and thought little about it until I was in Hollywood one day passing a movie theater that was advertising the film. The marquee boasted that it was an X-rated film! And there was my name on the marquee with the rest of the actors. I quickly contacted the filmmaker and suggested it might be well if they kept my name off the marquee from then on.

I appeared in *Bunny O'Hare*, a movie with Bette Davis that was shot in the Tijeras area. I played the part of a state policeman and was sitting in a state police car when a real state police car approached. One of the officers approached, looked in and said, "I thought somebody was out here impersonating a state police officer, but that's all right, governor, go right ahead."

I was also in *King Gun* a.k.a. *The Gatling Gun*. Others in the film included Guy Stockwell, Woody Strode and John Carradine. It was about a cavalry raid and some Indians being killed. But before I got a chance to take a shot at anyone, I was hit in the back by an arrow and killed. That didn't stop Wendell Chino of the Mescalero Apache Tribe from going after me charging that I was slaughtering Indians. I explained that "I never fired a shot, but if it will make him happy I will transfer a fire truck to the reservation, and he can have it free of charge." Actually, it was surplus property. But he got a new fire engine and apparently was happy.

Another controversy erupted when Warner Brothers was

filming *Flap* starring Anthony Quinn and produced by Jerry Adler. The problem was that the original title of the film was *Nobody Loves a Drunken Indian*. I immediately remonstrated with the filmmakers saying that the title was inappropriate. They eventually changed the name to *Flap* and we had a special premiere in Albuquerque with all the proceeds going to a $75,000 scholarship for Indian students. Quinn made a personal appearance at the premiere, which was held at Cinema East Theater. The scholarships were available to Indians who wanted to pursue a career in the creative arts, including cinema. That eased the tension and we had no more difficulties with the film.

In 1970, Burl Ives came to Santa Fe to do *McMasters*. I had known him before, but really got to know him during the filming. We became longtime friends and I eventually became his attorney. I represented him for many years, and he helped in my campaigns. Ives ultimately built an adobe home near Galisteo. Many times Burl and his wife Dorothy and Ida Jo and I would meet at his home and Burl would perform for us. He didn't simply entertain us. We became dear friends, and I was with him right up until his death.

I tried to encourage filmmaking in the state by advocating that filmmakers be exempt from the gross receipts and the inventory taxes. On July 1, 1970, the exemptions became law.

Another film that brought a great deal of attention to the state was *Butch Cassidy and the Sundance Kid*, starring Paul Newman, Robert Redford and Katherine Ross. It was filmed in Taos and Chama.

In addition to going to Hollywood, we tried to get as many producers to come to New Mexico as possible. We once held a conference in Santa Fe and invited producers. They came out in force. Those who came included Jack Ballard of Paramount Pictures; Burt Kennedy, who at the time was associated with United Artists; Brad Dexter and Sydney Furie, whose films were released through Paramount; Keith Larsen of Larsen Productions; Albert Jaeger and Jules Schermer of National General Corp.; Oscar Nichols of Oscar Nichols; Emit Emerson of Samuel Goldyn Studio, Inc.; Cornell Wilde of Theodora Productions; Herman King of King Productions; Francis Alyon of United Pictures; George Montgomery, an independent producer; and David Dortort, another independent producer.

They came and indicated they would invest up to $10 million in filming in the next three months in New Mexico. Dortort was especially impressed and said, "If Governor Cargo's committee on film entertainment, with assistance from the Albuquerque Chamber of Commerce, continues to expand the state's motion picture program, it will create the most attractive production package ever offered in the industry by any state in the union." That was a big step in bringing film industry people to New Mexico and letting the public know how important the effort was.

I decided to attend the Academy Awards to be held in Hollywood on April 7, 1970. I was invited by Gregory Peck, who was president of the Film Academy. I knew him quite well and he had been to the state several times to film. Ida Jo decided not to attend, so I took Burt Kennedy because he couldn't get tickets to the event. This proved to be fortuitous because John Wayne, Kirk Douglas and Johnny Cash decided to go to the show with us.

In Hollywood, I made a nationwide appearance on TV and again was given the opportunity to tout moviemaking in New Mexico.

Also during that visit, Charlie Cullen, who was the Commission Liaison Officer, was able to set up a meeting with top Hollywood figures. That eventually resulted in bringing over $40 million additional dollars in movie projects to the state. We had a luncheon and were accompanied by some very prominent people in the film industry. Burl Ives hosted the event. Included among the guests were representatives from *Life Magazine*, the *Wall Street Journal*, *Los Angeles Times*, the *Hollywood Reporter Daily*, *Variety* and the *San Francisco Chronicle*.

Others in attendance were Charles Borne, executive vice president of the Motion Pictures Association; John Mather, executive producer of *Gunsmoke*; Ray Stark, producer of *Funny Girl*; Fred Engle of Brian Production; William Castle of W.C. Enterprises; A.C. Lyles of Paramount Pictures; John Sturges, president of Goldwyn Productions; Ed Muhl, vice president in charge of production for Universal City Studios; William Sullivan of Columbia Studios; Lindley Parsons Jr., vice president of production for MGM Studios; Hail Wallace of Universal City Studios, Inc.; David Wolper of 20th Century Fox; and Carter de Haven Jr., of Warner Brothers Seven Arts Studio.

This all meant that we had hit it big time in getting the attention of the top people in the motion picture industry. On my way back to New Mexico I went to Sacramento and spent a few days with Governor Reagan. We had long talks about the film industry and he said that we were attracting more films than they were in California.

Then I had a luncheon in Sacramento and entertained the following people: John Goff of the *Hollywood Reporter*; Orlando Suervo of Globe Photos; Kevin Thomas of the *Los Angeles Times*; Dick Kleiner, NEA; Todd Everett of *Box Office* magazine; Jeanet Muzurki, Copley New Service; Digby Diehl of Freelance Film Critics; Dick Skrondahl, who represented *Daily Variety* and *Billboard* magazines.

The trip to Sacramento was an added success. Reagan again launched into a discussion about how amazing it was that New Mexico was able to attract all of the attention in California when it came to motion pictures. I was thrilled that he had done so. Reagan and I then concluded the day with a press conference that was centered around the movie industry. That got a lot of attention and was covered on the evening news by the three major networks. Ralph Looney was especially complimentary when I returned to Santa Fe. He wrote at great length in the *Tribune* about the trip. He said, "Taking the governor to Hollywood was important. That really impressed them. Politicians are not all that revered, but Cargo made an impact. That resulted in a steady procession of movies, and lot of the credit goes to him. It produced a gold mine for the state, and it all stemmed from the creation of the Film Commission and its efforts and trips to California and activities in New Mexico to attract productions."

As a direct result of the Film Commission's activities while

I was in office we brought in almost $1 billion to the state. The effort stretched into the administration of Governor Bruce King, who followed me as governor. King was very sympathetic and used to call me now and then for advice. I must admit that he was the only governor who ever really spent much time talking to me about the venture.

In all, the formation of the Film Commission brought in about $3.5 billion in film projects to the state. It was a worthwhile venture. Other states must have thought so, because now every state has a film office, and most major cities in the nation, including Albuquerque and Santa Fe, have film offices.

It was a good idea and it was good for New Mexico. It was also good for me in that I appeared in over a dozen movies. Today, I still receive small checks from those appearances.

Executive Orders

On January 1, 1967, I signed Executive Order Number One which dealt with conflict of interest. This was a two-page document which set forth various statements on conflict of interest in doing business with the state.

My Executive Order Number Two, signed on January 17, 1967, covered the minimum pay for New Mexico State Hospital employees, which went to $220 a month. That particular order was largely directed at the state hospital in Las Vegas. At that time they had not been paying employees anything more than the minimum wage which was not much. I signed Executive Order Number Three on the 23rd day of January 1967. This addressed certain forms of racial discrimination; it covered a code of fair practices governing the executive offices of the state and prohibited discrimination in appointments, assignments and promotions of state personnel. The third order also dealt with state services and facilities, employment services, licensing, public contracts, personal assistance at the state level and the patient training and apprenticeship programs.

Executive Order Number Six Hundred Seventy, which I signed on the 16th day of July 1970, created a governor/student committee to communicate with all branches of state government as well as various legislative committees and the boards of regents of the state universities. I did that as a response to the campus disturbances that we had been having.

Educational Commission

On the 15th of May 1969 I appointed Cleo Fernandez to the educational commission of the state. Cleo was the widow of Congressman Antonio Fernandez. I also appointed the Reverend Father Albert Schneider to the educational commission of the state in June of that year.

Board of Regents of the Various State Universities

These were some of the appointments I made to the Board of Regents of the Highlands University: Roberto Armijo, 25th day of January 1967; John D. Robb Sr., sixth day of March 1967; Stewart Beck, 31st day of December 1968; and Dr. José Maldonado, 23rd day of May 1970. To the Board of Regents of New Mexico State University. I appointed Reginaldo Rodgers Aston of Roswell on March 11, 1967; I also appointed Avelino Gutierrez to the Board of Regents of New Mexico State University. For the Board of Regents of University of New Mexico, I appointed Thomas R. Roberts on the second day of March, 1967; Arturo G. Ortega on the 15th day of March, 1967; and Norris Bradbury on the 10th day of December 1970.

Fair Employment Practices Commission

I appointed Alex Archuleta to the commission on the 14th day of March 1967, the Reverend J.H. Horton of Artesia on the 29th day of April 1968, Alfredo Abalos on the 31st day of December 1968 and Albert N. Johnson of Las Cruces on the third day of January 1969. Other members were Ricardo M. Montoya and Monsignor William T. Bradley. Clarence Acoya was executive director of the New Mexico Commission on Indian Affairs, and I appointed him to the New Mexico Advisory Council on Human Rights and Employment.

State Investment Council

For the State Investment Council, I appointed Frank Rand in February, 1967; Robert McKinney in December, 1967; Nathan Greer in March, 1968; and Charlie Vigil of Dulce in December, 1968.

State Fair Commission

I made the following appointments to the State Fair Commission: In 1967, Dan Burguete; in 1969, Fern Sawyer and G. T. Hennessee, Jr. During my tenure I also appointed T.D. Neal, Leo Smith and Jim Barber.

Human Rights Commission

I appointed Jonathan B. Sutin as Chairman of the New Mexico State Citizens Committee on Human Rights. He gave me a copy of the bill that he was proposing on human rights. The bill contained an appropriation of $73,246 for the 1968 fiscal year for salaries and expenses. The Human Rights Bill in the House was House Bill 142. It was sponsored by Representative Raymond Garcia and was enacted into law in 1969.

I also appointed to the commission Reverend W. C. Trotter

who was the pastor of a Baptist church. I named Byron L. Stewart, former president of the union at Sandia Corporation, as executive director, and I appointed Kay Bennett, and Leon Rubin of Raton. I also offered to appoint Michael Sutton.

Port of Entry

This is in regards to a letter that I received from Senator Clinton P. Anderson that was mailed on April 22, 1970. I was asking about the Port of Entry in Anapra. He replied that the chief beneficiary of the Port of Entry would be a wholesale liquor dealers and that they would not have to pay taxes license fees, so he declined to be of any help to me on that particular project.

Clean Air and Water

In 1970 I made a concerted push for clean air and clean water legislation. On January 21, 1970, I had a meeting in my office with the Wildlife Society, and the Riders Association. I asked for their help in pushing the environmental legislation. I sent executive messages to both the House and Senate in their sessions in 1969 and 1970, and I got the Health and Social Services Department to write air and water pollution control regulations.

Vocational Education

In 1968 the State appropriated $1,045,784 for vocational education. In 1969 we appropriated $1,728,500. It was a big step forward because in 1966, before I took office, a total of $795,000 had been appropriated.

Civil Rights Legislation

I sent out an invitation to meet on civil rights legislation that I was preparing for the legislature. We met on January 8, 1969. Lots of people said that they would support me on it. One was state Senator Jack Eastham. But the president of the Senate, R.C. Morgan, said it was impossible for him to attend or support it. Then state Representative F.L. Finis Heidel said he couldn't attend. Archbishop Davis said he could.

When Robert F. Kennedy was assassinated I called for prayer and set aside three days of mourning. I was shocked by his death. On April 8, 1968, the Archbishop and I held a service for the assassinated civil rights leader, Dr. Martin Luther King Jr. More than 500 people attended.

Government Reorganization

I was very much interested in the whole matter of government reorganization and especially in view of the fact that I had obtained a Masters Degree in Public Administration at the University of Michigan prior to my obtaining a Doctorate of Law. I had worked on issues of government reorganization in Michigan. Oddly enough, my principal professor of government was Ferrell Heady who then was teaching at the University of Michigan. When I told him I was moving to New Mexico he patted me on the shoulder and said "Stick to it, son. If you work hard you will be successful, I am sure." Nine years later during my first term as governor, he came into my office and I advised him that he would be appointed as president of the University of New Mexico. Then I added, "If you work hard I am sure that you will succeed."

Very early during my term as governor I formed a Government Committee on Reorganization of State Government and appointed the members of that committee. The chair was former governor John Simms, and Ferrell Heady was selected as vice chair. Charles Campbell served on that committee, as did Fabian Chavez, Tom Carr and former governor Edwin Mechem. The committee was authorized by the Laws of 1967 Chapter 157 and was approved by the legislature and I signed it into existence March 28th 1967.

There were 263 agencies of executive government that existed on April 24th 1967 and there were hundreds of appointed boards, commissions and advisory committees. It didn't make for *good* government, never mind *efficient* government. Some of the changes proposed by the committee I was able to accomplish by executive order. For instance, I created a combined Hospitals Board and also merged the Department of Public Health and the Department of Public Welfare into a single Department of Public Health and Welfare. I also got the legislature to create a Motor Transportation Department during the legislative session of 1967. I got the legislature to establish a special Hospitals Board and made an attempt to create a strong Labor Department. I especially wanted to set up a Labor Department because not only was such a department sorely needed, but I also had received strong support from organized labor and this was one of the things I wanted to accomplish for them. I put Paul Cruz, who was head of the Employment Security Commission, in charge of the entire project of creating a Labor Department. He had been president of the Professional Employees Union at Sandia Corporation and had wide experience in labor relations. I also wanted to consolidate the activities of the various institutions of higher learning. They all vied for funds and money in opposition to one another. It was not a very efficient operation.

The legislature, and most particularly my future opponent for the governor's office, Fabian Chavez, was interested in these endeavors. Fabian was a valuable member of the commission, but he was also getting ready to make a campaign for governor and felt he should represent a good many interests that were opposed to government reorganization either in part or as a whole. He filed a dissenting opinion, which I have quoted here. In addition to a special dissent he also opposed, along with Ferrell Heady, the matter of changing the situation as far as higher education was concerned. I included their comments in the reorganization documents. The objections were as follows:

Comment:

"The recommendation concerning higher education involve major constitutional changes, and raise important organizational issue it will require further study. We agree that the question of separating a single governing board for the institutions of higher education should receive serious consideration, but we are not prepared to advocate this as preferable to our existing system of separate boards of regents with coordinating functions assigned to the Board of Educational Finance. Also, we have reservations about combining public education and higher education in a single cabinet-level Department of Education as proposed, as against the alternative of separate cabinet-level departments for public and higher education."

S/Ferrell Heady
S/Fabian Chavez

Governor's Commission on the Status of Women

These are the individuals that were appointed to the commission: I set up the first Commission of the Status of Women on the February 15, 1967, and appointed the following women to that commission: Mrs. Louise Bundy, Mrs. L.G. Fiorina, Mrs. Geneva Clements, Mrs. Hannah Best, Mrs. Alberta Miller, Mrs. Margaret Garcia, Mrs. Winona Magoosh of Mescalero, Mrs. Fern Porter of Las Cruces, Mrs. John T. Parker, Mr. Ed Foreman, Mr. Joe Benites. Later I named the following women to the Commission: Ramona Brusseau, Mary Pena and Robin Bishop.

Absentee Voting

I tried to get an absentee voting provision section through and it was on the ballot on November 7, 1967. We had a proposal to amend the New Mexico Constitution to allow absentee voting and to remove the restrictions on the rights of women and Indians to vote, but three counties defeated it so it went down to defeat. We had to go back and redo it. I also set up a Spanish Heritage Day program at the State Fair with Roberto Mondragon.

Capital Punishment

We got Senate Bill 154 passed. It abolished capital punishment except for the crime of killing a police officer or jail guard while in the performance of their duties. Archbishop James Peter Davis supported it.

Old Time Politics

When I ran for governor in 1966, a number of Hispanic counties were dominated by political leaders, whom the press labeled, "Absolute Political Bosses." In those days there were generally no limits, until shortly before I ran, when it came to political hiring and patronage. Politics was a game played by people who were on the payroll, and it didn't matter who they were. They ended up in plush jobs and didn't have to work. Many of them held political positions in the Democratic Party. The political boss in Santa Fe County was Johnny Vigil. In Rio Arriba County it was Emilio Naranjo. In other counties, equally potent politicians dominated Democratic Party politics. In Socorro County, George Baca was the county chairman, and in San Miguel County Tiny Martinez was the chairman. In Mora County, Fermin Pacheco was the county chairman who ran things.

In all of the Hispanic counties the pattern was the same. County bosses chose candidates to slate. The organizations were strong, and their candidates usually won. I therefore employed a tactic which was a little unusual in that I took the time to get to know each and every political boss in each county. The late Senator Dennis Chavez taught me one thing. He said, "If you have an enemy that's calling you an SOB in Gallup, go visit him, he may not ever support you, but at least he won't call you an SOB because he feels that he knows you and that would be disrespectful." I took his advice to heart and I proceeded to do exactly that.

I would visit George Baca in Socorro and he would tell me where I needed to campaign and what I needed to do, and then he would provide dinner or lunch. Several times I sat in his home while he was discussing political affairs either with officeholders or party officials. Those conversations told me exactly what they intended to do. I therefore ran very strongly in Socorro County.

On one occasion I went down to Valencia County where Filo Sedillo held forth. We were sitting in his office when Gene Lusk went by in his car, which was followed by the usual stream of six Cadillacs. He never slowed down or contacted Filo while he was in town. As Lusk's convoy turned a corner and disappeared into traffic, Filo turned to me and said, "that is why he is going to lose this county." Then he gave me a figure that came within 10 votes of being exactly what the result would be in the county.

Every time then I went to Las Vegas I would always go to Mama Lucy's restaurant and meet with Mama Lucy, Mayor González and Tiny Martinez. We would sit and plot away about how the election was going to go. They enjoyed having me stop by, and after I was governor they enjoyed it even more because they liked to be able to get out and ask everyone passing by if they had said hello to the governor. They would call me over and we would shake hands. It was interesting to do that because it not only neutralized the other side, but in many instances it converted them to my cause.

A good illustration of conversion was in Mora County where Fermin Pacheco and his wife Mary would always serve up lunch when I came into Mora. Then when I had rallies there the Democratic women would prepare all of the chili and beans and other items for huge barbecues. The rallies we had in Mora were significant. Several times we had 10,000 people show up. The press didn't report it—they weren't there—and they couldn't understand why I would carry these areas by such large margins. Had they bothered to show up and do some real reporting they would have known.

Another event—long after my terms as governor—occurred on Thursday, November 18, 1999, when I went up to Espanola for a dinner at Northern New Mexico Community College to honor longtime Rio Arriba political boss Emilio Naranjo. Naranjo had served as sheriff, county manager, U.S. Marshal, state senator and Democratic Party Chairman during his 50-year political career. In attendance were such political figures as Senator Jeff Bingaman, then Secretary of the Department of Energy Bill Richardson, Congressman Tom Udall and former governor Bruce King. There were dozens of other current or past office holders present. I got up and recalled Naranjo's support in my earliest elections and thanked him for helping me. I said that I had appreciated receiving his seal of approval despite my Republican Party affiliation.

The evening continued and various dignitaries got up and fondly recalled their association with Naranjo. Then it came Naranjo's time to speak. He got up and surprised them all. He said that in all his years he had known presidents, senators and congressmen, but his favorite was a governor. At that point Governor Bruce King started to get up and there was a great deal of applause. Then Naranjo turned to me and said, "He is a Republican and I'm a Democrat, but we are friends. He is my friend and will always be my friend." He got a little emotional about the whole thing and continued, "I can't tell you how much I have appreciated his friendship through the years." It came as a surprise to most everyone there except those who knew Emilio best.

As Speaker of the United States House of Representatives Tip O'Neill once said, "All politics is local."

Indeed it is.

Ida Jo and Dave at his first inauguration party, December 31, 1966 at the La Fonda hotel in Santa Fe.

Ida Jo and Dave at the inaugural ball on January 1, 1967 at the La Fonda.

Miss Indian at Dave's first swearing in, 1967. Ida Jo and former Governor Jack Campbell look on.

Filming of *The Good Guys and the Bad Guys* in Hollywood, 1967. Dave is in the foreground in the glasses. In front of him is Marty Balsam. In back are George Kennedy and Robert Mitchum.

Celebrating the return of Blue Lake to the Taos Pueblo, May, 1970. Kim Agnew, daughter of then-vice president Spiro Agnew is next to Dave. Beside her is John Rainer from Dave's office. Next to Dave is Taos Governor Quirino Romero.

Anthony Quinn and Dave in 1967. Quinn had raised $75,000 for an Indian scholarship fund.

John Wayne and Dave at the 1967 Academy Awards dinner in Hollywood.

Dave on the set of the TV show *Bonanza* in March, 1968, with actor Dan Blocker and producer David Dortort.

Campaigning in 1968 in Taos County. This man was plowing the fields with a horse.

Dave at a 1970 fundraiser in Santa Fe with Congressman Gerald Ford of Michigan.

California Governor Ronald Reagan came to New Mexico in March of 1967. He stayed with the Cargos at the governor's mansion.

Ida Jo and Dave in 1967 with radio star Paul Harvey. He also stayed with the Cargos at the governor's mansion.

Ida Jo and Michael Landon on the set of *Bonanza* in March 1968.

Hollywood producer Bill Castle and Dave in 1969.

OFFICE OF DWIGHT D. EISENHOWER

October 17, 1952

Dear Mr. Cargo:

I am intensely gratified to learn that you are holding your vitally important position in the Citizens organization. This makes us members of the same team. I personally can do only so much; the important task of organization, of securing workers, and of getting out the voters who will vote for our team must rest upon your shoulders.

I am asking a good deal of you, I know, but I am confident that having accepted with me our positions of responsibility, you will do your utmost to obtain the results that we must have to win.

Walter Williams has explained very graphically to me the fine work which you are doing in your state on behalf of the Eisenhower-Nixon ticket. I know and keenly appreciate more than anyone else that if our ticket is successful in November, that success, in large measure, will be due to your efforts.

The Citizens for Eisenhower-Nixon movement, acting as one horse of a team pulling the Eisenhower-Nixon campaign wagon, has the tremendous job ahead of it to point out to over 10,000,000 Independent and Democratic necessary voters in our country why they should support our team. The accomplishment of that job is necessary for our victory in November.

I know you feel as strongly as I do that we must work day and night and personally sacrifice far beyond the normal call to duty to succeed in this crusade. We must put party lines and all personal prejudice behind us, and go forward to victory.

Sincerely yours,

Dwight D. Eisenhower

Letter from soon-to-be President Dwight D. Eisenhower.

Dave in Dublin, Ireland in 1970 with Irish President Eamon de Valera and the governors of New Jersey, Wisconsin, Missouri, Connecticut and Maine.

Dave in front of the new State Capitol building in January 1967.

Christmas, 1967. Son Patrick is in Ida Jo's lap. David is next, and then Veronica.

Ida Jo and Dave in 1967.

Dave with Mexican actor Antonio Aguilar and his wife, Flor Sylvestre and Pepe Aguilar.

In front of the White House with other governors in May of 1967. LBJ had told Dave to stand next to him. LBJ said the photo of he and I talking would make the others jealous.

```
CLINTON P. ANDERSON, N. MEX., CHAIRMAN
RICHARD B. RUSSELL, GA.        MARGARET CHASE SMITH, MAINE
WARREN G. MAGNUSON, WASH.      CARL T. CURTIS, NEBR.
STUART SYMINGTON, MO.          MARK O. HATFIELD, OREG.
JOHN C. STENNIS, MISS.         BARRY GOLDWATER, ARIZ.
STEPHEN M. YOUNG, OHIO         WILLIAM B. SAXBE, OHIO
THOMAS J. DODD, CONN.          RALPH T. SMITH, ILL.
HOWARD W. CANNON, NEV.
SPESSARD L. HOLLAND, FLA.

JAMES J. GEHRIG, STAFF DIRECTOR
```

United States Senate

COMMITTEE ON
AERONAUTICAL AND SPACE SCIENCES
WASHINGTON, D.C. 20510

November 23, 1970

Honorable David F. Cargo
Governor of New Mexico
Santa Fe, New Mexico 87501

Dear Governor:

    It is my pleasure to send you an autographed copy of my book, Outsider in the Senate.

    You have been so kind to me during your Administration that I am happy to do this for you.

    With every good wish, I am

Sincerely yours,

Clinton P. Anderson

CPA:O

Letter from Senator Clinton P. Anderson.

Clinton P. Anderson
with Milton Viorst

OUTSIDER IN THE SENATE
Senator Clinton Anderson's Memoirs

To my governor — fine citizen and friend — with every good wish —

Clinton P. Anderson

THE WORLD PUBLISHING COMPANY
New York and Cleveland

Senator Anderson's inscription to Dave in his book.

From the 1968 campaign. Cartoon by Mac McGinnis of the *Albuquerque Journal*.

Taking on the Democrats. Cartoon by Mac McGinnis of the *Albuquerque Journal*.

From the 1966 campaign. Cartoon by Mac McGinnis of the *Albuquerque Journal*.

Democratic County Powerhouses

I always made it a point to try and win over Hispanic and Democratic voters, and I can say that I was successful. I think this story by way of the late George Baldwin, then managing editor of *The Albuquerque Tribune*, illustrates that.

One day Baldwin told me of an August 27, 1968, phone call he had with Filo Sedillo. Sedillo, a Democrat, had served as Valencia County Democratic Party chairman, and was a potent vote-getter. The story went like this:

Sedillo said that Valencia County, just south of Albuquerque and heavily Democratic, would go my way in the re-election campaign. He told Baldwin that in 1966 I was the only Republican to carry the county, and one reason was that I had married into a Democratic family.

"The Trinidad Anaya family is both well liked and respected in Belen. Ida Jo, the governor's wife, is the daughter of Mr. and Mrs. Anaya. Ida Jo's grandfather was one of the county's leading Democrats. He was the mayor of Belen, the sheriff, a businessman and president of the school board in the county. He was the Republican county chairman, as well as the Democratic county chairman. Ida Jo has lots of cousins and uncles who are Democrats, and naturally they are Cargo votes. So add in that Governor Cargo established himself in Valencia County during the time that he was an assistant district attorney in Grants in the early years of his career.

"You simply can't sell Governor Cargo short in Valencia County. He has strong support from people who work for the railroad and belong to the Railroad Brotherhoods, and also from the uranium miners in Grants. Most of the Hispanic county chairmen didn't like Governor Jack Campbell and this was their way of making the Democratic Party take notice of the Hispanic counties."

Sedillo went on to tell Baldwin that most of the Democratic Party leaders in Valencia County would be supporting my re-election bid. He also said that the late Senator Dennis Chavez's family was supporting me.

They did support me.

Party Registration and Election Results

People often forget how lopsided the registration in New Mexico was when I first ran for office. For instance, in 1966 there were 298,864 registered Democrats and only 114,321 Republicans, yet in the general election in 1966 I received about 20,000 more votes than there were registered Republicans, while my opponent received 148,000 fewer votes than there were registered Democrats. In the 1966 election I beat Gene Lusk 134,625 to 125,587 votes. In the general election in 1968 I beat Fabian Chavez 160,140 to 157,230. Thus I carried about 46,000 more votes than there were total registered Republicans. You have to assume that all of the Republicans certainly did not vote, and of course all of the Democrats didn't vote either. But Fabian Chavez received 131,000 fewer votes than there were registered Democrats, so it gives you some idea of the odds that I faced in that election. It is interesting to note that in many counties I received three or four times as many votes as there were registered Republicans. It was not an easy task in what was essentially a one-party state.

Registration figures taken from the *New Mexico Blue Book* (1960, 1962, 964, 1966, and 1968) are as follows:

	Democrat	Republican	Independent	Other	Total
Bernalillo					
1960	66,501	36,618	3,982	4,292	111,393
1962	64,406	35,705		7,983	108,094
1964	79,611	42,327		8,996	130,934
1966	76,079	38,976	345	7,755	123,155
Catron					
1960	1,170	452	29	42	1,693
1962	1,118	443	28	27	1,616
1964	1,153	497	30	31	1,711
1966	1,023	471	27	25	1,546
Chaves					
1960	15,385	4,792	592		20,769
1962	14,284	4,879	555	1	19,719
1964	16,757	6,326	636	6	23,725
1966	15,241	5,716	547	5	21,509
Colfax					
1960	4,956	1,924	407		7,287
1962	4,873	1,761	362		6,996
1964	4,955	1,661	350		6,966
1966	4,633	1,499	303		6,435
Curry					
1960	11,099	1,925	93	671	13,788
1962	10,614	1,945	76	504	13,139
1964	11,712	2,514	108	524	14,858
1966	10,488	2,270	86	338	13,182
De Baca					
1960	1,492	249	2	14	1,757
1962	1,415	224	4	11	1,654
1964	1,455	207	6	6	1,674
1966	1,422	172	7	6	1,607

	Democrat	Republican	Independent	Other	Total
Doña Ana					
1960	15,391	5,291	705	537	21,924
1962	14,684	4,793	909	248	20,634
1964	17,075	5,995	1,183	300	24,553
1966	15,944	5,541	1,042	267	22,794
Eddy					
1960	19,356	2,515	401	6	22,278
1962	19,138	2,581	337	4	22,06
1964	20,775	3,212	432	3	24,402
1966	20,003	2,910	368	5	23,286
Grant					
1960	8,117	1,286	32	203	9,638
1962	7,480	1,092	48	99	8,719
1964	8,307	1,228	89	103	9,727
1966	7,608	1,086	70	91	8,855
Guadalupe					
1960	2,338	1,284	41	51	3,714
1962	2,288	1,189	85		3,562
1964	2,571	1,230	102		3,903
1966	2,703	1,232	100		4,035
Harding					
1960	783	565	13	30	1,331
1962	810	524		41	1,375
1964	681	474	7	23	1,185
1966	623	430	8	17	1,078
Hidalgo					
1960	2,006	213	30		2,249
1962	2,002	203	29		2,234
1964	2,023	216	31		2,270
1966	1,905	192	24	198	2,319
Lea					
1960	18,574	2,006	104	286	20,970
1962	17,299	2,163	96	179	19,737
1964	19,508	3,309	80	165	23,062
1966	16,903	3,001		205	20,109

	Democrat	Republican	Independent	Other	Total
Lincoln					
1960	2,917	1,655	187		4,759
1962	2,979	1,644	184		4,807
1964	3,264	1,795	200		5,259
1966	2,761	1,635	180		4,576
Los Alamos					
1960	3,846	2,153	497	185	6,681
1962	3,567	2,002	401	185	6,155
1964	4,109	2,356	436	227	7,128
1966	3,715	2,265		198	6,367
Luna					
1960	3,921	649	102		4,672
1962	3,807	742		76	4,625
1964	4,171	924	57	38	5,190
1966	3,715	852	68	28	4,663
McKinley					
1960	9,311	4,362	982		14,655
1962	8,620	3,492	771		12,883
1964	10,394	3,749	370	471	14,984
1966	10,054	3,066	310	388	13,818
Mora					
1960	1,680	2,307	88	1	4,076
1962	1,654	2,352		43	4,049
1964	1,726	1,888	16	34	3,664
1966	1,944	1,664	16	29	3,653
Otero					
1960	8,912	3,407		854	13,173
1962	8,726	3,317	127	568	12,738
1964	9,922	3,736	130	639	14,427
1966	8,796	3,176	98	518	12,588
Quay					
1960	5,529	908	282	2	6,721
1962	4,917	827	112	2	5,858
1964	5,040	906	36	81	6,063
1966	4,901	850	38	65	5,854

	Democrat	Republican	Independent	Other	Total
Rio Arriba					
1960	9,891	5,044	168	380	15,483
1962	10,353	4,871		566	15,790
1964	11,720	4,876	192	476	17,264
1966	11,903	4,421	146	334	16,861
Roosevelt					
1960	6,575	797	68	146	7,586
1962	5,968	826	52	112	6,958
1964	6,560	1,070	75	102	7,807
1966	5,683	1,062	95	95	6,935
Sandoval					
1960	2,917	2,036	325		5,772
1962	2,979	1,913	329	1	6,010
1964	3,264	2,030	298	1	7,181
1966	2,761	1,930	290		7,245
San Juan					
1960	11,270	7,148	475	380	15,483
1962	11,321	7,090	424	566	15,790
1964	12,539	7,796	192	476	17,264
1966	10,923	6,851	146	334	16,861
San Miguel					
1960	8,434	3,810	552		12,796
1962	8,091	3,968	505	1	12,565
1964	8,004	3,564		501	12,069
1966	7,874	3,163	472		11,509
Santa Fe					
1960	13,927	7,437	1,323	732	23,419
1962	14,297	7,074	1,192	666	23,229
1964	15,936	7,070	1,361	642	25,009
1966	15,813	6,436	1,214	563	24,026
Sierra					
1960	2,685	1,481	119	154	4,439
1962	2,583	1,360	114	118	4,175
1964	3,818	1,530	152	128	4,628
1966	2,438	1,380	122	98	4,038

	Democrat	Republican	Independent	Other	Total
Socorro					
1960	4,099	2,224	355		6,678
1962	4,187	2,282		466	6,935
1964	4,609	2,470	287	173	7,539
1966	4,938	2,472	264	216	7,890
Taos					
1960	5,588	2,708	151	133	8,580
1962	6,003	2,911	148	135	9,197
1964	5,739	2,975	168	100	8,982
1966	5,386	2,529	141	90	8.146
Torrance					
1960	2,388	1,453	114		3,955
1962	2,373	1,414	111		3,898
1964	2,480	1,433	52	60	4,025
1966	2,682	1,459	58	70	4,269
Union					
1960	2,592	859	118	1	3,570
1962	2,431	806		86	3,323
1964	2,319	796	39	45	4,199
1966	2,224	706	25	42	4,997
Valencia					
1960	11,433	5,250	1,042		17,725
1962	11,720	4,964	1,049		17,733
1964	13,697	5,305	1,121		20,123
1966	13,268	4,908	977		19,153
Totals					
1960	285,577	114,748	13,379	9,561	423,265
1962	277,775	111,357	6,914	13,952	409,998
1964	316,462	125,465	8,123	14,861	464,911
1966	298,864	114,321	7,480	12,493	433,158

In 1964 the Republican candidate for governor had been Merle Tucker, running against incumbent governor Jack Campbell. That year's election results were interesting. Jack Campbell received 191,497 votes statewide and Merle Tucker received 126,540 statewide. It is also interesting to note 1964 was a presidential election year and in Bernalillo County Tucker lost the county by 9,000 votes; I later won there by 21,000 votes—a switch of 30,000 votes in Bernalillo County alone. Given here are the comparative figures for each county and the results. Gene Lusk of course was the Democratic Party candidate in 1966 and Fabian Chavez was the Democratic Party candidate in 1968.

Bernalillo County
1964 election: Tucker 42,284 votes, Campbell 53,047 votes
1966 election: Cargo 50,274 votes, Lusk 29,431 votes
1968 election: Cargo 50,801 votes, Chavez 49,570 votes

San Miguel County
1964 election: Tucker 3,212 votes, Campbell 5,074 votes
1966 election: Cargo 4,134 votes, Lusk 3,623 votes
1968 election: Cargo 4,140 votes, Chavez 4,066 votes

Valencia County
1964 election: Tucker 4,117 votes, Campbell 7,340 votes
1966 election: Cargo 5,221 votes, Lusk 4,895 votes
1968 election: Cargo 5,381 votes, Chavez 6,336 votes

Rio Arriba County
1964 election: Tucker 3,165 votes, Campbell 6,300 votes
1966 election: Cargo 3,209 votes, Lusk 4,843 votes
1968 election: Cargo 3,816 votes, Chavez 4,948 votes

Santa Fe County
1964 election: Tucker 6,021 votes, Campbell 12,116 votes
1966 election: Cargo 7,945 votes, Lusk 8,369 votes
1968 election: Cargo 8,788 votes, Chavez 10,427 votes

Socorro County
1964 election: Tucker 1,738 votes, Campbell 2,352 votes
1966 election: Cargo 1,963 votes, Lusk 1,843 votes
1968 election: Cargo 1,882 votes, Chavez 2,315 votes

Taos County
1964 election: Tucker 2,058 votes, Campbell 4,036 votes
1966 election: Cargo 2,670 votes, Lusk 3,010 votes
1968 election: Cargo 2,908 votes, Chavez 3,260 votes

McKinley County
1964 election: Tucker 3,018 votes, Campbell 6,315 votes
1966 election: Cargo 3,069 votes, Lusk 3,375 votes
1968 election: Cargo 4,342 votes, Chavez 4,630 votes

Doña Ana County
1964 election: Tucker 6,755 votes, Campbell 10,710 votes
1966 election: Cargo 6,568 votes, Lusk 6,969 votes
1968 election: Cargo 9,182 votes, Chavez 10,214 votes

Grant County
1964 election: Tucker 1,707 votes, Campbell 5,272 votes
1966 election: Cargo 1,969 votes, Lusk 4,091 votes
1968 election: Cargo 3,440 votes, Chavez 3,822 votes

Los Alamos County
1964 election: Tucker 2,198 votes, Campbell 3,450 votes
1966 election: Cargo 2,646 votes, Lusk 2,185 votes
1968 election: Cargo 3,886 votes, Chavez 2,856 votes

San Juan County
1964 election: Tucker 5,818 votes, Campbell 7,507 votes
1966 election: Cargo 5,734 votes, Lusk 4.918 votes
1968 election: Cargo 8,086 votes, Chavez 5,413 votes

Eddy County
1964 election: Tucker 6,053 votes, Campbell 11,460 votes
1966 election: Cargo 5,297 votes, Lusk 8,191 votes
1968 election: Cargo 7,589 votes, Chavez 6,921 votes

Lea County
1964 election: Tucker 6, 070 votes, Campbell 9,400 votes
1966 election: Cargo 4,226 votes, Lusk 6,553 votes
1968 election: Cargo 7,383 votes, Chavez 7,114 votes

Just for the record, in Grant County in the 1968 general election I received 1,700 more votes than any other GOP candidate. This was a result of heavy campaigning by Chano Merino and Local 890 in Bayard.

Constitutional Convention

During my first term in 1967, we held a Constitutional Convention—the first since statehood. There had been periodic prior attempts to amend the state's constitution along with various other tries to modernize it, but this was the first real attempt to fully revise it. In many respects, the effort was inspired by the reapportionment lawsuits I had filed. It was designed to bring about some real change in state government.

Jack Campbell, who was governor from 1962 to 1966, had made constitutional change one of his top goals while in office. The project got started and carried over into my first term. The effort was pretty much under Campbell's direction from the beginning to the end. I had some input, but it was limited at best.

Bruce King served as the convention's chair, while Filo Sedillo served as vice chair. A number of outstanding citizens from around the state served, including future House Speaker Raymond Sanchez from Albuquerque.

The Constitutional Revision Commission submitted a report that suggested a number of important constitutional changes. The commission spent a lot of time on reapportionment. It said that the state Supreme Court had to approve any report from the Reapportionment Commission. However, it said the governor was supposed to appoint the commission's members. It removed the federal and state courts from the process, which I thought was unconstitutional. Lawsuits had already decided that federal law was supreme by reason of the supremacy clauses of the federal and state constitutions. They spent a great deal of time discussing my reapportionment case. I had also participated in the federal court case as counsel for the legislators. The report said that both the House and Senate were to be apportioned on population and population alone. It also said that the governor was to fill vacancies in both houses unless the legislature said otherwise.

The report said the governor should be elected in non-presidential years and should have two four-year terms unless otherwise determined by the convention. It also provided for a full-time lieutenant governor. Then they changed and said their preference was for a single, four-year term for the governor, and then indicated that they might favor two terms. I thought this was kind of a split decision, but in any event, it's what they recommended.

The one bit of input that I had was that I suggested that for the first time in the state's history, segregation in the public schools should be abolished. I made a personal appearance and pleaded with convention members to abolish segregation in the schools. I linked the issue to human rights legislation that was pending in the legislature, and also made reference to the fact that the legislature had already passed a human rights law and had formed a Human Rights Commission. The Revision Commission agreed and recommended an end to segregation.

Once rewritten, the proposed constitution was put to voters. I asked several times if I could help in getting it approved—I wanted to campaign for it—but I was told that my help wasn't needed. Well, apparently it was, because the constitution was rejected by the voters. It lost decisively in the northern counties where I had received a very large vote.

Father Roca

Whenever I would go into a town, especially a small town, I would go to the local church and talk to the pastor or priest and tried to establish a relationship. Most of the time I would go by myself. One of my longstanding contacts had been Father Casimiro Roca, who for years cared for Santuario de Chimayo. Father Roca had been a priest for about 10 years when I first visited, and he has now been a priest for about 40 years. He became a good friend, and I would attend his anniversary ceremonies and other special events.

One of the more interesting incidents that took place during our long association was that while I was governor he was temporarily transferred out of the state and he was most unhappy about it. He contacted me and said that the next time the archbishop stayed at the mansion he would appreciate it if I would discuss the possibility of bringing him back to the area. I promised to do what I could.

Shortly thereafter the priest that was in Chimayo died. I talked to the Archbishop about bringing Father Roca back. This created a unique situation and they returned Father Roca to Chimayo. Father Roca called to thank me, saying "You didn't have to go that far—but in any event, thank you!"

I had some powers as governor, but I was unable to take credit for that sudden job opening.

Reies Lopez Tijerina and the Courthouse Raid

Many people who have no other knowledge of New Mexico and its history are aware of the chapter in our history that is referred to as the "Courthouse Raid." The background of this incident was complicated and very much tied up in politics. In the northern part of New Mexico there is a belief in the prevalence of economic Darwinism: in effect this means that we were talking about the survival of the richest. I might also point out that so long as our society is more concerned to prevent strife than to prevent humiliation its moral status will be depressing indeed. A case in point was the political situation that existed in northern New Mexico in the 1960s.
The Duke of Wellington once said of his troops, "They may not scare the enemy but by God, Sir, they frighten me." As governor, my "troops" included people such as District Attorney Alfonso Sanchez and Senator Edmundo Delgado. I still see Alfonso Sanchez with some regularity after all the years since the June 5, 1967, raid on the courthouse. We see each other every so often and have lunch or converse amiably, but he was one of my troops, I guess. Edmundo Delgado who is now deceased, ultimately also became a reasonably good friend.

By way of background, I should point out that the problem of land grants in New Mexico had existed for a long time and had been the subject of much controversy. Many of the grants were quite old, having been established by the Spanish and Mexican governments before New Mexico even belonged to the United States of America. To this day many land grants still exist in New Mexico and are now recognized by state law. By the 1960s a number of land grants had simply disappeared because the land had been eventually taken over by other groups and passed into private ownership. For example, the Tierra Amarilla Grant dates from the summer of 1832 when Manuel Martinez received an original grant through the local representative of the Republic of Mexico. The grant was grounded in Spanish law and custom but guaranteed by the Constitution of Mexico. Later, in 1846, General Stephen Kearny came to the Territory of New Mexico and proclaimed himself governor of this area. Approximately two years later the Treaty of Guadalupe-Hidalgo would complete the takeover of New Mexico. This Treaty guaranteed all of the civil and property rights of Mexican citizens in what would become American territory. However, after the Civil War many of the land grants, including the Tierra Amarilla Grant, were broken up; there were a good many irregularities in the actions of various surveyors involved in fixing the boundaries of the grant. The so-called Santa Fe Ring ultimately gained control of vast amounts of land at the northern part of the state and they retained it for their personal use.

The loss of title did not bring with it any immediate loss of use. It was only with the development of large working ranches and the establishment and management of the national forest system in the 20th century that this happened. Gradually, the grazing and woodcutting rights on much of the land of the original grant were done away with.

It was into this charged environment that Reies Lopez Tijerina, at that time an evangelical minister, came to New Mexico and took an interest in the problem. In 1963 the Alianza Federal de Mercedes was formally established with Tijerina as the leader.

My first real contact with Reies Tijerina came about when I addressed the fourth state convention of the Alianza Federal de Mercedes, held in Albuquerque's Civic Auditorium in early September of 1966. There was a crowd at the convention of probably 1,500 people. I had been invited to attend by Eduardo Chavez who was secretary of Alianza, and also by Reies Tijerina. Santiago Anaya and Roberto Salazar encouraged me to accept the invitation to speak. They were both very active Republicans and I didn't see anything sinister in attending the convention. Many of the supporters of the Alianza were in fact old-line Republicans and came from counties up in the north of the state. Many of them came from Rio Arriba, Taos and San Miguel Counties. The invitation seemed innocent to me, although it proved to be more exciting than I ever anticipated. My opponent Gene Lusk declined to appear after having been warned by the governor, Jack Campbell, that they would want to talk about Hispanic land claims. Campbell warned against this saying that it would not be a good idea for Lusk to become involved in an argument like that with me. In any event, I attended the convention and spoke for about a half hour.

At the convention I was extremely well received because of the fact that Gene Lusk had turned down the invitation and had refused to even talk to any of the members of the Alianza. This gave me a bit of an advantage and I spoke in some length about the economic difficulties that people had in the northern counties and also referred to the poor condition of roads, schools and governmental infrastructure. I pointed out that if promises could be used as paving material that the northern part of the state would be covered with black top from top to bottom. I did not mention land grants or go into that subject matter at all. I spoke of the dangers of a one-party system and urged that they make politics competitive in the north. I also pledged that I would give a lot of attention to that area.

It was shortly thereafter that fairly lengthy articles and appeared in both *Newsweek* and *Time* magazine outlining exactly what was taking place in New Mexico with the Alianza and what their claims were. This came as a real revelation to people in New Mexico because the local press here hadn't given any coverage to them at all. As a matter of fact, most people didn't even know that the Alianza and land grants existed, let alone that they were creating a considerable stir throughout the state. It was only after the national coverage that the press in New Mexico began to discuss the situation. I managed to generate a fair amount of support from the delegates to the convention just by reason of being there. It was the first time that anyone running for statewide office had given them any respect at all.

There are a number of things that were highlighted in the Tijerina affair.

The first event that took place was the occupation of the Echo Amphitheater, located on Highway 84 between Espanola and Tierra Amarilla. The occupation took place in October of 1966 and involved a number of individuals led by Tijerina. There were two court trials stemming from the raid and Tijerina was acquitted in the first and convicted in the second. The group was also involved in the destruction of U.S. Forest Service signs near Coyote, about 15 miles west of Highway 84 between Abiquiu and Cibola. This also led to a conviction in Federal Court for Reies Tijerina.

The next major event and controversy was an incident which involved the raid on the Rio Arriba County Courthouse and Tierra Amarilla on the 5th day of June 1967 in which about 20 or more men were armed and involved in a shootout at the courthouse. Several police officers were assaulted and two were shot and critically wounded. One of them was Nick Saiz, a New Mexico State police officer who received a wound to the chest. The other was a Eulogio Salazar who was shot in the face when he attempted to escape from the courthouse by jumping through a window.

The next major incident involved Eulogio Salazar. Reies Tijerina at that time was the president of the Alianza. During the 1967 courthouse raid he was charged with several felonies and a preliminary hearing was scheduled for the 12th day of January 1968. Eulogio Salazar was to be a chief prosecution witness and was expected to testify, among other things, that Reies Tijerina had shot him in the face when Salazar attempted to escape from the courthouse. However prior to that preliminary hearing, on the second day of January, 1968, Salazar was abducted in front of his house and was brutally beaten to death. Eulogio Salazar had personally told me in the governor's office that Reies Tijerina was the one who shot him in the courthouse. I attended Eulogio Salazar's funeral on a cold winter day. It was interesting that when it came time to take communion, Salazar's wife, Casilda, and I were the only ones to go forward. After some delay, others followed, indicating that they were intimidated.

The investigation into the Salazar murder took place in 1968 and 1969 and was handled by the New Mexico state police. The case was investigated for more than a year with no results.

It was not until August 15, 1977, that an attorney general's report was issued by the attorney general, Toney Anaya. This was in response to a request by Governor Jerry Apodoca asking the attorney general's office to investigate the murder of Eulogio Salazar Sr. The findings of the report were interesting and are not generally known to the public. The attorney general found specifically that Reies Lopez Tijerina was not responsible either directly or indirectly for the Salazar's murder. Parts of the report were never released to the public, and fourteen pages labeled as confidential were excluded and blanked out of the report.

In that report it was noted that Tijerina took a polygraph and passed the test without any problems. The finding of a polygraph test was specifically that he did not participate or order the murder of Eulogio Salazar Sr. and that he was not aware of the killing until it was brought to his attention by the press. This is an interesting finding and something that weighs heavily on the situation. Governor Jerry Apodoca had requested a full investigation on the 22nd day of July 1976, and the investigation was reopened. Another thorough investigation of the matter took place but no real finding or solution was found in connection with the murder. It should also be noted that Tijerina stated that on the evening of January 2, 1968, he had been at home in a residential portion of Alianza office building which was located at 1010 Third Street Northwest in Albuquerque. He stated publicly that his wife and his young child were with him at the time and that an individual by the name of Bill Hicks was also there with him. Tijerina also stated that he had never been interviewed by state police in connection with his alibi for the night of the murder and there are no known state police reports or records indicating that there had been such an interview.

The Alianza and Reies Tijerina received a great burst of publicity in New Mexico and a considerable amount of national coverage as well. It was a trying situation in that Reies Tijerina was a Bible-belt fundamentalist turned political insurgent. He arrived in New Mexico and in a fairly short time grew the Alianza from a membership of about thousand followers in 1964 to 14,000 a year later. Then all of a sudden he was caught in a flood of publicity. Pictures appeared in many newspapers throughout the nation in which tanks were photographed in Tierra Amarilla and a shell-riddled courthouse was displayed along with it.

Oddly enough, the two people who were aligned with the Alianza that I knew best were F.M. Casaus and José Maria Martinez. I had a lot of earlier contacts with José Maria Martinez who is a descendent of a Spanish settler who was first awarded a Tierra Amarilla land grant. Martinez was active in politics and was a member of the Alianza, although he was actually fairly conservative. I first ran into him when I was campaigning in the Tierra Amarilla area and he became a person who was in a regular attendance at political meetings that were held up there. As a matter of fact he was a principal figure at a political rally that we held in the old theater in Tierra Amarilla. The main speaker was Bert Prince, who was a Santa Fe politician and longtime district attorney and at that time was practicing law in Santa Fe. He was the main speaker, along with me, at the political rally where José Maria Martinez appeared. There was a huge crowd there and he stood off to the side. After a while he rose and made a speech on my behalf and then sat down. I noted at that time that he was wearing a large horse pistol which I immediately observed. As the meeting progressed my primary opponent, Cliff Hawley, entered the room and then quite loudly stated that he was going to speak whether invited or not and he intended to take me apart from one end to the other. I said that I would be perfectly happy to debate him if that's what he would like. He said no, that he was there to disrupt the meeting and he was going to do it. At that point José Maria Martinez arose in a menacing manner and patted his horse pistol and said "No kidding." That was the end of the intrusion and Hawley hurriedly left and I think he was very happy to get out of the place. I used to see José with some regularity after that as he was active in the Republican Party.

F.M. Casaus was also active in the Republican Party. Casaus was the one who got my wife to pay six dollars in dues to the Alianza. He'd gone with a large group of people to my house one afternoon while I was out campaigning and told my wife that as an heir of the Atrisco Land Grant they all thought that she should become a member of the Alianza. They told her that the dues were only six dollars and that it would be a great deal of help to me politically if she would join up. They evidently spent several hours with her and eventually she gave them six dollars for the membership dues to cover six months. I was not aware of the fact that she had joined until the list was seized during a roadblock. At that point she had become delinquent in her dues. Cristobal Tijerina, the brother of Reies Tijerina, was stopped at a roadblock four miles east of Coyote by the state police captain Hoover Wimberleyn, and when they searched the vehicle they found a receipt book along with a card and original membership card made out to J. A. Adelaida Cargo. They had not delivered the card to her so she could never actually have been called a card-carrying member, but she had paid a half a year's dues.

Needless to say, I was not too happy about it, but I did mention to her that the only organization that I knew of that she belonged to was the Catholic Church. I didn't know that she was that much of a joiner. She never attended a meeting of the Alianza, and didn't receive any literature from them and never got her membership card. But the press painted her as wild eyed revolutionary and one that had to be watched. The press throughout New Mexico made mention of her membership more than a few times. I was very unhappy about that, but so be it. It was one of those things that happened.

The district attorney, Alfonso Sanchez, was credited with having designed an effective "bust" of the situation and that was fine with me. Sanchez was on the radio constantly, as was State Representative Bobby Mayfield who said that he "thought that all of them involved in the meeting at Coyote had automatic weapons and hand grenades and machine guns."

I didn't know whether that was a fact, but Sanchez backed Mayfield up somewhat in his efforts along that line and added that he had some evidence that some of the people had been training in Cuba and that surely some of them were Communists. However, a number of the people involved had been arrested and that didn't help the situation one bit. As a matter of fact, Sanchez chastised me rather strongly, saying they "had been coddled too much already." He then continued, saying, "My job is to carry out the law made by the legislature. I will not tolerate people being killed or property pilfered and that is communism." He then suggested that the Alianza members should all go to Cuba. This was before the courthouse raid.

In the meantime, after being assured that there wouldn't be any more arrests and things had quieted down considerably, I thought it was safe to take a long anticipated trip to Michigan. I traveled very infrequently outside of the state by reason of the fact that the press was more than willing to criticize me whenever I did leave the state. Early in my first term I was asked to take a group of 30 people to Spain on a trip for nine days. I was scheduled to be gone for nine days but the press raised so much hell about it that I finally canceled it. They said that governors were not elected to be out of the state. They were highly critical of me, and finally I simply decided it wasn't worth all the bother so I canceled the trip. Since that time they have become much more tolerant of the out-of-state travel; one governor spent a fourth of his time out of state promoting the legalization of drugs, and another seems to have spent almost 95 percent out of the state promoting himself. There's been little criticism of either one of them, so apparently times have changed.

However, I had long planned a brief trip to Michigan for five days. I was being honored in my hometown of Dowagiac, Michigan, where I grew up, and in Jackson, which was the birthplace of the Republican Party and where I graduated from high school. I went to Michigan and appeared jointly with Governor George Romney at several events with Lieutenant Governor Bill Milliken who later served 14 years as governor of Michigan. I also entertained Congressman Gerald Ford in Jackson and he was an overnight guest at my parents' home. I was scheduled to go to Grand Rapids for an event which was labeled Cargo/Ford day in Grand Rapids. I suppose if they'd known that Gerald Ford was going to become President they would have reversed the order of appearance. They had a large crowd in Grand Rapids and Governor Romney and Lieutenant Governor Milliken both appeared at the dinner. I was standing in the receiving line before the main event when a state police officer came in and approached Ford and Romney and began conversing with them in an excited manner. I asked what it was all about and Ford told me that there had been a uprising in Northern New Mexico in some small courthouse in the northern part of the state. A judge had been killed and the district attorney had been shot but was expected to live, and further that the town was generally shot up. I couldn't imagine what was going on, so I went to a telephone and tried to contact my lieutenant governor, E. Lee Francis. I finally ran him down at the New Mexico Armory in Santa Fe. Francis told me that there had been a raid on the courthouse in Tierra Amarilla and that two people had been wounded. Larry Calloway, a United Press reporter, had been kidnapped. I asked him what was being done and he said he was meeting with the state police and the National Guard to decide on a course of action. He said he would keep me posted. I commented, "I hope you don't do anything drastic. I will keep in touch." However, I was to be placed in a position shortly after where I couldn't be in touch with anyone.

I tried to arrange transportation to New Mexico and had some difficulty as I obviously couldn't catch a commercial plane. I called the governor of Ohio, Jim Rhodes, who was a close friend of mine, to see if I could get a National Guard plane to take me from Grand Rapids to Albuquerque. However, this didn't work out. So finally I had to settle for a Michigan National Guard plane that flew me to Albuquerque, posthaste. I had no idea that the lieutenant governor had called out the National Guard; I thought that only the state police were involved in the Tierra Amarilla situation. Once I boarded the plane I had no way of making contact with anyone because in those days we didn't have mobile phones. In any event, we proceeded to New Mexico, and when we flew over Santa Fe I looked out of the plane and could see two tanks going up the highway along with a long convoy of national guardsmen. I frankly was appalled. I couldn't imagine that at that time we were at war in New Mexico. I arrived in Albuquerque and Red Pack, my security state policeman, was there to meet me along with several others members of the state police. You should remember that during my time in office there were only three officers that were attached to the governor's security, and some of them were part time. I think that number now is something like twenty-seven.

Anyway the three of them were all there and we got into the state police vehicle and went to Santa Fe. Upon arriving I immediately went to the National Guard armory. There I learned directly from Lieutenant Governor Francis that he had ordered Adjutant General John P. Jolly to send 450 guardsmen and two tanks to Tierra Amarilla. I was distressed over the whole matter, especially when I was advised that Eulogio Salazar and Nick Saiz had both been wounded. Salazar was an employee of the sheriff's office in Rio Arriba County and Saiz was a state policeman on temporary duty out of Farmington, serving in the Tierra Amarilla courthouse. I was also very alarmed to hear that Larry Calloway, a press service reporter, had indeed been taken hostage. I made a comment to the press that I probably shouldn't have, noting that the Echo Amphitheater really shouldn't have resulted in the number of arrests that it did because the gathering was probably inconveniencing no one but some wandering sheep and perhaps a few passing tourists. I shouldn't have let that go because apparently people thought I meant it was not an important event. It stirred up a number of people up and was rather bizarre in nature but, anyway, it had blown into something that was far beyond that.

The matter of Reies Lopez Tijerina and the Courthouse Raid became widely publicized nationally and resulted in a number of books being written on the subject. Unfortunately, some of the people that became involved and wrote about the event were not entirely objective or accurate in their reporting.

The John Birch Society took an immediate interest in the case and assigned a so-called reporter to New Mexico for a period of six weeks. He conducted his own investigation into the matter. To say the least he was not entirely objective in his analysis of the situation. Basically his conclusion was that the whole thing was communist-inspired and the leading provocateur was no less than my wife Ida Jo. He claimed that she was actively involved in the raid and that she was actively involved in the Alianza. The problem with that was that at the time of the raid she was seven months pregnant and I doubt that she was in any condition to carry a rifle into the courthouse or to plot any of the events that led up to the courthouse raid. It was a complete fabrication and we eventually had a confrontation. He came into the governor's office uninvited and proceeded to walk through the office unattended and entered my office. He then sat down and started talking about the courthouse raid and to accuse my wife of being in effect a communist. I told him that if he didn't leave that I was going to throw him physically out of the office. He then wanted to know if the state police were on their way and I said,

"No, but something far more menacing than that is about to take place and that is that I am going to personally toss you out of the office." He left under the circumstances and did not return. However, he continued the exchange for many months and did not give up on slandering and libeling my wife. I thought that it was a disgusting event, and needless to say I wasn't very happy about it.

Richard Gardner, in his book *Grito: Reies Tijerina and the New Mexico Land-Grant War of 1967* dealt with much of Reies Tijerina's earlier life but likewise didn't add much historical material or anything by way of original inquiry or thought to the matter.

Peter Nabokov, a journalist with the *Santa Fe New Mexican* for a short period of time, was commissioned by the University of New Mexico press to write an analysis of Tijerina and the courthouse raid. He published a book entitled *Tijerina and the Court House Raid*. This book was a little more thorough, but again it was somewhat lacking when it came to research. For instance, he stated that he had done a thorough job of researching for the book, but oddly enough he had never approached me for an interview. As a matter of fact I didn't receive a correspondence from him and I didn't have any conversations whatsoever with him about the background of the Tijerina matter. I thought this was a little odd under the circumstances. He had a number of factual errors in the book, some of consequence and some that were not so important. For instance, he described having to find out the telephone number to the mansion by threatening Larry Prentice, and then Larry Prentice supposedly secured a phone diary in which he revealed the secret number at the mansion. I thought this was interesting in that during all the time that I was governor I had the number published in the phone book and maintained a public number all during my two terms of office.

Nabokov likewise went into great detail explaining why I supposedly took certain actions and why I refrained from making other actions without ever verifying any of it. It was also of some interest to me when he commented that during a visit in my office one day somebody asked if Tijerina could be contacted. At that I supposedly went over and pulled out a notebook and sorted out the phone number of Tijerina and called him on the telephone. The only problem with that was that the phone number was listed in the telephone book and I never had to resort to any secret documents to locate that phone number. All I had to do was pick up the phone book and look it up. He also referred to the congressional hearings, although he was neither present nor did he read them. I think that you can tell that because he clearly did not understand what took place at those hearings.

There were factual errors in the book when he repeatedly misrepresented efforts that I had made to improve road conditions in Canones and also how I dealt with the education crisis in that community. Overall he did do a fairly credible job with the book, but it certainly would have been helpful when it came to accuracy if he had taken the time to talk to me about the situation. However, I suspect that Nabokov's is probably the best of the books that have been produced in connection with Reies Tijerina and all of the problems that emanated from his raid on the courthouse. In any case, his book comes a lot closer to the actual factual situation than did the book by Rudy Busto entitled *King Tiger*. In that book the claim is that I ordered the tanks to be at the ready and assembled 450 members of the National Guard to prepare for a trip to Tierra Amailla. I obviously didn't do that, but in any event the Nabokov book was a rather interesting discussion of the case.

In passing I would note that Bruce King and his memoir, *Cowboy in the Roundhouse*, which consists of 353 pages, includes not a single mention of either the Alianza or Reies Tijerina. Also, in Fabian Chavez's book *Taking on Giants* there is only one brief mention of the Alianza and that amounts to a single line making reference to a quote from me in connection with Alianza and Reies Tijerina. His book covered 281 pages and that was the only mention contained in it. So these two political figures were not particularly interested in the general situation created by Reies Tijerina.

Victims of the Courthouse Raid

Judge James Scarborough had expected that District Attorney Alfonso Sanchez would be present for the court hearings on June 5, 1967. However, Sanchez sent his chief assistant Norman Neel in his place. The court proceeding had been going on during most of the day but by mid-afternoon the audience of approximately forty people had dispersed and Judge Scarborough had indicated that he would not be back in court again in Tierra Amarilla for about three weeks. Everyone started to leave the courtroom, and at that time things quickly developed. United Press International reporter Larry Calloway was talking on the phone to his editor in Albuquerque and all of a sudden armed men in army fatigues were filling the courthouse. Calloway indicated to his editor that a raid was taking place and that he would report back. His telephone went dead. Shooting started and state policeman Nick Saiz was wounded. He was taken to Presbyterian Hospital in Albuquerque and I drove down from Santa Fe to visit him. They were stabilizing him and he was very much concerned about his condition and I didn't blame him. I used to see Nick Saiz with some frequency after the raid, and for many years he would stop me on the highway and we would talk. He did that several times while he was stationed in Socorro, New Mexico. I knew him very well and I was deeply distressed that he'd been wounded. I tried to comfort him as best I could and finally he told me that as a result of his being in the hospital that he was going to have some financial difficulties. I told him that we would keep him on the payroll and that he didn't have to worry about that and that his hospital bills would be taken care of, but he was still concerned.

Finally, as I recall, I told him that I would help him any way that I could. He said that his family still lived in Farmington and that it was going to be a hardship even for them to come down and visit him. I then gave him $350 out of my own pocket and told him that I hoped that that would help, and he said that it indeed would and that he would repay me. I told him never mind, I don't need to be repaid. I said you had done your duty and that was the least that I could do.

    The other individual who was injured in the courthouse raid was Eulogio Salazar. I knew Eulogio and his wife Casilda quite well. Casilda worked in the laundromat in Chama, and whenever I was in Chama I used to stop and see her, and as a matter of fact, I used to stop and see her for years after Eulogio's death. I of course was quite concerned about his being wounded. About a week after the raid I arranged for both him and his wife to come to the governor's office in Santa Fe. They did. Once he arrived, he told me that he was fired from the sheriff's office the day he was wounded and that he had no way of having an income. I noted that his son-in-law had worked for the state forestry camp near Chama and that we used to have prisoners working in the forest. I offered to temporarily put him on the payroll and would see to it that he had an income. I also arranged for him to have medical care as well as securing his employment at the facility. It was at this time that he told me what happened in the courthouse, stating unequivocally that he'd been shot by Reies Tijerina. This startled me.

Resnick Hearings On the Effect of Federal Programs in Rural America

During June and July of 1967, Congressmen Joseph Resnick of New York held full subcommittee hearings on the effects of federal programs in rural America. The hearings were held before the Subcommittee on Rural Development of the Committee on Agriculture, House of Representatives 90th Congress. The reason for the hearings was the national publicity arising from the courthouse raid in Tierra Amarilla. Resnick called a number of witnesses, including some whose testimony pertained directly to the situation in New Mexico. They were Bert Corona, president of the Mexican Political Association; Father Robert G. Garcia, director of the Division on Economic Opportunity, part of the New Mexico State Technical Assistance Office, Office of Economic Opportunity; Dr. Clark Knowlton, Professor of Sociology, University of Texas; Alex Mercure, director of the Home, Education and Livelihood program; and the Honorable E. S. Johnny Walker, U.S. Representative from New Mexico.

All of them essentially testified in support of what I said before the subcommittee. I will not include all of their testimony here since it would run to more than 600 pages. Dennis Chavez Jr., the son of Senator Dennis Chavez Sr., also made a statement to the committee. His mother, Imelda Chavez, was a longtime friend and supporter of mine. Off the record, she advised the subcommittee to treat me with the greatest of respect, explaining that I was her favorite governor and that she didn't want any of them to be discourteous in any manner whatsoever. She stayed to hear all of the testimony that was presented. I find it interesting because there has been some question as to whether or not the Chavez family supported me in my campaign for governor. I can assure you that they did. As a matter of fact Dennis Chavez Jr. testified to that effect and I quote from his testimony.

"Now, I want this statement understood as nonpartisan," Dennis Chavez, Jr., testified, "because we have supported Republican governors in New Mexico, to our sorrow. In this respect, I would compliment the chairman of the subcommittee for what he said about the administration from the state level of federal programs. It was the neglect of the use of federal programs by the governors, Democrats or Republicans, which my father did not like, and for that reason, he tried to change it. It was for that reason that I supported a Republican in the last election, David Cargo who appeared before this committee."

He then went on to clarify his position on the rural programs in New Mexico. After the committee hearing, in an aside to the members, Mrs. Chavez expanded upon the reasons why they had supported me in the governor's race. She said that Ida Jo's grandfather, Ignacio Aragon y Garcia, was a cousin of Dennis Chavez and that they both had been raised in Los Chavez in Valencia County. At various times Ignacio Aragon y Garcia had been the sheriff of Valencia County, the mayor of Belen, the president of the school board and had served as chairman for both the Republican and Democratic Parties of Valencia County. She said that this was a close relationship that she could not forget. In addition to that that, she had thought that it was time for a change in New Mexico and that the whole family had supported me.

On Wednesday, June 14, 1967, I appeared before the subcommittee and testified at length. Here is a transcript from some of my testimony:

Governor Cargo. Well, first of all, I want to thank you for inviting me here and to begin with, I would like to explain just a few things by way of background.

Now, we were asked to prepare a two-page statement when

I came in today and it is very, very difficult to condense 400 years of history and put it together on two pages. But, there are several things that I believe should be pointed out. One is that in New Mexico, at least in the northern part of the state, the population of that area that we have been essentially concerned with is Spanish-American, and I think we should make this clear because they are not in that area of the state Mexican-Americans. They are Spanish-Americans. And much of the language that they speak is not the Spanish that is spoken in Spain or in other parts of the country. It is Spanish that goes back to an early period in our history. And I think that we also have to realize that in the area which has been under discussion recently, that is, the Tierra Amarilla area, or Chama, that these people have a different culture. They have problems that are *sui generis*, and it is something that frankly, I do not think that our poverty programs have dealt with adequately.

It is not just a matter of land grants, and I know that many times you have read in the paper and you had seen a discussion to the effect that it is all involved in land grants, and nothing could be further from the truth than to say that only land grants are involved.

All that Reies Lopez Tijerina did was to articulate the type of frustration that has been built up in the people of this area over 100 years, and as I said, it does not involve just land. It involves a hundred other problems, and some of them I know seem maybe a little strange to some of you.

While Congress has been talking about mass transportation, rapid transit, and all of the rest, in northern New Mexico the problem that is critical to them is the fact that they cannot use work animals on the national forest.

Now, I know this sounds silly, but one of the reasons behind what happened in Tierra Amarilla is the fact that they do not permit work horses and work animals on the national forest.

Now, you had several other problems which I think should be referred to. Another one involves roads, and those that are not familiar with what has happened in northern Rio Arriba County in the past few months should only reflect back a very few months when in a place called Canones they indicted the parents of most of the children within that village because they refused to send their children to school over an impassable road. They were indicted. They were given a year in the penitentiary and the sentence was suspended.

I went up to Canones and was the first governor in 300 years to ever go there, and this was a very frustrating experience for these people because they are concerned about their roads, and they simply do not have roads. It is just as simple as that. The roads are bad.

There are school board elections up there and we have had some burnings in this part of the country. For many, many years they've burned haystacks. They burned homes. They burned barns. We had eight fires in a five-week period this year. And for those that say that this was all a part of a pattern of terrorism in this part of the country, I would just respectfully point out that each and every one of those fires took place after a school board meeting. So, I doubt that it had anything to do with the land claims. As a matter of fact, I doubt it very seriously.

But, some of the other things that bother these people and believe me, they are bothered, is the fact that for many years no one would ever listen to them. Nobody ever takes the time to go and listen to them. All they do, they go into the northern counties, and the OEO [Office of Economic Opportunity] is guilty of this on occasion as anyone else, they go in and promise them something. The only difference that exists with OEO is that they are having really an election every day of the year up there whereas the politicians are only having an election every two years, and believe me, if you could pave roads with broken promises, they would have black topped all of northern New Mexico years ago.

Mr. Resnick. *Why is that?*

Governor Cargo. Because the local people do not have enough animals.

Mr. Resnick. *And neither the Department of Agriculture nor the Forest Service has done anything to help these people get any more animals?*

Governor Cargo. We have had meetings after meetings with them. The Archbishop of Santa Fe and myself have met with them time and time again begging them to go again and let these people graze on the national forest. We have had a lot of problems along this line. And frankly, they have not corrected the situation.

Now, I am not saying you can graze everything you want to graze on the national forest, but you have got to give the first opportunity to the people that live there.

Mr. Resnick. Absolutely. If I can interrupt you again, because this is I may say so, boggles my mind. In other words you are saying that the forest service, instead of helping these people, have been putting up roadblocks by saying let us get somebody from the outside who has gotten more capital, who can, instead of raising 10 cows or sheep or whatever, bring in 50 or 100, and then we do not have to deal with this many people.

Governor Cargo. That is exactly right. And, another thing that has happened is that slowly and gradually the people in the northern part of the state are losing their land. They have been losing it ever since United States acquired the territory. They have been steadily losing it. And people come in from the outside. They buy it up for tax purposes. They put it into ranches that are large and really not used productively in many cases, and this is one of the reasons that the Rio Arriba County, which is the county in which Tierra Amarilla and Chama are located, out of the 23,000 people that live in the county today, 11,000 of those people are receiving some form of welfare. Now, this is an awful lot of people and—

Mr. Resnick. Give us those figures once again.

Governor Cargo. Yes, Sir. Out of 23,000 people living in Rio Arriba, 11,000 of them receive some form of welfare.

Mr. Resnick. In other words 50 percent.

Governor Cargo. Almost 50 percent. And the only thing that strikes you when you go through Rio Arriba County and through all of the northern counties is that you have living there only the very old and the very young. Those in between cannot make a living. And there is a reason for their leaving. They do not have jobs, and I know some people say, well, fine, give them vocational training. This is great. If you have 22 people in a class at the end of their period of instruction you have got 23 people unemployed because the instructor cannot find a job either. So this is a very real problem. You have got to have a place where they can go to work.

Now, we also have had some welfare laws in the State of New Mexico that have been extremely unfair. We have what is known or did have—we repealed it in the last session of legislature—a relative responsibility law. We have have old age lien law.

Now, the Spanish have a very special feeling for the land and they do not believe that you should alienate the land freely. They do not believe you should sell it. You should hand it down from generation to generation.

What happens is that by reason of the peculiarity of our laws, we have not only visited poverty upon each succeeding generation but we had deprived them of the one thing that they hold dear in life and that is land, and if the federal government is going to intervene on anything, I would strongly suggest they do away with this type of law.

Mr. Resnick. *Right. Could I interrupt there again?*

Governor Cargo. Yes, sir.

Mr. Resnick. *Now this is, it seems to me, a function of the Department of Agriculture, the Agricultural Soil and Conservation Service, and also the County Extension Service. Now, do they not do this work? I mean, what is the Department of Agriculture doing there?*

Governor Cargo. Nothing that I can see. And I will be very—I would just be as blunt as I can and maybe I should not be.

Mr. Resnick. *You might as well.*

Governor Cargo. I will say it just as bluntly as I can. I think when the federal government quits conducting studies and quits counting outhouses we are all going to be better off because they go out there and they count outhouses many times.

Now, I can tell you how many outhouses we have got in Mora County. Just take the number of families and multiplied by one and if they are well off, they have got a two-seater, and that is just exactly what it comes down to. So, I say save your money and spend it on something else.

Mr. Resnick. Now, what I would like to ask is this. We heard the testimony about the lack of educational facilities up in these northern counties, lack of roads, and we are pretty well documented it. As to the resources available to the state of New Mexico from local tax sources, would you say that they are pretty well exhausted or that you are doing as well as you can in raising local funds?

Governor Cargo. Well, we have some problems in that we have a 20 mill limit on the *ad valorem* tax, which means that frankly, land owners do not always pay their share. You have a very regressive tax system. We lean heavily on the sales tax. 46 percent of our revenue in state government comes from the sales tax.

Mr. Resnick. So again, the poor are penalized.

Governor Cargo. The poor are paying again. It is like a fellow told me in Mora one time. He said, happy day, you increase our taxes—I did not, I voted against it—he said you increased our taxes. You built a brand-new capital in Santa Fe and I am paying for it, and that is the way he felt about it.

Mr. Resnick. You have no state income tax?

Governor Cargo. We have a state income tax, too, but it also is regressive. It is a very regressive. And although we have raised the exemption, it hits the family that is in the $5,000-$7,000 bracket the hardest.

Mr. Resnick. I would also like to ask you this. Of the OEO money that is coming into the state, limited as it is, is it a fair proposition of it getting out into the rural areas?

Governor Cargo. Most of it is not getting out of the hands of the administrators. They are paying it all in salaries. This is what has happened. You have some people that really—and we have some that work very hard. Do not get me wrong. But, what has happened with a lot of this is that they are chewing it all up in administrative salaries.

Mr. Resnick. We had testimony from Mr. Mercure. He said that his overhead ran about 6 percent, which is not bad.

Governor Cargo. Well, Mr. Mercure is most unusual because he is a very, very able administrator and he is probably one of the sharpest people that you have in the HELP program and they have been the most effective. But, what I am talking about are some of the people that have been drawing salaries which are far in excess of what they ever made before in their lives.

Halfway to my testimony on page 184 congressmen Resnick warmly commended me for my testimony before the committee and then went on to say:

Mr. Resnick. Oh, I absolutely agree with you, Governor. I want to congratulate you on your forthright statement. I think it is an outstanding one and I certainly will use it as the days go by. Thank you for your willingness to operate with the federal agencies and the government to get these things going it's wonderful. Unfortunately, were there are the opposite example where governors are vetoing badly needed, governors who are worried about the poor are going to and vote against them and that sort of thing.

Governor Cargo. But, you are developing more responsibility on the state level and we should have a part in the poverty program.

Mr. Resnick. Governor, I say amen, but the problem is that you, I might say, are unique and I would like to point out, particularly for the etiquette of the gentlemen of the press that a month ago I set one letter to fifty governors. Now, I do not have the exact figures but I do not think more than ten or fifteen had ever bothered to answer me so far.

If that is how much they care about the problems of their rural residents—I do not know of any other governor beside yourself who is coming. Some are sending representatives. This is the problem, that the governors did not even care enough to answer the letter. Fine, say you are not coming, not even to answer the letter—I would imagine that the problems that you have in your state are a little unique with that particular special ethnic group, but certainly all states have the same disparity in living conditions between their rural sections and their urban sections.

I would like to ask you another question and then I would yield to my colleagues. It is my feeling that the problem we seeing today on the front pages of every newspaper, the urban ghettos which are exploding—it is my feeling that what is happening, people are leaving the rural areas, going into the urban ghettos. They are untrained. They are unsuited for that life. No jobs, welfare problems, crime, and of course, you see the whole thing and then go up in flames.

Now, I see this problem as two sides of the same coin, that the people leaving the rural areas are crowding into the cities and the cities have this intense pressure put upon them.

Would you care to comment on that?

Governor Cargo. Well, I think it is obvious what has happened in the state of New Mexico. Between 1930 and 1950 in Mora County they lost 40 percent of their population. Between 1910 and 1960, the population of Mora fell off almost 70 percent.

Now, what happened to these people? What has happened in the northern counties of New Mexico, the rural part of New Mexico? It's very simple. They either sold their land or they lost it or they began to starve and they moved into the city, or they sought opportunity. We do not need some guy sitting on a chair drawing a big salary.

If we have the money in community grants, we would rather have to repay it. They do not want a gift. We do not want gifts. We will pay the money back, but we have got to have it available so that we can use it. You have got to go in and, for instance, things that you would really pay off, to go in and line your irrigation ditches or your *acequia* projects. If you could go in and line them to save your water this is far better than somebody coming out and just simply drawing a salary. Although many of the people that are involved in the poverty program are very dedicated people and their hearts are in the right place. I know virtually all of them and they are very capable and work hard at it.

Mr. Resnick. Governor, I agree and I would hope that during your visit here in Washington, that in your meeting with Mr. Shriver and other people, something could be set up in order to accomplish this. I would like to ask a couple of other questions. Before I ask them, though, on balance, and if you were sitting here in Congress, either as a congressman or senator — I do not want anybody to think you are after their seat, but —

Governor Cargo. Do not say that too loudly.

Mr. Resnick. Would you vote for the war on poverty?

Governor Cargo. Well —

Mr. Resnick. The one that is coming up.

Governor Cargo. I think that selectively I most certainly would, and as a general proposition I am very much in favor of the program.

Mr. Resnick. In other words, you feel it has helped ease problems that must be worked out?

Governor Cargo. Yes. It is moving in the right direction, but I think the big difficulty with the program is that, number one, you have not fixed a focal point of responsibility, and I believe that the states should be playing some part in this. In other words, I think that the states as well as having rights have responsibilities.

Mr. Resnick. Oh, I absolutely agree with you, governor. I want to congratulate you on your forthright statement. I think it is on outstanding one and I certainly will use it as the days go by. Your willingness to cooperate with the federal agencies and the government to get these things going is wonderful. Unfortunately, we have the opposite example where governors are vetoing badly needed projects, governors who were worried that the poor are going to rise up and vote against them and that sort of thing.

Governor Cargo. That is right. So do I. I believe that the state has a basic responsibility. But one of our problems has been that the federal government has pre-empted most of the tax sources and it becomes difficult for the state to embark upon the programs that are needed. But I do believe that if you can get these things closer to home, that you are far better off. I can go out and visit, and have, virtually every little village in New Mexico. I doubt that Sargent Shriver will ever make it because he cannot. He cannot conceivably do it. But you have got particular problems in each one of those villages.

I can give you a good example. There is a place called Villanueva, which is a little village up in San Miguel County. Now, I went up there during the campaign and said if I were elected governor I would come back and visit Villanueva because they have never had a governor there. Two years prior to that, our candidate for governor did not get a single vote up there and they came back after the election and they had 1,500 people out to meet me and they came out on horseback, lots of them walked, and the reason they came out on horseback is because they do not have a road that you can drive over.

I cured that, too, because—this is maybe not the way to do things, but we have a provision in the law that says that you have to build roads to state parks. So, I created a state park in Villanueva, and they built a road up there. That is exactly what we did. Now they have got a road. They have also got a state park. And it is beautiful state park.

Mr. Resnick. Mr. Mathias?

Mr. Mathias. Governor, it seems like you have things well in hand. I think you should make it a state park in every part of New Mexico.

Governor Cargo. Frankly, I am thinking of it. I have got several of them picked out right now and this is exactly what we're thinking of doing. Yes, sir. If this is the only way we can get roads. I will build a few state parks.

Another exchange with Congressman Resnick appears later in my testimony:

Mr. Resnick. I would like to ask a couple of other mechanical questions, you might say. What is your authority vis-à-vis the forest service? As governor?

Governor Cargo. None.

Mr. Resnick. In other words, all you can do is talk to them and talk to your congressman and ask them to talk—

Governor Cargo. I took a little unfair advantage, you see. I took along my archbishop and some people believe in redemption, and if those people in the forest service are of our faith, they may have to go to confession one of these days, and the archbishop has a lot to say about it. So, I took along the archbishop, but many people in the forest service are sympathetic and they are good people and they want to do what is right, but so many times they do not understand the problem.

Mr. Resnick. *Well after your testimony today and after the testimony the other day, we are issuing this afternoon an invitation to the forest service, because I think they certainly ought to explain their stand in this matter to the satisfaction of the subcommittee. I will be perfectly honest, I find it very difficult to believe in this day and age that they would do things like that, but obviously they have and I want to hear their side.*

Governor Cargo. I will tell you a very funny one. Up in San Miguel County they have a wilderness area, between San Miguel County and Santa Fe County, and they turned it into a wilderness area but they allow limited grazing, and some of these sheepherders had some old shacks up there. So they told them that you have got to tear down the shacks and buy tents and move up in the woods. Well one of them told me, he said any time you see sheep it is not wilderness and I do not know why I should live in a tent up in the woods. And I have to agree with him. I am all for the wilderness areas, but by golly, if I am a sheepherder I would like to go in style and live in a shack.

I was also asked if the people involved in the courthouse raid were radicals. Congressman Goodling of New York asked me the following question:

Mr. Goodling. *Can anything be done about that to help your people? I mean, can you not do anything to help yourself?*

Governor Cargo. Well of course, this land has been split up now. Much of it has been split up. There is not anything that can be done about it. This is what the Alianza was talking about. They wanted all the land back, but you cannot do that because they have sold it and it is no more fair to take property from people who have a chain of title now that it was when they took it from their ancestors. So, there is not much you can do about it.

But here is the thing that strikes a lot of these people, and most of them are uneducated in the ways of the world. They do not understand a lot of these things and, of course, under the old land-grant system they did not pay taxes. There was no such thing as a tax within a land-grant. You took your taxes in kind. In other words, you turned — or military duty, something like that. So it is very difficult to get across to these people that they no longer have any hope of getting their land back.

But, here is the thing that strikes them as being funny, and you talk to them in their homes and they will tell you. They say, well, by demanding this land they say we are communists, and we have had people call them back down there. They say you are communists because you want this land or you want a part of it. And yet, they can look out at their neighbors who have had huge settlements in land claims, the Indians out there. I have done a lot of work for the Navajo tribe. It is awfully difficult to explain to a guy that has had his land taken away or his ancestors had it taken away that he is a revolutionary because he thinks that he should be compensated when the guy right over the fence gets paid many millions of dollars.

I am not saying they had our right in the way they look at it. But, I am saying that it is a factor. And, the only way we are ever going to get their minds off of this thing is to develop some kind of viable alternative for them. We have got to give them schools. We have got to give them opportunity. We have got to give them a chance to get ahead. We have got to do all of these other things so that they will forget what happened a long time ago. It is the only way you can do it.

Mr. Resnick. I understand the situation is bad. But, it seems to me, it was not that desperate, was it?

Governor Cargo. Well. No; it was not. And, I am not being critical of the people that were involved. But I have been greatly disturbed and I have also been very widely criticized, number one, because I have listened to these people. This is, I think that it is one of the duties of every public official to quit talking now and then and listen, and so I think it is my duty as governor to listen to the problems of these people and I have done it. And, of course, they have charged me with coddling. They say you are coddling all of them.

Then, I became most disturbed about the violations of the rights of these people. Now, I was the one that withdrew the National Guard, of course. I was not in the state when this happened. I was gone on a day trip. And, when I came back, of course, the National Guard had been called out. I was not saying that they should not have been called out. But it disturbed me greatly because I began getting phone calls from people who said you ought to shoot all of those Mexicans up there.

Well, this is not my job as governor. My job, as the governor, is to see to it that every man has his right protected and that every man is equal before the law. And this is what I am trying to do. But when I saw these pictures on television—and they worried about my safety, I was less worried about my safety that I was some others—when I saw people being herded together and all the rest of it, it bothered me. It bothered me a great deal. And justice in the state of New Mexico does not and should not function that way.

We are going to see to it that every single person that is charged gets a fair trial.

Now, I am not condoning any violence. When you shoot a policeman, and they shot two of them, and both of them were Spanish-Americans, when you shoot them you're going to be prosecuted. You should be prosecuted and I am going to see to it that they are. At the same time you have got to protect their rights. You have got to see to it that they have adequate legal counsel. You have got to see to it that they have a change of venue so they can get a fair trial. You have got to see to it that they are treated fairly in every respect. And, I will do everything within my power to do that. But, I had been subject to a great deal of criticism.

After my testimony Dr. Clark Knowlton, professor of sociology at the University of Texas was called. He gave very extensive testimony and during his comments to the subcommittee made some positive remarks about pertaining to my position:

> *Mr. Resnick. Do you think the state of New Mexico can do more?*
> **Dr. Knowlton.** Yes, very much so.
> *Mr. Resnick. Do you think they are straining their resources?*
> **Dr. Knowlton.** No. In fact I do not think they are doing hardly anything. I think Governor Cargo is one of the very few governors who has had a feeling for Spanish-Americans and is interested in them. As you pointed out, the governor of New Mexico does not have control other than agencies of the state government, and so by himself a governor can do very little, but to my knowledge he is one of the first governors in New Mexico who has ever been in the villages, let alone know what is going on. Maybe because of his wife, but he does have a feeling for these people. It comes out and the people respond to this and it is a situation resolving itself in land, water, grazing rights, poverty, lack of employment, these are traditional things. They're found in many parts of the United States. But in New Mexico they reach a special component because the language and the culture and because of the feeling among the Spanish-Americans that they are conquered, that their will was trampled on and it has been persistently trampled on since New Mexico became part of the United States. I submitted to your office a whole series of studies in which I tried to analyze this detail but I do feel we have reached a crisis point in northern New Mexico and this unless, and I say unless, very soon, the state and federal government address themselves realistically to the programs, there will be more violence. There will be more violence even though these are very gentle people.

The reaction in Washington to my testimony and to the hearings in general was largely one of approval. They thought that my testimony had been fairly well balanced. In fact, a number of people congratulated me in connection with what I had said. In New Mexico it was a far different story. A large number of people did not think that civil rights were really the issue. The cry was that the activists, as simple lawbreakers, should be summarily shot. The reaction of some people shocked me, but it was obvious that there still existed a great deal of bias. Personally I have never condoned what happened in the courthouse raid—I felt very strongly about that—but I think that we must protect the civil rights of everyone involved. They certainly were entitled to a fair hearing and a fair trial. One newspaper in Hobbs faulted me and was deeply critical of me saying that it all started while I was governor during the events at the Echo Amphitheater in Rio Arriba County, even though that incident occurred well over a year before I became governor. That was the type of criticism that I received; some of it was neither balanced nor rational.

Black Churches in New Mexico

New Mexico had, and still has, a small African-American population. Because of the community's small size, many politicians ignored them. Not me. I paid attention to them and went to their rallies, events and to their churches.

I think the thing that endeared me to the Black community was that I invited Black ministers to the mansion for dinners twice a year—the first time in the history of the state that they had been invited there as a group.

I regularly attended NAACP meetings, which I always enjoyed. I also enjoyed the Ms. Black New Mexico contest, which was held in Roswell. I was the first governor to attend the pageant. Ernestine Hodge, who was very active in the NAACP, told me that she was especially proud that I attended the contest. In fact, she sent a letter of all African-American organizations lauding my efforts and the attention I paid to the Black community.

Community Meetings

When I was campaigning for governor in 1966 the incumbent senator representing Santa Fe County was Jose Ortiz y Pino. He headed the group Democrats for Cargo. After I went into office I took him on board my staff and he began to plan community meetings. We went essentially to small towns in northern New Mexico like Canones and Peñasco. He would plan the events and then would make sure that they were properly conducted. The number of people attending would range from 300 to in Truchas to over 1,000 elsewhere. They were very successful because I took most of my top administrators with me and we would devote an entire day to a community and attempt to solve their problems. Usually they wanted improvements to roads. I would have the chairman of the state highway commission, Reynaldo Espinosa, with me. He would explain what needed to be done.

The residents also talked about education and schools, and we would have an explanation in connection with that, and usually Leonard Delayo, head of the Department of Education, would talk.

Another problem many communities faced was that of clean water. I got the legislature to appropriate money for water systems. When we would hold a community meeting and they would ask what could be done about total failure of the system to provide clean drinking water, I would say that we could do something immediately about it. Normally, I would announce that on the following Monday I would have a crew up there. The village or town would then proceed to drill for water and set up a system where we would hook up to the main line and have water.

I also dealt with sewage systems, and many times the state would provide sewer systems. It was always interesting because there was one meeting we had in a small village where I indicated we could put in a water and sewer system. But I needed to know what size the system would have to be. At that point one gentleman got up and said that it depended on how much they were able to feed the crowd that day. He then said he would adjust it by way of support from the state, and also by how much they could afford to contribute in the village. I thought that was a rather interesting response.

Governors in Support, 1968

One thing I did to prepare for the election in 1968 was to secure endorsements from my fellow Republican governors well ahead of the primary and general elections. They were almost unanimous in endorsing me. Of course, Governor Nelson Rockefeller of New York, and Governor Winthrop Rockefeller of Arkansas, led the way, but I also had strong endorsements from governors like James A. Rhodes of Ohio. He did a long endorsement for me by saying that he was surprised that a primary was necessary and that he couldn't understand why I would have any opposition at all. He took a strong position in supporting me and offered to come to the state to campaign for me.

Governor Tom McCall of Oregon did the same thing, as did Governor Dan Evans of Washington State. Governor George Romney of Michigan had added his endorsement. In any event, I received the endorsement of virtually every governor. I think there were only one or two who didn't endorse me, and that was simply because they had been difficult to contact and I wasn't able to catch up with them.

Much has been made of the fact that President Nixon had a larger majority in the general election in 1968 in New Mexico than I did. I think that people should be aware of the fact that George Wallace, who was the third-party candidate, drew more than 26,000 votes in his race for president here. He drew 99 percent of his votes from registered Democrats. He got a lot of votes on East Side and in San Juan County, but his campaign here was headed by Democrats and there wasn't a single Republican that I know of that endorsed him. So you have to figure that into the equation as well. I had a lot of issues on my hands because the Democrats were in a huge majority in this state, including those who were supporting George Wallace.

Fabian Chavez

Fabian Chavez was the Democratic Candidate for lieutenant governor ticket with Gene Lusk in 1966, but it is worthy of note that in the primary he was opposed by Jack Jones who owned Ford dealerships in Santa Fe and Albuquerque. U.S. Senator Joe Montoya was very active in the primary, and he got Robert McKinney, who owned the *Santa Fe New Mexican* newspaper, to endorse Jones. Montoya then cornered a number of his political associates to oppose Chavez in the primary. He didn't succeed because Chavez beat Jones in the May primary, 76,609 votes to 47,386.

Fabian further stirred up Montoya when he was quoted as saying, "Joe Montoya's fingerprints were all over it." He put it out that Montoya's group had gotten "Jack Jones to file for lieutenant governor and he heavily supported him." This did not make for a cordial relationship between Chavez and Senator Montoya. It's no wonder that Montoya didn't support him either for lieutenant governor for governor in 1968.

Also in 1966, Gene Lusk had attacked a number of people personally, which was a mistake. He attacked Harold "Fats" Leonard, Paul Case, Victor Salazar and Tom Montoya—the senator's brother—directly by calling them "the Four Horsemen of the Apocalypse." He also then went on to dump all over people like Charlie Davis, Alonzo Gonzalez and even John Burroughs.

In the 1968 primary election for governor, five big-name Democrats filed. They were all convinced that I would be easy to knock off. Running were former Lieutenant Governor Mack Easley, House Speaker Bruce King, former House Speaker Calvin Horn, state Representative Bobby Mayfield of Mesilla Park, and former Assistant Attorney General Harry Stowers, Jr. That gave Fabian an easy race because they were all Anglos. Even though Senators Montoya and Clinton P. Anderson did not look on his candidacy with much favor, Fabian had an easy time of it in that he was the only Hispanic in the race.

In the primary, which was held on August 27th 1968, Chavez got 41,348 votes; King, 24,658; Horn, 24,376; Easley, 21, 436; Mayfield, 19,528; and Stowers, 2,543.

In the Democratic race for lieutenant governor, Albuquerque state Senator Michael Alarid defeated Albuquerque attorney David Kelsey by a vote of 31,764 to 29,584. This was a close election, and oddly enough, Alarid had been a longtime Republican before going to the state senate. Actually, he pretty much supported me when I ran in 1966 and was very favorable towards my candidacy that year, but it brought about a ticket which Senator Montoya called the "Tortilla Ticket." The "Tortilla Ticket" did not do as well as it might have in the northern counties where they lost the election.

In 1968, Fabian had the support of Ed Romero, who at the time was a regional manager for a direct sales company based in California. Romero would later go on to become Bernalillo County Democratic Party chairman and, even later, the United States ambassador to Spain. Ed was a very shrewd politician and a good friend, but he helped Chavez a lot. He was Chavez's campaign treasurer, but he said publicly a number of times that Senators Clinton P. Anderson and Joseph Montoya worked the hardest against him in Chavez's election against me.

I also got the support of a number of Democratic county chairmen, including Filo Sedillo from Valencia County, George Baca of Socorro County, Emilio Naranjo of Rio Arriba County, Johnny Vigil of Santa Fe County, and Andy Vigil, chairman of Taos County Democrats who was active in my campaign and who took me around Taos County to canvass for votes.

Some of my strongest support came from Santa Fe County Democratic Chairman Johnny Vigil and Santa Fe Mayor George Gonzalez. Johnny was Democratic County Central Committee chairman on the Sunday prior to the election and he invited me to speak to one of their gatherings. It was funny because during the meeting, Victor Salazar and Alonzo Gonzalez came in. They were running the state campaigns pretty much for the Democratic Party, and they arrived with stacks of dollar bills and put them on a table in the front of the room. Then Johnny got up and gave me a big pitch and Mayor Gonzalez spoke on my behalf. Then I got up and made a speech that actually brought them to their feet. Chavez claimed that some of them got mad and started leaving the room, but they didn't.

The New Mexico Young Democrats also held their convention in Albuquerque. David Branch, who was the state chairman of the Democrats, and I appeared. They quietly endorsed me. They didn't say anything about it in the press, but they quietly worked for me and were very effective.

Fabian Chavez Apology

On October 7, 1968, in the gubernatorial campaign, Fabian Chavez made a number of charges at an Espanola rally that were reported by the *Santa Fe New Mexican* newspaper. I asked that he either issue an apology or a retraction for what he said.

According to the newspaper, Chavez told a group that I had made a statement during a recent speech in the northern part of the state, saying, "Is Fabian ignoring you just because his name is Chavez?" I indicated that I had never made any such statement and I said, "It is pure demagoguery, and especially in view of the fact that he could furnish no proof therefore he should retract his remarks."

I also cited another part of the story where Chavez again accused me of making a statement that I never made. This story said that Chavez told a group that I had called "the Rio Grande Gorge Bridge Campbell's folly and the biggest payoff in history." I countered by pointing out that in the 1966 campaign I had fully supported construction of the bridge and supported the Republican Party in Taos and a resolution that they had passed and early 1966 supporting the bridge. I stated at the time that I supported the project but I also supported completing the road on Highway 64 and said that it should be paved so that the bridge would be useful. At the time I had indicated that it was a bridge to nowhere if it didn't have the road leading to it. I supported both the bridge and the road leading to it, and during my first term in office had pretty much completed Highway 64 all the way across northern New Mexico. I also charged that Chavez should have been aware of the fact that the highway had pretty much been completed and that it was completed during my term in office.

Another issue that arose during the campaign was that Fabian Chavez was supporting liquor sales and that he indicated that I was being supported unanimously by liquor dealers and that he could prove this because he had seen Cargo literature in bars in Grants the week before. This was during the second week of October and he said he had been to a number of bars in Grants and had seen the literature. I thought that it was unusual that he would be campaigning in so many bars around town.

My campaign manager, State Senator John Eastham, an Albuquerque Republican, said that "Chavez's remarks were completely ridiculous and unfounded and apparently designed to hide his own past and present support of the liquor industry and its support of him." Eastham then continued that "Chavez had for years lobbied for the liquor industry and supported legislation favoring the industry and that he later switched over after admitting that he was wrong and he fought for the repeal of the Fair Trade Law."

Eastham cited an article from the *Santa Fe New Mexican* which quoted Chavez as saying he had "supported the liquor industry for about 10 years until I could see where it was all wrong." Eastham also added that "I had never done a flip-flop on the liquor industry like Chavez and that I hadn't had to apologize for 10 years of being on the wrong side of the issue."

Treatment of State Employees

I used to make it a regular practice whenever I went to a town or villages outside of Santa Fe to stop by and visit with any state employees that happened to be headquartered in the town I was visiting. State police officers used to shuttle me across the state. One officer would take me from Santa Fe to Albuquerque, and another would take me from Albuquerque to Socorro and so forth. That way I could learn about the problems of state employees. Early in my first administration I pledged to try and help them with their many problems.

State employees had long been neglected in New Mexico. They were often ignored because they were political appointees. There was no personnel system in New Mexico until late in Governor Jack Campbell's second term. It didn't function effectively until I took office. Very little had been done to improve state employees' salaries or work conditions.

In the state Capitol, employees were governed by a Capitol Buildings Commission, which was comprised of the secretary of state, the attorney general and me. They were working six days a week and I reduced their work week to five days with no work on Saturday and Sunday. I would be promptly overruled by the attorney general and the secretary of state, who were of the opposing party. Then I would go and move to try to increase their salaries, and I was overruled on that as well. Finally, I decided that I would resolve it by issuing executive orders. I asked Attorney General Boston Witt to file suit to change the situation. This ultimately made for a very interesting political situation because almost all the state employees employed at the Capitol and in state buildings in Santa Fe were former Democratic precinct officials or activists in the Democratic Party. There were almost no Republicans.

I quickly established a good working relationship with them and regularly used to have parties for them and their families at the mansion. I also increased their wages and improved their working conditions. I often went down to the lunch room in the Capitol and eat with the custodians. They would bring things from home and they would entertain me at noon. Frankly, I enjoyed that much more than being lobbied by people who simply wanted something out of me by way of favors.

About two weeks before the election in 1968, the Capitol staff came to my office and said they wanted to meet with me in the basement. All employees were there and they said that they had met and decided that were going to support me for re-election even though they were Democrats. They said that they could see no reason why I shouldn't be re-elected because I wasn't very partisan, and was liberal enough that they all agreed with me on most of the issues. They did support me and that accounted for much of the margin that I had in Santa Fe and Santa Fe County in the election. I used to regularly inquire about their families and their living and working conditions. I genuinely enjoyed talking to them.

Campaign Tactic

There is a story that the late attorney Jim Toulouse used to tell about me. It was that as a young lawyer new to New Mexico and working in Jim's office, I was sent one day to cover a court hearing in Los Lunas.

As I was racing down Broadway on my way to Los Lunas, the story went, I saw a funeral procession, screeched my car to a halt, jumped out, joined the procession and became, in Jim's words, "an instant mourner."

I have to say that it is mostly true. I was detoured by the funeral, but I did *eventually*, make the court hearing.

I guess I couldn't help myself. Shaking hands, talking to people and going to funerals seemed to be in my genes.

I did a lot of handshaking and went to a lot of funerals and every gathering I could. If there was someone breathing, you can bet that I would have been there.

One of my most unusual campaign tactics came courtesy of the New Mexico State Legislature. During my first term, the wise lawmakers decided that they were going to cut back on the budget for services. One of the things they wanted to cut was the mailing of false teeth and eyeglasses to welfare recipients.

I took an immediate interest, and used the situation to my advantage. Every time I went out to drive around the state, and in particular, when I went by myself, I loaded up my car or the truck with false teeth and eyeglasses. Then I would personally deliver the glasses and dentures to people.

It was effective because I would knock on their doors and tell them that I was going to save them a trip to Santa Fe. I didn't ask for anything in return. I would chat with them and sometimes they would invite me in for a meal or to just sit down and talk. I would then give them their glasses or false teeth and leave. I think they were impressed that the governor had personally delivered this stuff to them.

I delivered those things all over the state. I never pressured anybody, or openly campaigned, but it was an opportunity to do a lot of personal, one-on-one campaigning. I did this for more than two years before the legislature caught on and realized that they had handed me a great campaign tool.

Finally they issued a directive to the Department of Health that from then on they wanted eyeglasses and false teeth mailed to welfare recipients. That solved the problem for the recipients, and I didn't have to fight with the legislature over it. A lot of people gave me credit for forcing the legislature to recognize how greatly they had inconvenienced those people by forcing them to drive to Santa Fe to get their glasses and dentures. It was an interesting twist and probably a first in political campaigning.

Continuation of the race in 1968

One of the highlights of my 1968 campaign was the support I got from the Rockefeller family. Governor Winthrop Rockefeller of Arkansas, attended a September 21, 1968, at a $125-a-plate fundraising event for me at the Western Skies Hotel in Albuquerque. About 500 people showed up. It was a roaring success.

Rockefeller endorsed me by saying, "It takes people like Dave Cargo to push to get elected where a party is far outnumbered. We need Republican governors who can get along with Democratic legislators!"

After the dinner I got a call from Governor Nelson Rockefeller of New York. We talked about TV advertising for the campaign. He had a group of people that worked on his TV ads who were headquartered in Dallas, Texas. He sent them to Santa Fe and they went through a number of prototype ads. They cautioned me against advertising too much on TV. Their reasoning? It was mostly ineffective and a waste of money.

I didn't have any money to waste, so their advice was welcome. Eventually, Nelson Rockefeller personally picked up the tab for some of my ads. They were highly effective in that they were centered on conservation and the environment. Rockefeller and I had been heavily into environmental issues.

S. Q. Chano Merino, president of Local 890 of the United Steel Workers of America union, had announced at the end of the Democratic Nation Convention in Chicago that he was going to return to New Mexico and support me for re-election. I had fully expected that he would do it because I had tried to get his union's support in

1966. I failed that year, but I kept up the effort throughout my first term.

In 1966 I went with future state representative Murray Ryan and asked Local 890 for their support. I told them that I had a far better labor record than Gene Lusk did and that they should support me. Chano and Nacho Morales, the local's political director, let me address the membership. I pulled out our voting records and explained them very carefully and said they should endorse me, not Lusk.

Nacho got up and said they had promised Lusk their endorsement. I said I thought they were dead wrong, but that I respected their views and would be back. I said, "When I run for re-election I hope that I will get your support, because I will earn it." I also told them that Lusk had the worst labor voting record in the legislature. No matter, though, I couldn't get their support.

In 1968 it was a different story. On Friday, October 26, of that year we had a spectacular rally at the United Steel Workers of America Local 890 Union Hall in Bayard. The place was packed, so packed that in early 400 people were outside because they couldn't get in. Ida Jo had come along. So did state Senator Junio Lopez, who wound up addressing the crowd.

I had also lined up an airplane tour that day that started at 9:30 in the morning. We met 75 people at the Santa Fe airport, flew to the union hall in Bayard and had a private meeting with all of the incumbent office holders in the county, including the district attorney, sheriff and all of the county commissioners. We included the county officials because they were all endorsed by the union and therefore were supporting me. After the meeting we toured the New Mexico State Hospital. I also went to Western New Mexico University for a lunch that was sponsored by the school's Political Science Club. We had a capacity crowd and all of the student leaders were there.

At the union hall rally I discussed my labor record and the long copper strike, which had gone on for almost nine months.

Union officials talked about how I helped them during the strike. They described my dealings with President Lyndon Johnson and noted how I was able to persuade him not to issue an injunction requiring them to return to work. They also described how I had gotten Johnson to settle the strike on the Monday following our White House conference regarding the strike. I also told them that I had increased the state's minimum wage every year I was in office but one. I talked about how I had fought for improvements in the workers and unemployment compensation programs.

State Democratic Party Chairman Penrod Toles was also the subject of discussion at the rally. Toles had been selected by Fabian Chavez as the chairman, and that did not go over well with organized labor. Toles strongly opposed labor. His voting record on labor issues amounted to a big fat zero, I said. In addition, Senator Joseph Montoya was adamantly opposed to him. The so-called "Young Turks" didn't like him either because of his ultraconservative votes in the state Senate. He was probably the most conservative man they could have selected for the job. It didn't help Chavez one bit to have put him there because he antagonized many elements in the party, including people like Tiny Martinez and others who were more progressive.

The union hall rally lasted for more than two hours. One by one, Democratic Party officials stood up and endorsed me. The Chavez candidacy was pretty much dead in Grant County.

There was a lot of shouting and laughing. The funniest thing, though, was when two guys showed up and held up signs that said Local 890 was unfair to Chavez. The sheriff and the district attorney told them to leave. They said they were going to stay on union property no matter who asked them to leave. Finally, the sheriff grabbed both of them and said he was going to place them under arrest. I thought it was a little extreme, but anyway, that's what he did.

The sheriff hauled the guys into the union hall. Nacho Morales was the presiding magistrate judge and said he was going to arraign them on the spot. They said they were going to disqualify him and asked that a bond be set. Morales said he couldn't set bond because he had been disqualified and that they would have to sit in jail until a designated replacement judge showed up. When the two asked how long it would be before they could find a replacement judge, Morales said it would be up to the state supreme court and that it would probably take several months. At that point I asked that they be released, and they were.

We had a campaign barbeque that was sponsored by a local rancher. I had met the rancher about six months earlier in the La Fonda Hotel in Santa Fe. He was sitting on a bar stool as I was walking by and he stopped me and said, "I didn't vote for you." I said, "Well, that's all right. There were 100,000 others who didn't vote for me either." He laughed and said, "I would like you to have dinner with me." I said, "Why not? I'm in no rush."

We ate and talked for an hour and I hadn't seen him since. When he heard that I was coming to Bayard he donated the beef for the barbeque and supervised everything. He also turned out 1,500 people. He stood up at the barbeque and said, "I didn't vote for him last time, so I just wanted to tell him that I'm supporting him this time around."

The Chavez campaign tried leaking information to the *El Paso Times* and the paper bit. It reported that there was dissension in the union ranks and that predominantly union precincts were going to turn in substantial majorities for Chavez in the election. That turned out not to be the case. Chavez was almost wiped out in Grant County. I ran about 1,700 votes ahead of the Republican ticket in the county.

An interesting note to the matter was that Chano Merino faced opposition in the union election that was held in late December 1968. He was opposed by Juan Chacon, a former president of Local 890 of the International Union of Mine Mill and Smelter workers. The El Paso Times reported that Chano was strongly opposed for re-election. Once again, they got it wrong. He was re-elected by a vote of 465 to 184.

The rest of the ticket, which included Alfredo Avalos, local vice president, Ruben Rodriguez and German De Luna, who was the treasurer, also prevailed. They didn't win by as much as Chano, but it was close.

I had put Avalos on the state's Human Rights Commission. He and Chacon supported me and were very vocal about it. The *El Paso Times* said they were targeted in the election "in reaction to their having supported Dave Cargo." In his home precinct Chavez got one vote. The *El Paso Times* got it all wrong.

Education was another issue that came up in the 1968 campaign. On October 4 of that year Chavez and I collided over the public school funding formula the state had. In my second term I had managed to get the formula changed by getting the legislature to approve what was known as the P.I.E. Formula.

The previous system had favored rich counties over poor ones. Counties on the state's East Side, particularly the oil-producing counties, had lots of money, while schools in Albuquerque and in the northern counties didn't have adequate funds. Many East Side schools had carpeted classrooms and plush furnishings, while those in the north had two or three classes in the same classroom.

Chavez appealed strongly to the East Side, and in order to woo them, he had to defend the old distribution system. I lashed out at him for defending the indefensible, faulty funding formula. In a published statement he said he would "take care of school needs under the present distribution formula for education." He was also quoted as saying, "There is a need of $20 million to $40 million in additional revenue."

I responded to Chavez by saying it would take ages to raise that kind of money and that it would be of little use to places like Albuquerque, Las Cruces and the poorer school districts. I was in Farmington that week and said, "With a $40 million tax increase it means that more money is going to be poured into the old formula, which by his admission, is a faulty formula. In other words, you would have the relentless pumping of money into a faulty and unworkable system." I added that "by taking this position he stands by himself, because the legislature has unanimously recognized that the present system is indefensible."

I added that for the present formula to meet Albuquerque's needs, "$450 million at least would be needed just to bring it up to the barest minimum." I also charged that his idea for school funding would scuttle the adoption of a progressive foundation for a new funding formula.

Then I said, "If you go ahead with the old formula and pump in an additional $40 million, plus adding a hold harmless clause so that next year no district would be cut, it would meant that we would be, therefore, effectively prevented from going into a foundation program.

"Likewise, putting that kind of money into the old formula would mean you would give the same amount to the richest districts and the poorest ones. It isn't based on need, and his proposal would be an extremely wasteful process."

Then I accused him of adopting an anti-Albuquerque attitude. He responded by saying that I was "emotional" about the issue. I countered by saying, "Chavez wants to go back and repeat the same mistake they made in 1962 and 1963 when he presided over the largest tax increase in the state's history as majority leader of the Senate."

The following week I addressed a convention of educators and school administrators in Albuquerque's Civic Auditorium. I outlined a school financing formula that I thought was viable and that would result in sizable pay increases for teachers throughout the state. The *Albuquerque Tribune* made my proposal front-page news and then went on to support me on the issue.

I thought that that might get me the *Tribune*'s endorsement again, but the paper's new editor, George Carmack, thought differently.

I had gone to Carmack's office earlier during the State Fair so he could interview me in connection with the campaign. He said very bluntly that he was a horse racing fan and that he expected me to extend the racing season at the track on the fairgrounds by two weeks. He asked my position on the matter. I said, "I don't intend to do so because I don't want to be placed in a position of getting between the *Tribune* and the *Journal*, which is adamantly opposed."

The Journal didn't want any extension at all. Carmack then said in a loud voice, "If you don't extend the season and I can't go to the races, then I'm going to editorially oppose you for re-election. I said "fine" and left. Sure enough, I didn't get The Tribune's endorsement.

Chavez's position on education jibed perfectly with that of his East Side manager, state Senate President Ike Morgan. At a meeting in Carlsbad, Morgan said he was adamantly opposed to any changes in the school funding formula. He attacked me for wanting to change it. State Senator Robert E. Ferguson was quoted in the Carlsbad Current-Argus as saying, "A school foundation program as proposed by Cargo would be very costly to a few counties in New Mexico, including Eddy and Lea." He added that he "could not support the foundation offered during the last legislative session by the governor because it would cost Eddy County taxpayers over $1 million in additional taxes, with $340,000 less returned to the county schools than is the case under the present money distribution formula." It was an interesting twist, and it showed very clearly why Chavez was doing so much to please East Side legislators.

On October 30, 1968, a group of senators and representatives who were taking a caravan tour of the East Side and who were promoting Chavez's campaign, met at the Stevens Hotel in Carlsbad. They had a news conference at the hotel and spent the entire time criticizing me. Morgan, a Democrat from Portales, led off by saying that I was a "misplaced, displaced juvenile delinquent from Michigan."

He didn't like me because I had gotten into a dispute with him about membership in the F.E.P.C. Commission. He came to my office one day and dumped on me about the commission's makeup. He said that, "On this commission you have appointed a Rabbi, a

Catholic priest, a Mexican, a Black and an Indian." He ended by adding, "Why haven't you appointed any Americans?"

I took exception to that statement and we got into a loud argument. I obviously didn't like his approach or ideas.

Senator Mike Alarid, who was a candidate for lieutenant governor, accused me of "placing proposed legislation before the state legislature with no hope of having it passed." He also said that, "the governor, during the legislative session, consulted the editorial pages of the *Albuquerque Journal* and the *Albuquerque Tribune* and then formulated his legislative program of the day from those pages."

All the East Side legislators campaigned hard for Chavez, who was making a big pitch to carry the area. In the process, though, he neglected the northern part of the state, and that proved to be fateful.

I also got support in the re-election bid from Senator Clinton P. Anderson, who helped me in many ways. He was a close friend and later sent me an autographed copy of his book, *Outsider in the Senate*, along with a warm letter addressed to "My Governor."

A week before the 1968 election, Senator Anderson took me as his guest to Rotary Club luncheon at the Albuquerque Country Club. His son Sherb came along as well. At the luncheon, Clinton introduced me by saying, "He is my guest and I'm supporting him for re-election." Afterwards he handed me a $500 contribution and said, "I hope that this helps." He also made calls to his many friends on my behalf, and that helped.

Anderson called me on election night to say that Senator Joseph Montoya had also called a good many of his supporters as well. Anderson and I agreed on many issues, including reapportionment, conservation and civil rights.

Labor Support

During the third week of September 1968, the AFL-CIO had their endorsement convention in Albuquerque. About 250 delegates attended, in spite of the fact that we had made an effort to secure the endorsement of the AFL-CIO and that the union's Executive Committee had decided that no endorsement would be made. A union spokesman said that "the decision to withhold endorsement arose because, both men have good labor records and it might have been impossible to get a two-thirds majority for either man."

I spoke first at the convention. Fabian Chavez followed me. We both received standing ovations, although the applause was somewhat more sustained I think in my case than it was in his. For the first time a good many Republican candidates appeared and tried to get endorsements from the Committee on Political Education, which held its convention on Sunday following the Saturday convention.

The unions represented 17,000 New Mexico voters, and even though they were not going to make an official endorsement, I figured I could at least try to get their unofficial endorsement and their votes.

My address to them was rather lively in that I spent some time talking about former state Senator Penrod Toles of Roswell. Toles was Chavez's campaign manager and was picked by Chavez to be the Democratic Party's state chairman. I told the crowd that "I wouldn't pick Toles, who, when he was in legislature, sponsored the right to work bill and fought for it hard and long." I also said that he had a record that was anti-labor at every turn. That drew a standing ovation.

I went after the rest of his record when I said that "I didn't vote for the Lusk anti-picketing bill and I didn't vote to cut the Workers Compensation Act." Chavez defended his vote for the anti-picketing law in 1957 by saying "all the Senate voted for it and I did too."

Likewise, I attacked Chavez's voting in the 23rd legislature where he opposed anti-discrimination legislation, which prohibited discrimination based on race, color, religion, ancestry, or national origin in public assisted housing. That bill failed by a vote of 11 to 20. Thus, he was on record as opposing anti-discrimination in public housing. He also voted against an Equal Employment Opportunity Act amendment which would have strengthened the existing act. Senator Carr killed the bill, and they carried by 19 to 13 vote with Chavez leading the way. Those votes didn't help him with either labor or with minorities.

Chavez did come back by saying that Toles wasn't on the ballot with him and that Anderson Carter somehow was involved in my campaign and that Carter wasn't running so he didn't have that much to say about my campaign.

I also added that it seemed to me it was an anomaly when it took a Republican governor to get good social legislation passed in spite of the fact that the Democrats had long dominated the governor's office and had a stranglehold on the legislature. The legislature would still be dominated by ultraconservative elements of the Democratic Party if it hadn't been for the reapportionment lawsuit that I filed. And I said that even with the passage of partial reapportionment the Democrats still had a stranglehold on the leadership in the legislature, which they did.

At the conclusion of my address I received another standing ovation. It was clear that most of the individual unions were going to support me rather strongly. I had a lot of support from former officers of the various unions and also current ones. Jim Price, a former president of the AFL-CIO, and then the executive treasurer of the New Mexico Building and Construction Trades Council, wrote me a letter on May 29, 1967. I'm going to quote it in full because

I think that he was speaking on behalf of the federation pretty much, and he was certainly speaking on behalf of James J. Fanning, the council's president. Both of them endorsed me publicly in the campaign. Here's the letter in full:

> *Dear Governor Cargo:*
>
> *Be advised that I have had conversations with several of the local unions concerning the many appointments that you have made from your office.*
>
> *Paul Cruz, Director Employment Security Commission*
>
> *Leon Dobson, Labor Member Employment Security Commission*
>
> *R. M. Montoya, Commissioner, State Labor and Industrial Commission*
>
> *James A. Price, Labor member, State Labor and Industrial Commission*
>
> *James Fanning, Planning and Development Commission*
>
> *Elmore Hipsky, Park and Recreation Committee—and others.*
>
> *I have also had time to evaluate actions of the past legislature and had made note of the many changes that will directly and indirectly help both organized and unorganized laboring people.*
>
> *The defeat of the so-called "right to work" bill was a major victory, and I feel sure that you as governor had quite a lot to do with the defeat of this bill.*
>
> *The improvement of Worker's Compensation and minimum wage will help a large number of New Mexico citizens.*
>
> *Many of us from the trade labor movement are well aware of these improvements and wish to express our gratitude and appreciation for any effort you might of put forth in the improvement of these laws.*
>
> *I am sure that I speak for the group who will also be writing letters expressing their appreciation for your help and recognition of the above mentioned appointments.*
>
> *If I can be of service to you or your administration in any way*

please feel free to call on me at your convenience.

In closing, I wish you continued success while serving as governor of the state of New Mexico.

Respectfully,
James A. Price

Then I also sent letters to all of the state's labor organizations. Here's the letter in full:

Dear Union Members:

The AFL-CIO C.O.P.E. convention did not endorse gubernatorial candidates, feeling that most candidates on both parties, including myself, were friends of organized labor. I respect and appreciate that decision.

My purpose in writing to you now is simply to relay to you personally, for what it may be worth, my observation and impression of what I consider to be a good and friendly working relationship with organized labor during and prior to my administration as governor of the great state of New Mexico; all of which concerns union leaders, the membership, prospective members and, in total, the wage earner as well as myself.

During my tenure as state representative in the legislature between 1963 and 1966, and now as governor, I have supported and introduced labor legislation that would enhance the goals and objectives of organized labor and the wage earners, recognizing that a lot of work remains to be done. The legislative records confirm my position on the issues important to the wage earner of New Mexico.

For your information, I have attached a compilation of some of my contributions in the area of (a) labor law, (b) civil rights and (c) public welfare; also, my appointments of union members from the ranks of organized labor, made in accordance with the recommendations of this state's AFL-CIO. Significantly, the narrative does not reflect unfinished business on issues such as the Department of Labor, teachers' salaries and fringe benefits, private employment agen-

cies, public employees' bargaining rights, and industrial safety and other issues that hopefully will be resolved in the 1969 legislature.

I have always acknowledged and respected the purposes and aims of organized labor in that it is devoted and dedicated to promoting, protecting and championing legitimate struggles of the working people. The results of your systematic efforts certainly benefits the wage earner in securing good working conditions, and fair working hours and wages. These are the basic principles that favorably stimulate the economy and provide the union member with a decent living, protection for his family and job security, which are the keys to maintaining our dignity.

If you and the other citizens of New Mexico see fit to nominate and re-elect me as governor for another two-year term, I will continue to work with organized labor to further your goals and objectives.

With best personal regards, I am,
Sincerely yours,
David F. Cargo, Governor

Labor Legislation:

Appointments:

Mr. Ricardo M. Montoya to the Labor and Industrial Commission.
Mr. R. C. Brooks reappointed Assistant to the Labor and Industrial Commission.
Mr. Boren W. Wilkinson appointed Assistant to the Labor and Industrial Commission.
Mr. Paul J. Cruz appointed Administrator of the Employment Security Commission of New Mexico and Chairman of the Commission.
Mr. W. Leon Dobson appointed Labor Member of the Employment Securities Commission.

Mr. James A. Price appointed Labor Member of the Labor and Industrial Commission.

Brother August Raymond appointed Public Member of the Labor and Industrial Commission.

Mr. John B. Carrillo appointed member of the state Arbors Association.

Mr. Neal Gonzalez appointed to the Electrical Board of the Construction Industries Commission.

Mr. Luther Sizemore appointed to the Judicial Standards Commission.

Mr. S. Q. Charo Marino appointed to the Mine Safety and Advisory Board.

Labor Law:

Right to Work (1963, 1965, 1967). As a state representative, I voted against and, as governor, opposed publicly the right to work law which would have prohibited the signing of a union shop agreement. Workers know that Right to Work Laws are intended to weaken strong unions, destroy weak unions and make it harder for unorganized workers to form a union and bargain successfully.

Municipal Employees' Collective Bargaining (1963). Favored both permissive collective bargaining and signing of contracts in all branches of state, county and municipal Governments (1965). I opposed this legislation as introduced (1967). Recently appointed Advisory Committee to present to me recommended draft legislation on the subject of public employees' unions and bargaining.

Agricultural Labor Act (1965). Prohibiting picketing of farms, ranches, or orchards.

Teachers Activities. Prohibiting discrimination in hiring, dismissals, discharge, transfer and demotion of teachers because of membership or not membership in a teacher's organization. Also, provided for equal opportunities and privileges for members of teacher's organizations.

Civil rights:

Discrimination in Employment (1963). Favored by a vote. Law provided for equal employment opportunities regardless of race, color, creed or national origin (1967) as governor, personally appeared before the Finance Committee and urged them to give favorable passage in committee to the New Mexico Act Against Discrimination. The act also created a state Human Rights Commission.

Fair Housing Act (1965). Favored by a vote to prohibit the practice of discrimination in housing because of race, color, region, national origin or ancestry (1967). As governor, issued an executive order prohibiting discrimination in employment because of race, color, religion, national origin or ancestry.

Public Welfare:

Minimum Wages (1963, 1965). Favored by a vote raising minimum wages to employees in the various occupations (1967). As governor, strongly supported increasing minimum wages of employees and signed the Minimum Wage Bill into law, providing for up to $1.60 per hour for non-service employees and up to a $1.30 for service and agricultural workers, effective during a one and one-half year period.

Minimum Wage for State Employees (1967). As governor, I issued an executive order setting state minimum wage at $220 per month for all state employees. On July 25, 1968, I requested the state Personnel Board and state Personnel Office to review all salaries for employees in the classifieds service and to take positives and prompt action to assure comparability as with salaries paid by private industry and the federal government.

Unemployment Benefits (1963). Favored by vote a bill to increase weekly unemployment benefits raising the minimum and maximum rate (1967). As governor, supported and signed the bill into law a raising the maximum weekly benefit to $40 per week and other pertinent adjustments.

Public Works Minimum Wage (1965). Favored by vote minimum wages for labor and mechanics employed by contractors.

Occupational Disease Disablement (1965). Favored by both increasing the benefits for the total disabled and death (1967). As governor, supported and signed into law increases in benefits for disability to $45 a week for 500 weeks, with death and medical benefits provisions.

Worker's Compensation Benefits (1965). Favored by vote increases to compensation benefits with the disabled workman during a period of disability (1967). As governor, supported and signed into law increasing the disability benefits to $45 for 500 weeks, increasing the total benefits from $20,000 to $22,500 and increasing the medical benefits from a minimum of $5,000 to $25,000 maximum and facial disfigurement from $700 to $2,500.

Some People I got to Know

I got to know President Lyndon B. Johnson extremely well. He used to coach me on political matters with a great regularity. Once he took me all the way through the White House showing me all kinds of things. He had a sense of humor that was really most unusual. He told me once when we were being photographed with a host of governors and lawmakers:

"Stand next to your president because when the photographers come around they are going to take pictures with all these governors standing around us. And your president will be looking at and listening to you and it will appear in all the newspapers and magazines and on the front page of the *New York Times*."

That picture was taken, and sure enough it appeared all over. LBJ was a character to say the least, and a person I greatly enjoyed.

I also knew President Richard Nixon very well. I met him at the Republican National Convention in 1952. He was shy by nature, and a good many times when I would go to the White House, he would call me aside and we would go into a separate room from where a crowd had gathered and we would talk quietly. Actually, he was far more progressive than people give him credit for. But we had some serious disagreements over political strategy. I thought that the party had become a very parochial one. Ultimately, I told Nixon, we would lose most of the support that we had at that time in the northern states. Sure enough, that's exactly what happened.

Likewise, I knew Ronald Reagan and Senator Everett Dirksen very well.

Probably the most attractive intellectually was Daniel Patrick Moynihan, who worked as a domestic advisor to Nixon. I got to know him well and really admired his intellectual abilities. He later became a longtime senator from the state of New York. He was among the most interesting of the people I met, and for many years I maintained a correspondence with him.

I've met a lot of wonderful, talented, smart and interesting people, and that's one of the blessings of my life.

Native Americans

I had taken an interest in Native Americans for a long time. I had represented, as an attorney, a number of individual Navajos and the Navajo Nation itself. I represented the Council on many occasions, as well as the tribe's chairman. In addition to that, I had done a lot of legal work for the Pueblos of Laguna, Taos, and Santo Domingo. Therefore, I had an rather extensive background when it came to dealing with Native American problems and the Native Americans themselves. In addition to that, during the time that I was governor I used to attend meetings of the All Indian Pueblo Council with great regularity. I was the only governor to do so, with the exception of Governor Toney Anaya, who came after me, and I think this helped me when it came to becoming familiar with problems that were unique to the pueblos and tribes.

Likewise, I became good friends with Miguel H. Trujillo of Isleta Pueblo. He was a great proponent of voting rights for New Mexico Indians. On June 14, 1948, he attempted to register to vote in Los Lunas and was refused by Valencia County Clerk Eloy Garley. The reason: "The Indians are not taxed provision" of the New Mexico Constitution. Trujillo then filed suit in federal court and was able to secure a favorable ruling on August 3, 1948. The presiding judge for a federal panel of judges ruled that those portions of the New Mexico Constitution and statutes (Article 7, Section one) that denied Indians the right to vote were unconstitutional and void. He further said that all citizens of Indian blood had the right to vote. This case was settled almost 36 years after statehood. Thus I had a good deal of background, which I had gained from Miguel Trujillo, and it proved to be indeed a starting point for guaranteeing the rights of Indians to vote. It is also interesting to note that I had written to U.S. Senator Dennis Chavez in the same year that the Federal Court case was decided in which I asked him about how Native Americans were going to vote and which direction they might lean. He most graciously responded and said, "They would vote as Americans." He was right.

I also represented the Navajo Tribe on polling places where various counties like Sandoval County were requiring the Indians to travel more than 60 miles to vote in spite of the fact that they could have voted easily in Cochiti, Santo Domingo pueblos, or in Pena

Blanca instead of having to go the northern end of the county. It was all designed to keep them from voting.

I held community meetings at each of the Chapter Houses on the Navajo reservation and visited all the Pueblos with great frequency. It paid off for me handsomely both in the election in 1966, and when I ran for re-election in 1968. In 1968 I was endorsed by scores of pueblo governors. They gave me a substantial majority of the votes cast by Native Americans. I also utilized the Navajo radio stations and got substantial support from them.

I likewise acted as a go-between between the federal government and the various tribes and pueblos. At that time they were having a difficult time communicating. One interesting incident took place at the Navajo Chapter house in Water Flow when a Navajo got up with a mischievous look on his face and asked me if I knew what the term BIA meant. I replied that I thought that I did but maybe he could enlighten me. He then stated that BIA meant a Boss Indians Around, and he wanted me to help them with their problems. I proceeded to do so.

My support of Taos Pueblo and their request for Blue Lake resulted in an official endorsement by Taos Pueblo. I also made a great number of appointments to various boards and commissions and put Indians in official government jobs for the first time in the state's history. This helped me a great deal. Especially important in connection with this endeavor was the appointment of John C. Rainer Sr., who not only worked in my office, but who also was my representative on the Governor's Interstate Indian Council. He was eventually elected chairman of that organization.

I also had an extremely good relationship with Robert Lewis, who was the governor of Zuni Pueblo. He had just gotten in a battle with the Democratic Party over various matters, in particular the case of *Lieutenant Governor Tom Bolack vs. Joe Montoya*, which was a case that went to the Supreme Court of the State of New Mexico and involved the question of whether or not Indians could vote in New Mexico state elections. He was very strong in supporting that particular case, and I assisted Bolack in his court case. The case involved the lieutenant governor's election in 1962. The Democratic Party filed suit to prevent Native Americans from voting in state elections. This also gave me a great deal of stature among Indian tribes and pueblos. In the case of *Montoya vs. Bolack* in 1962, the court ruled unanimously that the Indians did have the right to vote in state elections.

It was an important case and was not easily forgotten by Native Americans. As governor I also appointed Governor Joe H. Herrera of Cochiti Pueblo to several positions. He served on the State Advisory Council for Vocational Education and the New Mexico American Bicentennial Commission. He was a longtime friend and a strong supporter. I also made sure that Native Americans had an opportunity to serve in the legislature. Two Navajos, Jake Chee and Wilburt Begay, both served in the House of Representatives as Republicans, and Tom Lee served as a Republican state senator for many years.

I tried to give recognition and respect to Native Americans and attempted to bring them into government.

Blue Lake

For years I had been interested in the matter of Blue Lake and the surrounding 50,000 acres as claimed by Taos Pueblo. Back in 1906 — well before I had any involvement in New Mexico politics — President Theodore Roosevelt had signed an executive order creating the Carson National Forest. In doing so he ignored the rights of the native people and superimposed a national forest on land which is still known to the Taos Pueblo as *Na-Wha-Lo*.

The oldest of the nineteen Pueblos in New Mexico, Taos Pueblo has been inhabited for more than 800 years and was more than 400 years old when the Spanish arrived in 1540. They managed to attract little attention through the years, however, in 1620, the King of Spain set forth the boundaries of the lands of Taos Pueblo and presented a cane to the governor of the Pueblo. Likewise, President Abraham Lincoln gave a succeeding Taos Governor another cane during a visit to Washington, DC in 1863. It was not until 1923, with the introduction of the so-called Bursum Bill in the U.S. Congress that there was any question about the land and water rights of the Taos Pueblo. The bill would have severely curtailed those rights. Senator Bronson Cutting introduced a bill in 1932 which authorized a patent to Taos Pueblo for 30,000 acres covered by the act of 1928. This stipulated that the Forest Service should continue to manage and administer the acreage. In 1933 a U.S. Senate committee recommended that title be restored to the pueblo. This would result in a diluted act protecting some Indian use rights, finally issued by the U.S. Department of Agriculture in 1940.

Blue Lake became an issue again in 1951, when Taos Pueblo filed suit with the Indian Claims Commission. By the late 1960s, Blue Lake was a touchstone issue for Indian rights in New Mexico. The pueblo gained an ally in Congress, Representative James A. Haley of Florida, chairman of the House Subcommittee on Indian Affairs. He introduced H.R. 3306, which was designed to place in trust 48,000 acres of Taos land and the Blue Lake area. Predictably, there was loud opposition. Many legislators argued that in the past, Indians had lost so much land through legislation and action in the courts that restoration of the Taos land might set a dangerous precedent. Historically, politicians had relied on the old military saying "sacrifice the few to save the many." Recreation interests and the Forest Service also mobilized their forces against the Haley Bill, and it died in the Senate.

Opposition to the return of Blue Lake was led in Congress by the members of the New Mexico delegation, most particularly by

Clinton P. Anderson, the state's senior senator. Prior to being in the Senate, Anderson had been aware of the Blue Lake controversy, but he had become much more intensely involved after he left the House to serve as Secretary of Agriculture under President Harry S. Truman. Since the U.S. Forest Service is an integral part of the Agriculture Department, Anderson naturally sought to maintain Forest Service control over as much public land as he could. This most certainly included Blue Lake and the 50,000 acres adjacent to it. Anderson felt strongly about the matter; he was subsequently to lead the battle in Congress against legislation to return the parcel to pueblo control.

At first I was the only public official in New Mexico to support the return of Blue Lake and its surroundings to the pueblo. With the 1968 election of Congressman Manuel Lujan, Jr., I was to acquire at least one ally. In the early stages, however, I stood alone in my support of Taos Pueblo's claim to Blue Lake.

Anderson took an intense interest in the disposition of the matter and contacted me on a number of occasions to discuss it. Twice, in fact, he made special trips to Santa Fe to try and talk me out of supporting the federal legislation. This created a bit of a dilemma for me in that Anderson was a very close friend and supporter of mine. His support had been instrumental both in getting me elected in 1966 and in my 1968 re-election effort. I felt the need, therefore, to be extremely cautious, while I had to be fair in stating that I did fully support the legislation in favor of the pueblo. Anderson presented lengthy and forceful arguments for his contrary view. Of course I listened to what he had to say, but ultimately stuck with my choice to go forward with my support, with or without his agreement. This strained our close relationship, as illustrated in a November 23, 1970, letter he wrote me.

Anderson always referred to me as "my governor" and made it our deep friendship clear. He knew that I had done legal work for the Navajo tribe as well as for various pueblos in connection with the reapportionment case and in many cases involving politics. At the time of the reapportionment suit I had been determined to make sure we had Native American representation in the state legislature. Prior to the case, New Mexico had followed a moiety system giving each county one state senator and at least one state representative. In the event a county was entitled by population numbers to elect more than one representative, those representatives were chosen in an at-large vote. For a long time this system effectively prevented Native Americans from being elected. At the time I was elected governor, however, two Native Americans came into office from McKinley County, Jake Chee elected to the House and Tom Lee to the Senate. In addition, in San Juan County, Wilburt Begay was elected to the House. The presence in the legislature of these three Native Americans, all Republicans, provided me with additional political support in the Blue Lake decision and became an important factor when I first undertook to support Taos Pueblo in their claim.

In 1968, house legislation HR3306 was introduced by Representative James A. Haley, a Florida Democrat. It provided for return of the Blue Lake and 50,000 acres of land. The bill passed in the house but died in subcommittee largely through the efforts of Senator Anderson. In 1969, HR471 was introduced by Haley and the bill returned 48,000 acres to the pueblo; Blue Lake likewise was to be returned. That bill was approved in 1970 by the Senate and signed into law on December 15, 1970 by President Richard M. Nixon. Nixon had been involved in passage of the legislation, and stated that it was "an important symbol of governmental responsiveness to the grievance of all American Indians."

In spite of his initial failure, Haley was convinced the Taos Indians had been wronged by the government in having their aboriginal lands taken from them. Early in 1969, at a time when the plight of the Taos Indians was coming to light across the country, Haley introduced a bill on behalf of Taos Pueblo. The House held hearings and the Senate reviewed the bill. By July, the proposed legislation was receiving nationwide media coverage and more importantly, editorial support from influential newspapers and major magazines.

As a result of this media coverage, people across America came to know about Blue Lake. Most sympathized with the concerns of the Taos Indians. I have to admit that I personally contacted a number of newspapers soliciting their support. A few of the major newspapers provided editorial support to the Taos Indians were the *New York Times, New York Journal American,* the *Washington Post,* the *St. Louis Dispatch,* the *Minneapolis Star-Tribune,* and the *Denver Post.* The editorials emphasized the constitutional guarantee of freedom of religion and the return of the land to its rightful owners.

At long last, Taos Pueblo was gaining publicity and increased support for their cause. Many religious organizations also supported the pueblo. Some of the organizations that spoke out for the Taos Indians were the New Mexico Council of Churches, the National Council of Churches of Christ, and the American Jewish Congress. Meanwhile LaDonna Harris, the grand Indian lady of Washington, entered the fray and began doing her part to educate and persuade the stern and staunch opponents in Congress with her charm and knowledge. Harris, a Comanche, was president of Americans for Indian Opportunity, an Indian advocacy organization based in the nation's capital. She also was the wife of former Oklahoma Senator Fred Harris. Later, Fred Harris was to become professor of Political Science at the University of New Mexico.

To old-timers on the Indian scene, the situation was much like the fight against the Bursum Bill by Pueblo Indians in 1922 when they marshaled forces to defeat that destructive and unfair legislation. This time, however, a more experienced lobbying force of Indians and other individuals were working unceasingly for Taos Pueblo, visiting influential persons around the nation. In addition, key supporters like Kimberly Agnew, the daughter of Vice President Spiro Agnew, also visited the Taos Pueblo to show their support. She would return later for a victory celebration.

Early in 1970, a Taos Pueblo delegation attended the Executive Council meeting of the National Congress of American Indians (NCAI) in Washington, DC. John C. Rainer was vice president of this association and the chief Indian member of the National Council of Indian Opportunity under Vice President Agnew. The Taos delegation traveled to Washington hopeful that the NCAI would use its influence to convince the President of the United States to publicly support the return of Blue Land and the pending legislation.

Support for the Taos Indians also came from another source close to President Richard Nixon. Although he has not publicly been given credit, presidential aide John D. Ehrlichman, like Congressman Haley, was convinced that people of Taos Pueblo had been wronged. As a result of all these efforts, and ultimately because truth triumphs, on July 7, 1970, President Nixon announced his support of the Taos Pueblo claim. This pronouncement gave Taos cause a great boost at a critical time.

At this point, Senator Anderson introduced another bill that appeared to give Taos Pueblo use of some of the land. Closer examination of its terms, however, revealed that the legislation would have separated the grant into parcels for different purposes, including logging. It was quickly denounced by Taos Pueblo spokesmen. Nevertheless, the bill made it out of committee in 1970. It was challenged immediately by Senator Harris and by Republican Senator Robert Griffin of Michigan. Together, they moved to substitute Haley's M.R. 471 for the Anderson bill.

The Senate was scheduled to vote on December 2, 1970, on which date the bill would be adopted. To aid the Taos cause, Domingo Montoya, chairman of the All Indian Pueblo Council, sent a telegram to New Mexico's junior Senator, Joseph M. Montoya, asking him to vote for the House bill. Montoya replied that he could not go against the state's powerful senior legislator, Senator Anderson. As it turned out, Senator Montoya was conveniently out of the country on a trip to Mexico when the vote was called.

Taos Pueblo officials and their friends were tense as the vote was taken. They thought the numbers were on their side, but they could not be sure until the votes were counted. Anderson's bill was defeated 56 to 21. Then came the vote on the legislation that would give the site back to the pueblo. It passed overwhelmingly, 70 to 12.

During the tabulation, John C. Rainer was sitting with network broadcaster Roger Mudd at Vice President Agnew's seat in the Senate. That evening, Mudd was able to broadcast accurate information about the Taos situation given him by Rainer.

With the victory, the Taos Pueblo Council and their friends wept with joy. The jubilant news spread from Washington across the continent to all American Indians on this most momentous day when the David that was Taos Pueblo and defeated the Goliath of the U.S. federal government.

At 11 a.m. on December 14, 1970, in the state dining room of the White House, President Nixon signed into law H.R. 471 giving Blue Lake and its environs back to its rightful owners. Of the many pens on table, the one Nixon used to sign the document was given to Juan de Jesus Romero, whose Indian name was Deer Bird, a man who had devoted much of his life to the quest for the return of Blue Lake. With great dignity, Deer Bird accepted the pen and said: "Now when I die, I will die at peace." When Deer Bird died eight years later, the *New York Times* printed an obituary of this dedicated man with the headline: "Taos Tribe Leader, In West, At Age 103, Juan de Jesus Romero, a Spiritual Head of New Mexico Indians."

With Deer Bird at the bill signing ceremony in the White House were Quirino Romero, governor of Taos Pueblo; James Mirabel, tribal senior councilman; Deer Bird's constant companion, Paul J. Bernal; and John C. Rainer. At the ceremony Rainer was the only Indian wearing a war bonnet, which was worn to represent all American Indians. The war bonnet had belonged to Leo Vocu, a Sioux from Pine Ridge, South Dakota. Vocu had given it to Robert Jim, Chairman of the Yakima Nation, when Jim was going to South America as a representative of the American Indians. When Jim learned of the date of the signing ceremony, he flew from Yakima, Washington to the capital the day before to give the headdress to Rainer.

In my efforts on behalf of Blue Lake the most important figure was obviously John C. Rainer who worked directly for me in the governor's office and was also the director of the New Mexico Commission on Indian Affairs. Rainer had served as chair of the All Indian Pueblo Council and was the first vice president of the National Congress of American Indians and likewise was the first college graduate to come from Taos Pueblo. Rainer spent a lot of time with me and he made me familiar with the issue of Blue Lake. He took me on two trips to the pueblo and also took me up to Blue Lake. Another stalwart supporter was James Peter Davis, archbishop of Santa Fe. I met with Davis early during my first term as governor and acquainted him with the battle for Blue Lake. His support was invaluable and he consistently helped me with the issue. Congressman Manuel Lujan eventually stated his support for H.R. 471. Lujan said immediately after the hearings "I believe this achieves a settlement with which we can all live in the best of conscience."

R. C. Gordon-McCutchan in his book, *The Taos Indians And The Battle For Blue Lake,* pinpoints the importance of Lujan coming on board as follows on page 161, and I quote, "Lujan's decision represented considerable political courage, since he represented a state that was Democratic and often anti-Indian. Two highly placed elected officials in New Mexico now stood with the Tribe: Lujan and Governor Cargo. That both Republicans would prove to be important to the outcome of the summer of 1969 brought primarily good omens."

At the time President Nixon mailed out a letter to Republican members of Congress urging their support of Blue Lake. This was an interesting development and one that I would hardly expect them to do today, but in any event it happened. Likewise, Vice President Spiro Agnew, through my almost daily contact with his top administrative assistant J.D. Ward, was one of the really key supporters of the legislation. It was interesting because here again you would not have expected it. Nixon's chief White House advisor on minority affairs, Leonard Garment, was fully expected to come on board and did. I discussed the matter with President Nixon on a number of occasions and he was enthusiastic in his support of the legislation. I fully expected the White House to issue an announcement of support for the legislation. However, when no statement ensued the tribe felt they were in a very difficult position due to Senator Anderson and his opposition to the project. They then called upon Congressman Lujan and myself for information and advice. Gordon-McCutchan wrote, "Cargo continued to prove his friendship. In January he had written to the White House to declare his support for the Indians. In February, he made the first official visit to Taos Pueblo by a New Mexico governor in 123 years, for the express purpose giving H.R. 471 a widely publicized endorsement. Now he called the White House and learned that, while the president was planning to support H.R. 471, his announcement would be delayed for strategic reasons. Lujan informed the Tribe that the ABM/Jackson problem was causing Nixon's hesitation. Greatly disappointed the tribe decided that their only recourse was to increase the political pressure on Nixon."

I likewise directed Myra Ellen Jenkins, the state historian, to appear before Congress to testify in support of the bill. Her testimony was most instrumental in getting the legislation passed.

Not everything went as smoothly as that. At the Senate committee hearing Montana Senator Lee Metcalf was abusive towards the members of the Taos Pueblo delegation. As Paul Bernal put it, "Metcalf was under the influence of firewater, and said that the whole affair was a shameful behavior and a mockery to the hearing audience." I then got into a fight with Metcalf, saying that "he insulted all American Indians and that his comments during the hearing had antagonized Indians throughout the nation." I added, "If he has no more respect for these people than that he should disqualify himself. But to ridicule the pueblo before the committee is uncalled for."

Senator Metcalf then returned to the committee and said, "If Taos Pueblo was given Blue Lake and the adjoining land then every medicine man in America was going to rise up and demand the same for every tribe in the United States."

On December 2, 1970, at the close of a two-day debate, the Senate voted 77-12 for a bill which restored the land and the lake to Taos Pueblo. At the Albuquerque airport the following day, Deer Bird, spiritual leader and tribal cacique of Taos Pueblo, spoke for the delegation, saying, "Blue Lake wilderness keeps our water holy and by the water we are baptized. If the land was not returned to us it would have been turned over to the government for its permanent use. That would have been the end of our Indian life. Our religion would have been violated."

The delegation led by Council Interpreter Paul J. Bernal, one of the prime movers of the legislation, then returned to Taos Pueblo. News of their success in Washington was proclaimed at Taos with the ringing of the mission bell. At the church in Taos Pueblo the people gathered, crying and laughing, and the ninety-year-old cacique spoke for all when he said "We are going to enjoy the happy new year every year!"

The Blue Lake victory ceremony that followed in August 1971 was the most joyous celebration seen at Taos Pueblo in a very long time. Prayers of thanksgiving, songs, dances, speeches, and a buffalo feast marked the event. The celebration was open to the public, and the pueblo honored those non-Indians who had particularly helped them retain the land. Those honored included Secretary of the Interior Stewart L. Udall; Senator Fred Harris of Oklahoma; Senator Robert Griffin of Michigan; Representative Manuel Lujan, Jr.; and myself. When Paul Bernal, who had served as secretary to the Taos Pueblo Council for twenty-four years, and who had fought unceasingly for Blue Lake for many years, was asked who had led the battle from Taos, he said, "No one man, all together. The governor, the council, and the people."

Just as Metcalf and others feared, the return of Blue Lake to Taos Pueblo set a precedent for Indian nations throughout the country. As a result of this legislation, many other tribes that had not received compensation for, or return of, unjustly seized lands have demanded redress. Legal action has also been undertaken to return to the tribe's sacred relics, implements, and ancestral bones from museums and other collections. By 1990 the federal government had passed a Native American Graves Protection and Repatriation Act to provide a process for museums and federal agencies to return certain Native American cultural items—human remains, funerary objects, sacred objects, and objects of cultural patrimony—to lineal descendants, culturally affiliated Indian tribes, and Native Hawaiian organizations. This was all set in motion by the Blue Lake victory.

The legislation was supported organizations as varied as the National Council of Churches and various conservation groups. The real driving force behind it, of course, was Paul Bernal. He should be given credit where credit is due. Likewise, credit should be given to the late Senator Cutting's actions in the late 1920s and early 1930s. Joe Sando, in his volume entitled *Pueblo Profiles a Cultural Identity Through Centuries of Change*, at page 181 gave me credit:

> Among them was a local champion of Indian rights, New Mexico Governor David Cargo. Through his ties to the federal administration, and especially Vice President Spiro Agnew, the tribe was able to make broader contacts with politicians and media.

Sando's book provides a description of the final moments in the battle of Blue Lake:

> The Forest Service objected to the proposal; it would not take care of land outside National Forest boundaries, and no one outside the tribe came forward to support the bill. That for the time being ended, but not defeated, the Taos Indians did not give up. They learned the hard way that public opinion was one effective way to progress, and by that time the pueblo had gained support from outside the Tribe. Among them was a local champion of Indian affairs New Mexico Governor David Cargo. Through his ties to the federal administration and, especially, Vice President Spiro

Agnew, the tribe was able to make broader contacts with politicians and the media. For example, though the efforts of Vice President Agnew, Taos Governor Quirino Romero and John C. Rainer, Sr., appeared on the Dinah Shore television show to champion their cause.

Cargo, dubbed Lonesome Dave by the media, had for the first time in state government appointed a number of Indians to state committees and boards, giving them broader public exposure. John Rainer, Sr. of Taos Pueblo was appointed director of the State Commission on Indian Affairs making that office a valuable avenue of communications.

Taos Blue Lake
Chronology of the Fight for Justice

1300: Taos Pueblo Indians occupy the area and establish the central village as a permanent home.

1598: Spanish rule is established, under laws recognizing Indian possessory rights to territory used and occupied.

1821: Mexico assumes sovereignty and confirms Indian possessory right to occupied territory under the Treaty of Cordova and Mexican Declaration of Independence.

1848: Sovereignty passes to the United States under the treaty of Guadalupe Hidalgo, which guarantees protection of all property rights recognized by Spanish and Mexican law.

1906: United States Government takes Blue Lake Area and makes it a part of what is now Carson National Forest.

1933: Senate committee recommendation that title be restored results in diluted act providing for a permit to protect Indian use rights, finally issued by the Department of Agriculture in 1940.

1951: Pueblo files suit before the Indian Claims Commission, seeking judicial support from its rightful Indian owners.

1966: Legislation to return the sacred area to the Pueblo, S. 3085, is introduced in Congress by Senator Clinton P. Anderson of New Mexico "by request" to indicate the lack of his support. The bill dies without action in a Senate Interior and Insular Affairs Subcommittee.

1968: House Bill 3306, introduced for the Pueblo in 1967 by Representative James A. Haley, Chairman of the subcommittee on Indian Affairs, passes the House of Representatives unanimously but dies in the Senate Interior and Insular Affairs Committee.

1969: The Blue Lake bill is reintroduced as House Bill 471 on the first day of the 91st Congress by Representative James A. Haley.

January 26 1970: National Congress of American Indians Executive Committee endorses H.R. 471 and calls for presidential support as the cornerstone of a new Indian policy.

July 8, 1970: President announces support for H.R. 471 as the first element of his new Indian policy.

July 9-10, 1970: Hearings before Senate Subcommittee on Indian Affairs on H.R. 471, and Senator Anderson's alternative, S. 750.

August 27, 1970: Senate subcommittee favorably reports to full Committee on Interior and Insular Affairs both H.R. 471, which grants trust title to 48,000 acres comprising Blue Lake and access routes from the pueblo, and S. 750, which grants an exclusive use area of 1,640 acres around Blue Lake, but without exclusive access thereto.

September 30, 1970: Full Committee meets with majority favoring H.R. 471 but adjourns before vote is taken.

October 6, 1970: Full Committee approves a substitute measure which would deprive the Pueblo of control of its sacred lands and undermine its water rights.

December 2, 1970: Senate kills committee substitute, 46-21; approves H.R. 471, 70 to 12.

December 15, 1970: President Nixon signs H.R. 471 into law.

Potash

I had for many years followed political affairs in Canada and subscribed to *Maclean's* magazine, which is the *Time* magazine of Canada. I had also followed Canadian politics with great interest. For many years, *Maclean's* was published by Ted Rogers, who was a very influential person in Canada and who was also the largest cable television operator in the world. I got to know him rather well after I left the governor's office and eventually became a partner with him in setting up the cable television franchise in Portland, Oregon, in 1973.

Twenty-eight of us became financial partners with Rogers.

I got to know him well through this association. It also gave me a great insight into the problems in the potash industry in Canada, and more particularly in the Canadian province of Saskatchewan in 1969.

I must say that the potash industry in New Mexico was not covered particularly well in Albuquerque because the *Albuquerque Journal* did not think it was newsworthy. The *Albuquerque Tribune* didn't cover it either. The only coverage of the problems in the state's potash industry were various articles published by Associated Press and Bill Feather, their correspondent. Both Feather and Rodger Beimer accompanied me on a trip to Saskatchewan in 1969.

The *Journal*'s failure to cover the matter reminded me of a trip I once took to Belfast, Northern Ireland. I went to a Protestant section of Belfast where there was a huge sign that said "No Pope Here." Under that slogan was the notation, "Lucky Pope." Maybe I was lucky they didn't cover it, I don't know.

The only coverage that the *Journal* gave to the whole matter was a series of attacks that Senator Joseph Montoya directed at me by way of press releases in connection with the pending matters pertaining to the potash situation. The *Journal* carried a headline that read, Montoya said Governor Is Grandstanding. That was all well and good, but people in Albuquerque didn't really know what I was grandstanding about, if in fact I was. the *Santa Fe New Mexican* covered the matter rather fully as did *Current-Argus* in Carlsbad. The *El Paso Times, Portales News Tribune* and the *Lovington Daily Record* covered it as well.

I likewise received a lot of background material in a series of long, long letters from Gil Hinshaw, editor of the *Current-Argus*, whom I had appointed to the State Parks Board. He was a very active member of the board and I would see him with great regularity in Santa Fe when the board met. He was a wonderful source of information and certainly had a very strong interest in what happened to the industry.

Another thing that gave me some background on the local

feeling in connection with the potash situation was the fact that my opponent in the 1968 governor's race was Fabian Chavez. In 1957, state Senator Gene Lusk introduced a bill in the legislature to reduce the severance taxes on potash. He was very much interested in getting the bill passed. The House passed the bill, but when it came up in the Senate, Senator Fabian Chavez moved to table it. Not only that, but he carefully worked the Senate membership and got support from Republicans as well as a number of Democrats. When the roll call was taken the matter was tabled 22 to 10.

A few days later, Lusk tried to get Chavez not to oppose the bill on a motion to reconsider it and bring it out of committee. Chavez refused to and told Lusk, "Gene I am doing this just to teach you that it is a man that makes a Senator, not a seat to which he is assigned in the chamber. I'm giving you a message that I can defeat you."

Chavez did indeed prevail. The action prevented a reduction in the severance tax on potash. I appropriately used this against him in the 1968 election and defeated him decisively, even in Eddy County. I kept reminding the miners of what he had done and they agreed with me and I became the first Republican candidate running for statewide office to ever carry Eddy County. The only other Republican to carry it before was Caswell Neal, who did so in a local race. This made for an interesting situation. When I was running against Chavez I stopped by and talked to my 1966 opponent Gene Lusk and reminded him of Chavez's opposition to the bill. He looked at me, rolled his eyes and said, "it won't help him here," and indeed it didn't.

The situation in connection with the decline in the potash industry continued, and on Tuesday, November 14, 1967, Arthur Ortiz and I attended a meeting in Las Cruces concerning the possibility of a loan in order to put the US Borax potash mine back into operation. Eddy County was represented by Joe Gant as chairman and he was a strong supporter of mine. He later went on to become a state senator and was a very able public servant. I again went to Carlsbad in

January 1968, and met with the representative group of people from the community and assured them that I would try to help. At that point the economic health of Carlsbad was being severely threatened because the potash industry was in a depressed condition. US Borax and Chemical Corporation had shut down completely and 850 jobs were lost. International Minerals cutbacks severely injured the industry and 400 jobs were lost. Duval Corporation shut down its Wills-Weaver mine and 50 jobs were lost. Jobs in the potash industry were very well-paid. The annual gross earnings of one of those jobs was over $8,000 a year plus fringe benefits, which came out to an estimated $1,350 a year, or a total of about $9,350 annually. The potash jobs were stable, year-round jobs.

The cutbacks had cost the state 1,300 jobs. About 2,700 jobs remained in the industry. The remaining payroll amounted to approximately $22 million dollars a year. Of the royalties the industry paid to government, 37.5 percent of them went to state government. In 1960, the gross royalties were $4.75 million and the state's share was $1.75 million. In addition, they paid severance, ad valorem, income and gross receipts taxes to the state.

The potash industry also paid double the severance tax rate of the rest of the mining industry, which seemed extremely unfair to me. The industry paid an *ad valorem* production tax in 1966 that amounted to five times the state income tax paid by the industry. The gross income tax levied against the potash industry was 3 percent of mine salts and three-quarters-of-a-percent of the value of the finished product. The tangible property was valued at 38 to 40 percent of installed costs. Other locally assessed tangible industrial property in Eddy and Lea Counties was generally valued at 16 to 18 percent. Canadian companies employed only half as many employees per ton of product than New Mexico companies did.

In the early spring of 1967 I went down to Carlsbad and met with a large group of people. The meeting was packed with miners and business people and It included the following group from Carlsbad:

Carlsbad Group

Bob Boyd, Mayor
Dr. Ted Hauser, President Chamber of Commerce
Jimmy Hall, member City Council
H. C. Harvey, former Mayor, former President Chamber of Commerce
Joe Rose, County Republican Chairman, former Councilman
Gil Hinshaw, editor *Current-Argus*
Ed Dunagan, real estate and insurance, member Carlsbad School Board
Lewis Whitlock, manager Chamber of Commerce
All three potash unions represented:
Hollan Cornett, District Director Stoneworkers' Union
Neal Gonzalez, IBEW and Executive Director New Mexico AFL CIO
Henry Hudson, Machinists' Union and former Carlsbad mayor
Newell Ricer, Stoneworkers Union official
All Carlsbad potash producers were represented:
Tom Ferguson, President, National Potash Company
Houston Clark, Vice President, Potash Company of America
J. S. Mitchell, General Manager, Southwest Potash Company
Ted H. Pate Manager, Duval Corp.
Dr. John Hermann, Assistant Manager, Kermac Potash Company
Gene Pressnell, Manager Administrative Services, International Minerals and Chemicals Corporation
Roy H. Blackman, Resident Council, Potash Company of America
Jack Sitton, Public-Relations Representative of New Mexico Potash industry
Bill Darmitzel, Manager New Mexico Mining Association
James Russell, Prudentia

Early in the summer, by a fortuitous turn of circumstances, the National Governors' Conference was held in Jackson Hole, Wyoming. One of the invited speakers was Premier Ross Thatcher of Saskatchewan. Governor Nelson Rockefeller of New York immediately cornered him and told him that he needed to meet me. I was glad that I in fact had been in and that we had a chance to talk about the situation in the potash industry at some length. Later, Rockefeller took us to his ranch, which was on a 50,000 acre piece of land in the middle of the Tetons, and we had lunch. The Rockefellers had given the land to the federal government to create the Grand Teton National Park.

Premier Thatcher and I got to know each other quite well and he invited me to Canada a couple of times to go fishing. I got to know him and I became even more conversant with the situation in Saskatchewan and in the potash industry. His political background was that he'd been a leading member of Parliament while he belonged to the CCF Party and had crossed the aisle to become a Liberal and subsequently led a political revolt which resulted in his being elected Premier. I was also getting a number of petitions from various communities in southeastern New Mexico and the problem was coming to the forefront.

On November 27, 1967, Carlsbad Mayor Robert J. Boyd sent me a copy of City Council Resolution 339 which covered the plight of the potash industry in Eddy County. Other communities joined in and many adopted similar resolutions. On October 8, 1967, the Roswell City Council adopted Resolution 1301 which was sent to me by Roswell Mayor Gail Harris who also pleaded that I continue my interest in the potash situation.

On November 28, 1967, I instructed Maralyn Budke, my top administrative assistant, and Jim Robertson, head of the Department of Development, to commence a study of the potash industry so that we would ultimately could be kept informed as to what was happening in the industry.

On October 20, 1967, I meet in my office with J. S. Wright,

resident manager of US Borax, and Sherman A. White, general manager of International Minerals and Chemical Corporation. At that time they had warned me that there were going to be massive layoffs in the potash industry if somebody didn't act rather quickly. They had been working with the state's congressional delegation who were concentrating only on the matter of a punitive tariff. They had also been talking about doing something to prevent potash dumping under the tariff act. U.S. Senator Wallace Bennett was also in the forefront of wanting to do something by way of sharply increasing tariffs on foreign potash and in getting U.S. Tariff Commission to act concerning the potash dumping that was occurring. He was joined in by Senators Joseph Montoya and Clinton Anderson.

The problem with all of this was that potash was easier and cheaper to produce in Canada than it was in the United States. Canada, France and West Germany accounted for 90 percent of the potash imported into the U.S. 1968. The problem with the tariff issue was that almost all of the companies that operated in Carlsbad also operated in Canada, so it would have really penalized them in Canada and would not have particularly helped them in the United States. Also, 90 percent of the U.S. production, and 20 percent of the world's production of potash was in New Mexico. The companies were not at all enthusiastic about huge increases in the potash tariff.

I then contacted Mike Rosenberg, who represented the U.S. Potash Company, and explored the problem of declining production and tax revenues from the potash companies. This severance tax produced $491,371.77 in 1968, and $264,845.66 in 1969. Likewise, the processors tax had declined from $643,875.73 in 1966, to $253,372.87 in 1969. Compensating tax revenues had gone from $117,741.57 in 1966, to $24,670.88 in 1969. The withholding tax in 1966 was $195,427.39, and in 1969 it was $103,384.01. The gross receipts tax was even more dramatic in that the amount collected in 1966 was $13,691.01, and declined to $47.08 in 1969. The corporate income tax was a disaster in 1966 when the state collected $131,529.03. In 1969 that fell to zero.

I then requested that state Senator Joe Gant get figures of total potash of valuation starting in 1964 and running through 1969. The reduction in assessment and evaluation was dramatic. In 1964 the assessed valuation was $61,366,953, and in 1969 it was $35,183,507. This presented a dramatic picture of the situation that the companies were in.

On June 6, 1967, I met with S.A. White, who was general manager of International Minerals and Chemical Corporation. He had also given me a great deal of material to mull over. He then again returned to my office on August 21, 1968, to update me on information that pertained to the potash problem, and believe me, at that point it was a growing problem. He said he wasn't crying wolf when he said that the whole industry was going to shut down if action wasn't taken. By that time the prices had dropped to a low of $12 a ton, so the situation became desperate.

The situation was so bad in Carlsbad that the employment of miners was down to 2,721 by the first week of October 1969. It was then that I was notified by all of the companies that they were going to have to close down all of the mines permanently if something dramatic wasn't done. At that time the number of employees had declined by 1,188, or 30 percent, in a three-year period. The production of potassium salts had skidded by 21 percent in the past year, and the value had declined by 29 percent.

I then assigned Walter Kerr and Charles Cullen of my office to work full time on the potash problems. Kerr was a former editor of the Paris edition of the *Herald Tribune*, and had been former editor of the *Santa Fe New Mexican*. He had also been the Associated Press's Bureau Chief in the Soviet Union during World War II. He had covered Adolph Hitler and pre-World War II Germany and was a very knowledgeable and capable individual.

Senator Montoya then picked up the pace by introducing legislation that would allow duty-free imports up to 30 percent of U.S. domestic needs. Anything imported over 30 percent would be hit with a 40 percent ad valorem tax. He also increased his efforts to get the legislation passed in Congress. Unfortunately, he was not having a great deal of luck with it because the farm organizations, and more particularly, the Farmers Union and the American Farm Bureau were large stockholders in the potash companies. So they had mixed emotions about the whole thing, and they didn't want to see the price of potash to decline sharply. But at the same time they wanted cheap fertilizer and that made for an interesting situation.

This is especially true because 95 percent of all the potash mined and refined in Southeastern New Mexico went to fertilizer factories and farms because potash is one of the most important plant foods. If the potash industry disappeared it would have had a huge effect in that an industry that had been operating in Carlsbad since 1925 when the Snowden and McSweeny Company first discovered potash salt, was going under. It was not a very pleasant situation.

The problem essentially with potash production centered around an ever-expanding production that was taking place in the Canadian potash beds in the province of Saskatchewan. This was a vast deposit which was 300 miles long, and the ore beds were both thick and rich.

Finally, during the last week of September 1969, Premier Thatcher and I mutually set up a meeting in Santa Fe for October 9, 1969, to discuss the mutual problems of potash. He came to Santa Fe along with six members of his cabinet. I also invited Senator Anderson and U.S. Representative Ed Foreman. I also had Franklin Jones, head of the Department of Revenue; Ed Hartman, Secretary of Finance and Administration; Maralyn Budke, my administrative assistant; and Jim Robertson, head of the Department of Development.

It was obvious that the potash dumping investigation by the U.S. Bureau of Customs wasn't going anywhere despite the fact that in December 1968, Senator Montoya said that they had reached a decision. The fact was that they never did reach a decision and they were not likely to. Various public officials discussed ways that we could remedy this situation, but it was quickly decided that I was going to have to make a trip to Saskatchewan. I had not planned on going to Saskatchewan, but I didn't think we could resolve it without

Premier Thatcher. It was also clear that the tax proposals in Congress were not going to happen.

We then set up a meeting for October 16, 17, 18, 1969, in Regina, the capital of Saskatchewan. I took along a number of news people, including Feather of the AP, Rodger Beimer who covered it for television, Charles Cullen, Franklin Jones and Ida Jo. They really put out the welcome mat for us and had several banquets. We toured the Mounted Police National Academy in Regina. I made a short trip to Saskatoon, which was the center of most of the potash mining in Saskatchewan. We had a number of detailed discussions which involved Jones, Haskell Smith, the State Tax Commissioner, Department Director James Robinson and the State Mine Inspector William Hayes.

I had an opportunity to informally address the members of Parliament. I reminded them that both of my grandfathers been raised in Canada. So I had a lot of Canadian connections, and I think they were amazed that I was as conversant with Canadian politics as I was. It helps if you can read; it helps if you keep yourself informed. It was a very interesting trip and ultimately very productive. During my address to the legislators I indicated that they might adopt a program of pro-rationing for conservation purposes which was similar to what we did in New Mexico in connection with oil production.

One of the really interesting aspects of the press coverage of the potash matter while we were meeting in Regina was that the major Albuquerque newspapers crowded the potash news off the front page with a lengthy story about a Polish mule going to Arizona. Neither did they send along a reporter, and they didn't use the Associated Press either. Oddly enough, the Polish mule got all the coverage and the Associated Press report was thrown out the window. I talked at length in Regina and asked them to establish some kind of pro-rationing program. I also thought that the provincial government had the power to limit production. I didn't think that New Mexico could limit production because it might well violate antitrust laws. However, I thought that the natural course of events in New Mexico would take care of that problem. Refined potash had been selling for about $12.50 a ton, with top grades bringing in about $14. But I thought that a price of $18.75 a ton was the minimum that we could have as a breakeven point for New Mexico producers. In addition to that, I had pointed out I had a Report from State Tax Commissioner Jones which indicated most New Mexico mines would exhaust the economically feasible deposits within a couple of decades at most.

Another interesting aspect of the meeting in Regina was that Senator Montoya concluded that there would be a great increase in potash production in New Mexico only if a much higher tariff was passed by Congress. He was adamant that potash production would increase greatly with a much higher tariff. I think that it is obvious in reviewing the following meeting on potash in Canada and Santa Fe. Potash production wouldn't increase because production was much more difficult in the Carlsbad area, and there was a natural decrease in production that had to take place, and it did.

Montoya was adamant that the production of potash had to be increased dramatically in Carlsbad to be viable. I thought that was our major problem, that there was overproduction in Canada and in New Mexico. We were going to have a natural decrease, whereby Canada had to do something to keep from overproducing. Montoya ridiculed my contention that production levels in New Mexico should remain static, and he insisted that Congress was going to pass a dramatic tariff increase and that the Federal Trade Commission was going to rule that Canada was dumping on the market in New Mexico. The tariff never was increased and the FTC did not rule that Canada was dumping in New Mexico at that time. But in any event that was his position and it came right during the middle of our negotiations in Saskatchewan.

I also discussed the matter of dramatic increases in the tariff duties with Premier Thatcher, his Mineral Resources Minister A.C. Cameron and Attorney General D.B. Herald. They were aware of the fact that the same companies were operating in both Saskatchewan and New Mexico. That probably would have been a disaster for the potash companies and that most likely their political opposition in Saskatchewan, the New Democratic Party, would probably want to nationalize the companies. In fact they did, when Premier Thatcher lost a subsequent election. They were frightened that by erecting high tariffs the whole rescue operation would be scuttled. Thatcher and I issued a joint statement opposing any increases in tariffs.

In Regina, Thatcher indicated that the government of Saskatchewan would set a minimum price on potash produced there and shipped outside the province. He said that the price would probably be set at $18.75. He was giving a lot of thought to my suggestion of the pro-rationing system that would allow for continuing production and more stable price levels. Canadian government officials were insistent that even with a pro-ration system they were opposed to any increases in tariffs and said they thought it would set off a trade war between the two countries. I think it would have. They wanted me to take a strong position against Senator Montoya's proposals, and ultimately I accommodated them and issued the joint statement with Thatcher. I outlined our position on the case, and I think it was quite effective. Thatcher pointed out that U.S. businesses had $21 billion invested in Canadian enterprises and that it would have been devastating for them if the two countries got into a trade war. Thatcher said, "If Ottawa and Washington will leave us alone, we would have this thing settled."

On October 28, 1969, I went to Carlsbad and held a meeting in The Motel Stevens, which attracted an unbelievably large crowd. It was one of the largest meetings in Carlsbad in some time and it was attended by people from management, labor, government and just interested citizens. I tried to explain that the announcement of a program of strict production control, export licensing and a minimum price for Canadian potash was the direct result of the meetings in Regina and Santa Fe between me and Thatcher. It was one of the most interesting town hall meetings that I had held, and I talked about the dangers of increasing the tariff on potash by 40 percent. I said that we had a cash trade surplus of $1.5 million in the first three quarters of that year and that I thought that it was dangerous for us to pursue that particular remedy after the preliminary agreements that we had reached. I think the audience agreed with me in that I got a standing ovation when we got through. The *Current-Argus*, in a subsequent editorial, on Sunday, November 9, 1969, questioned Montoya's approach and said that they didn't think it would stabilize industry in Carlsbad. But they added that if it did, they would publish his picture in the paper the words "Our Hero."

I would find out belatedly that the U.S. Tariff Commission actually did find that New Mexico's potash industry was being injured by imports, but they did nothing about it and never pursued it really.

It seemed to me that we had come a long way from the announcement that all of the potash mines in Carlsbad would close within a week. I did my best to persuade the companies that they ought to wait until after we had actually gone up to Canada and had conferred with the Canadians and in Santa Fe as well before initiating the layoffs.

At least Carlsbad seemed to be satisfied with what we had done. On November 20, 1969, the *Current-Argus* ran an editorial that said, "If all goes well, Carlsbad has a reprieve. If we don't take advantage of it, we will have no one to blame but ourselves. In the meantime, our stock in Governor Cargo, who was heavily involved in the discussions which led to the Canadian price supports, has gone up 100 percent. Regardless of his political motivations, results are results, and we think that Carlsbad will owe a debt of gratitude to Governor Cargo if the Canadian proposals work as planned."

On November 17, 1969, Thatcher and his Minister of Mineral Resources, A.C. Cameron, finally issued their Regulations affecting pro-rationing. They included one Potash Producing License, two Potash Disposal Licenses and three Potash Production Allocations Formulas proposed for the first quarter of 1970. This effectively set up a pro-rationing system for the potash industry in Saskatchewan. It had also increased the minimum price of potash to $18.75 per ton.

It essentially set up a system that was designed to conserve and provide for the orderly development of potash resources in Saskatchewan. It was pretty much developed upon the lines that Thatcher and I had suggested in our first meeting. It eventually did save the potash industry in Carlsbad. The industry continued for many years in Carlsbad. Saskatchewan produces were subject to disposal licenses before they could export any potash.

During our first meeting, Thatcher and I suggested there be some mechanism to coordinate an international potash market. This didn't come into effect until much later, but Canpotex required that all producers join this organization or have their production allocation cut back. Canpotex was set up in 1970.

The interesting thing about all of this was that later, Alan Blakeny was elected Premier and he decided to expropriate all of the properties of the various potash companies in Saskatchewan and established the Potash Corporation of Saskatchewan, a Crown Corporation. This meant that the company was now publicly owned. I would add that the price of potash went from $75 a ton that year and that helped New Mexico, but it didn't do very much for the corporations in Saskatchewan that had been taken over by the provincial government.

I thought that the only way that we could deal with the potash problem in those days would have been to deal with them directly in a trade treaty.

I think that the potash saga had ended.

Trouble at the University of New Mexico

One of the things that I vowed to do if I became governor was to generally improve the situation involving the appointment of regents to the various institutions of higher learning in New Mexico. I felt that they had long been neglected and that they were normally appointed either for political or social reasons, but not for educational reasons. A few of the regents were outstanding in their pursuit of academic excellence. And, there were almost no Hispanic regents. The first time that I looked at it, out of 35 members of various boards of regents, Judge Paul Larrazolo was the only Hispanic. He was appointed by Ed Mechem and served with great distinction during his brief tenure at the University of New Mexico. I had made a pledge to former state Representative Lorenzo Chavez (the father of former Albuquerque Mayor Martin Chavez) that I would appoint highly qualified people to the various boards of regents. I told him I would appoint people of distinction and that they would represent the whole community. I think that I was largely successful in bringing about diversity and also bringing in distinguished individuals to serve as regents.

One of the first appointments I made was that of Chavez's law partner Avelino Gutierrez, who I named to the Board of Regents at New Mexico State University. I had no sooner announced his appointment than a large group of people came up from Las Cruces and advised me that this was probably not a very good idea. The group included the Democratic national committeeman and a good many other distinguished individuals from Las Cruces. They told me that many of the duties of a regent at New Mexico State University involved social gatherings and that they doubted that Gutierrez would be an appropriate individual to serve as regent because he might not be accepted into the community. There were approximately twenty-five people in the group and I listened to them for better than a half hour and finally I said, "Well I agree with you." I really didn't, but I wanted to see their reaction. I said, "I may not appoint Avelino because I think you've given me a lot of reasons why shouldn't do so." They then asked me who his replacement would be and I said well that I thought the one that would fit the bill was Don Perkins. Perkins, of course, was a former Dallas Cowboys football star, and he was Black. They immediately rose up and said that that would be equally unacceptable. I then said, "Well, in that event I'm just going to appoint Avelino Gutierrez." And I did.

The University of New Mexico was a special problem when it came to appointing regents because the Vietnam War was raging and it was obvious that we would have difficulty on the campuses throughout New Mexico and throughout the United States, and indeed we did.

I thought that I would seek out people who were really well qualified and I found them. Cyrene Maple was a holdover at UNM, so I simply left her in place. I then appointed some people that were truly outstanding. One was Tom Roberts, a former state representative, and an absolutely brilliant physicist at Los Alamos National Laboratory. His appointment was welcomed by the entire academic community. Even the press thought he was an outstanding selection.

Howard Bratton had long served on the board of regents, but had resigned to become a federal judge, so I had his position filled as well. Shortly after I appointed Tom Roberts, he died in a tragic incident, and so I had to replace him. I appointed Dr. Norris Bradbury, a world-renowned scientist and head of Los Alamos National Laboratory. I had also appointed Dr. Larry Wilkinson, well respected surgeon in Albuquerque. I did this out of deference to Dean Leonard Napolitano, who was head of the medical school. He wanted Dr. Wilkinson on the board because it would assist him greatly in developing the university's medical school, which was just coming into being. I also appointed Arturo Ortega, who was one of the top attorneys in Albuquerque and a person in whom I placed a great deal of trust. He turned out to be one of the best regents ever. I also appointed Walter Wolf, who headed the Legal Services Department for the Navajo Tribe. Walter and I had attended the University of Michigan law school together and he was a well known attorney and highly respected when it came to dealing with Indian law. He also helped develop a Campus in Gallup.

I appointed some equally qualified regents to the various

boards at the other institutions of higher learning throughout the state, but I thought that these appointments were really outstanding, and I think that any unbiased observer of UNM would admit that that was the best board of regents it had ever had.

We have had a variety of regents at UNM. Some were highly qualified and others highly unqualified. A great number of them had only graduated from high school, and very few of them were ever known for being particularly adept at dealing with university community.

The other problem that I had was that longtime UNM President Tom Popejoy was getting ready to retire. He was a favorite of mine and I was very fond of him because I thought he did a great job. I knew that he was going to be replaced and I asked the regents to very carefully consider whom they wanted as his successor. Late one afternoon Arturo Ortega came into my office and sat down and said, "I understand that you know Dr. Ferrell Heady, and I wanted to know if you think that he is qualified to be president of the University?" My immediate response was "heavens yes" because he headed the Graduate School for Public Administration at the University of Michigan and supervised my Master's thesis. He was an outstanding individual, and coming from the University of Michigan I knew that he had all of the academic qualifications that one could want in a president.

Arturo then asked me if I approved of his appointments. I said, "I am enthusiastic about his appointment." Heady became UNM's president on November 9, 1968. I attended his inaugural ceremony. However, he took over during troubled times.

There had been a long-standing controversy at UNM over regents, and I would respectfully point out that my successor Governor Bruce King appointed Austin Roberts, who was a former state representative from the San Juan County to replace Dr. Norris Bradbury, and Calvin Horn, who served prior to my going into office, to a vacancy that was created when King replaced Dr. Wilkinson. Many people in the academic community tried to persuade King not to replace these outstanding individuals, but he did. He also appointed Henry Jaramillo Jr., a small businessman from Belen, to UNM's board as a replacement for someone I had appointed. I thought I faithfully discharged my duty as governor by appointing an outstanding set of regents.

Another controversy that was brewing at UNM was the problem of academic freedom. Some people who had been invited to speak there, particularly U.S. Senator Strom Thurmond, had been prevented from doing so, and that caused a storm of protest from people who agreed with Thurmond. I said at the time that he should be allowed to speak even though I disagreed with him on many issues, including civil rights. Another senator who appeared and filled Popejoy Hall was Mark Hatfield of Oregon. I attended his lecture and introduced him. I introduced him because generally I agreed with his views on the Vietnam War, and we were some of the only politicians had stood up to President Lyndon Johnson on the War. He was extremely well-received by a capacity crowd of students. I thought that was a step forward, but I thought that Thurmond should have been allowed to speak. Why can't you hear opposing opinions?

The legislature, generally speaking, didn't have much sympathy for the anti-war movement, and not much sympathy for the university's faculty. Most of the legislators were Democrats, and I must say that at that time the Democratic Party in New Mexico represented a conglomeration of totally unrelated prejudices—they each had their own agendas. Some Democratic legislators were reasonably liberal, and some were probably members of members of the John Birch Society. But the Democratic Party was indeed inclusive.

The first storm of protests from the legislature came in March of 1969 in the fading hours of the legislative session by the Chairman of the Senate Finance Committee, Harold Runnels, who came into my office and deposited on my desk a copy of *The Love Lust*, a poem by Lenore Kandel which told of sexual intimacy, oral sex, copulation and everything else imaginable—and unimaginable! Runnels found this to be a shocking bit of prose. Worse yet, it had been presented to a freshman English class, and this made it more interesting. Another complication was that Lionel Williams was UNM's only Black teaching assistant, and he was in charge of that section of the freshman English class. It became required reading, and the students had to report back as to how they liked it. This set off a storm in the legislature.

Runnels also told me that he had sent a copy of the poem to every civic organization in the state. I had no idea what he was talking about I until opened the envelope and took a look at the poem. I can assure you that it was not iambic pentameter. It was the filthiest thing that I had ever read, and after having looked at it I gave it back and said, "I just can't understand why anybody would be distributing that in a classroom." That was when Runnels told me that it had been sent all over the state, and indeed it had.

I received, within a very short period of time, almost 15,000 letters, telegrams and petitions commenting on the poem and its lack of literary content. That "poem" set everything off.

I would point out that Lionel Williams ultimately was killed in a car accident in Washington State. He left the UNM under interesting circumstances. I was, to say the least, less than happy about the poem. I knew that Runnels was getting ready to run for Congress in the Second Congressional District, and that he was going to use the poem in his campaign. He was running against Congressman Ed Foreman, and he defeated him.

Calvin Horn, who was one of my severest critics, commented on the poem and said, "I found many moving and touching rhythms and images. I also was repelled by the gutter terminology that she used." He disapproved of it, but found support among some people at the UNM in that he found some parts of it "moving."

It went on. State Representative Brad Prince of Albuquerque stormed on the House floor and said, "The poem is terrible and I'd knock his block off if he shows such a thing to my college-age children." Most legislators felt the same, and they immediately began to demand that Lionel Williams be removed from the teaching faculty. They commenced a series of moves that placed me in a very difficult situation because it was a direct assault on the academic freedom. They moved to cut UNM's appropriation requests by $128,000, and $40,000 of that money was to be used to set up a Legislative University Investigating Committee. The principal target was the UNM President Ferrell Heady. I vetoed the bill.

Heady then appointed a special Blue Ribbon Advisory Committee of university leaders to make an inquiry into the matter and make a thorough investigation of the incident. He likewise suspended Williams and another teaching assistant, Kenneth Pollack, and put them on temporary leave. Pollack had gotten involved because he gave a guest lecturer in one of Williams' classes in which he used four-letter words. That happened on March 26. The following day I again went to campus.

I went to the university campus scores of times during the difficult time there and tried to show them I was interested in the situation and that I was aware of what was taking place. However, well over a thousand students and non-students attended a rally that was held in the mall in front of the student union building. This was UNM's free-speech forum. I attended by myself, and I did not have security with me. There are a good many vigorous speeches that were given by others demanding the reinstatement of Pollack and Williams and condemning everybody in sight, including Dr. Heady. Then, English professor Gene Frumpkin read the notorious poem to the crowd and received, to my great surprise, a standing ovation. Television cameras were rolling and they immediately focused on me. Then Frumpkin turned to me and said, "Why don't you take the microphone and maybe you can say a few words?" I went up to the microphone and said, "I am interested in academic freedom and knowing you can have a free university where teachers can teach theories without the legislature getting too deeply involved, but still protecting your university."

I then stated very strongly to them, "Don't let it go down the drain, and I will not, if I can prevent it." I added, "They shouldn't confuse academic freedom with filth." One co-ed standing in the front row shouted to me that she could decide what was filth was and wasn't. I said, "If you want to read the poem, be my guest." I received a fair amount of applause, but there were some scattered boos, and some of the protesters approached me. I was by myself and there were large number of people there and I didn't exactly know what to expect. Then six of them surrounded me and said that they wanted an explanation out of me. The problem was that the protesting students were all decades older than I was, and some of them were rather rusty. I didn't back down and I said I thought they were a disgrace and should look out because what they were doing was endangering the university.

One student said he came all the way from California to protest, and he damn well was going to do it, and that included in front of me. I said I appreciated him making the long trip but I wanted to wish him well on his trip back to California. I later returned for several meetings with the regents. On one occasion I was accosted by an individual who was dressed in a full suit of armor and had a long spear, which he put against my chest. Again, I was there by myself and I wasn't exactly sure what to expect of him. I leaned forward and quietly said, "If you don't get that damn thing off my chest I'm going to break it over your head—right now." He lowered the spear and retreated and I was thankful for that.

On my fourth visit, Jane Fonda appeared at the university. People gathered in great numbers. Later she made a call to the governor's mansion and spoke with Peter Fonda, who was having dinner with me at the mansion. She said that she was going to put a good word in for me. I dissuaded her from doing that, and I was glad that I did.

It was during this period that President Richard Nixon called all of the governors to the White House into a closed session. We were given a lecture by the attorney general outlining the direction that civil lawsuits could take. They were advising us to not be present on campus if any buildings were burned or if there were any demonstrations that involved violence. We were given a great number of instructions, and I remonstrated with the President and asked that some attention be paid to the disturbances that were taking place across the country.

Unfortunately, a National Governors Conference had been scheduled in a few weeks after the events at which Jane Fonda appeared. The conference was to be held in Santa Fe. Fonda and her crowd indicated that the university would be a great place to hold protests and get national television, radio and press coverage. They would have been correct except that most of the governors had to cancel, and the conference was greatly reduced in size and the press coverage wasn't there. However, at a reception held at the governor's mansion during the conference, a student appeared and came into the mansion and began looting liquor cabinets. I caught him. He had loaded up bags full of liquor and was getting ready to leave. I asked him exactly what he was going to do and he said he was going to take it because he thought that everybody should be able to have liquor available to both him and some friends that were in dire need of it. Sometime later he sued me over the incidents at the university. I appeared at a deposition, and when he walked in he took one look and turned red-faced and said, "I think we met before." I said, "I think we have too, I was just wondering if you were really serious about this lawsuit?" The next day I was dismissed from the suit, although it was continued against other individuals, including the State Police Chief Mark Vigil and General John P. Jolly.

Then students proceeded to occupy the Student Union Building for a number of days. They burned down the ROTC building, and returned to the SUB and began consuming food. They ate large amounts of food over the next few days, and they all had free meals.

President Heady had called me at the mansion and was very disgruntled. He said that he was going to request that I immediately put the National Guard on notice that they were going to have to enter the campus. He said that if the National Guard wasn't there he feared for the lives of people on campus. He was fearful that other university buildings would be burned. He had a few regents with him, and they were very adamant in demanding that I send in the Guard. I said I didn't want to send them in, and I certainly did not want to have them armed, and that my position was that I didn't think it was a very good idea. But they were insistent. They asked that I not tell anyone that they had made the request, and that I not disclose it as long as they were alive. Well, now they're not alive, but they requested the National Guard be sent in. They were insistent that the Guard would be needed. I kept silent about it all through the years and never did say anything until now. I had great admiration for President Heady, and still do, but I shouldered the blame and received all the criticism without a comment on that particular matter involved.

Another incident that took place was when the American flag was pulled down and burned. There were several football players who'd been hired to raise and lower the flag. Students were fighting with the Black football players. Three students were stabbed and several Black students suffered injuries. The whites may have suffered some injuries, but I can tell you that Black athletes called me and wanted to know what could be done about their being stabbed. I was irate over it.

On May 6, 1969, President Heady indicated he had conferred with me and that we agreed jointly to close down the university for the rest of the week. That we did.

University officials then met with Major Hoover Wimberley, who acted as head of intelligence for the state police. He recommended that they not attempt to remove the students from the Student Union Building but also said that there was probably going to be a lot of violence. He said he had intelligence that indicated that they would be involved in a violent situation.

On May 6 a group of 15 students drove to Santa Fe to meet

with me in the governor's mansion. They were led by Mel Eaves, who later became a state representative. William Pickens, president of the UNM Graduate Student Association and I had a long discussion with them. I said that "I would not permit the National Guard to go in unless there were serious threats to life or property." At that point I had no intention of sending them in at all. I was called by President Heady and the same regents as before. They said that it was imperative that I be prepared to do something and at that point I put State Police Chief Martin Vigil in charge of the overall operation of the State Police and the National Guard. I advised General Jolly that under no circumstances did I want any of the National Guard people to be armed. I said, "I don't want any bullets, I don't want any arms, I don't want anything or anyone to be injured." General Jolly assured me that would be the case, but that was not the case. They did not have bullets, but they did have bayonets, and that was how the injuries took place.

Most of the National Guard came from Belen, and they were Hispanic. The unfortunate result was that protestors threw urine at the National Guardsmen, and some instances even more than that. It became a bad situation and was in effect in many ways racial. It wasn't a very pleasant situation, and it's one that has bothered me a great deal over the years.

For almost three months every evening I was occupied until midnight by a constant stream of phone calls in connection with the disturbances and looting and other disturbing events at the university. I was totally sick and tired of it, and finally I called the city commissioners in Albuquerque and said, "Are you people going to take any responsibility for maintaining law and order in the City of Albuquerque?" Their response was, "We don't want any part of it." Consequently, the city police simply avoided the university area pretty much and didn't become involved. I called Pete Domenici, who was at that time a city commissioner, and asked him why the city would not become involved at least to some extent. He said, "I don't want to get mixed up in this." It was a situation where I guess those in charge of the state had to be looked to when it came to maintaining order and peace.

However, the National Governor's Conference in Santa Fe had concluded. President Nixon did not appear because of all the riots at the various universities throughout the nation, and everyone left except for a few news people. Bill Lawrence, a former correspondent for the *New York Times*, and at that time the political editor of ABC Television, was staying at the mansion. Lawrence and I were good friends and fishing companions, and he had asked me about going fishing while he was here. I asked both Lawrence and Mike Wallace if they would like to go up to Chama and do a little fishing. They readily accepted and said that they would like to make the expedition. I then called the Chief Vigil and General Jolly and asked them if there was any immediate danger in the next 24 hours as I had really wanted to get a little rest. They said they didn't think there were any great problems, although there had been a cascade of rumors about events to take place on campus and that buildings had been selected for burning or destruction. Finally I said I would take a chance on it and that's where I made a fatal mistake. I left for Chama. We went to the Chama Land and Cattle Company. Then I got a phone call from chief Vigil. He said things had escalated and that I probably should return. At that point Bill Lawrence had a heart attack, and as strange as it may seem, we never got to fish, never did any fishing, and got blamed for going fishing. We got into the car and immediately returned to Santa Fe. We took Lawrence to St. Vincent Hospital. I stayed with Lawrence until four in the morning and then went home to the mansion. In the meantime, my press secretary, Bob Beier, was asked where I was. Not knowing that I was at St. Vincent's Hospital he was a little flippant and said that I was out fishing. The fact of the matter was that I never did get to fish. But I did regret ever having heading in the general direction of Chama.

Lawrence's heart condition was such that he had to spend most of the rest of the summer at the mansion. He remarked to me repeatedly that he was willing to defend me in connection with the whole "fishing trip," but I didn't think that was a very good idea because he was in the news business and he had an extremely responsible position. I thought that he should shy away from defending me at all.

By that time the riot was in full force at the university and Chief Vigil the next day called a press conference and said that he wanted to defend the National Guard. "The National Guard was called in on my direction and all I can say is that use of the National Guard, in my judgment, was a necessary move," he said. He then continued, "Our primary interest was the protection of the students, and I think if we had not taken the necessary precautions and had the manpower that we did it would've been negligent really in trying to correct this thing."

I had given him the authority while we were on the way back from Chama to use his discretion in utilizing the National Guard, but I had cautioned everyone involved that I didn't want any violence whatsoever. However, I've been blamed for this for years. It was a rather strange twist in that I was one of the few governors who were opposed to the war in Vietnam. Dr. Heady and I were not very happy about the outcome. There just simply wasn't much we could do about it under the circumstances.

Several weeks later I had some more difficulties which landed on my desk and that was that a large group of students were proceeding down Central Avenue to go to the federal courthouse to protest the war. When they got as far as Albuquerque High School, which was then located on Central Avenue, a large group of African-American students who had family members in the military came out and commenced to beating them up. It turned out to be a rather messy situation and I again received phone calls saying that I had to intervene. They advised me that the city had no interest in becoming involved. So I had to call the state police in to try and break it up and prevent injury.

Prior to the aforementioned described events at the university, the legislature passed a series of laws that severely curtailed academic freedom at UNM. I vetoed each and every proposal with the exception of one, and then I began to catch it from legislators. They were unhappy, and a good many of them told me that they thought that if large number of students had been shot at it would've been a welcome sight. In any event I again was criticized, this time from the other direction. It was a no-win situation. In retrospect I almost think that if I had it all over to do again maybe I would have just let them simply burn the thing down. Maybe they should not have been prevented from doing so. But in any event I was sworn to protect public lives and property and I discharged my duty. Part of it was done knowing full well that I would have to take criticism for many of the incidents that took place and there was simply nothing I could do about it.

It was also interesting that there was a large demonstration shortly after I left office. I happened to be in Albuquerque and was near the university and watched as the marchers went by. Strangely enough, they began to applaud and cheer me. I couldn't understand why, but at least I got some applause out of the whole mess. After I left office and Bruce King became governor the destruction and rioting continued at UNM and a liquor store and several buildings were burned and virtually demolished. But nothing really came of it. It was like the 1980 prison riot in that some things catch the eye of the news people and some things don't. But in any event, that was the end of a very sad experience. One gratifying result of all this was that the *Albuquerque Journal*, in a long editorial, praised my efforts in connection with the problems at the university and said that I had done the only thing I could do and I had done the right thing throughout the course of events.

Dr. Heady came in for more than his fair share of criticism over the incidents. But I can assure you that to my mind he remained a good man and a respected academic.

There was an extremely troubling situation which was developing at Highlands University in Las Vegas and many people expected it to be a much more difficult thing to deal with.

Therefore I set up a meeting at Highlands and was formally invited by the president of the student body to come there and address an audience. We had a meeting that was held in the largest assembly hall at Highlands. I took the regents with me to the meeting. I addressed the crowd at length about the problems that I thought existed at Highlands. My speech was very well received, and when I opened it up for questioning, the questioning was sympathetic to say the least.

I not only answered all the questions that they posed, but then indicated that among other things I intended to appoint another Hispanic regent to the board. I had already submitted Roberto Armijo's name as a regent and I had already appointed Roberto to the Highway Commission. I ultimately appointed him to the New Mexico State Court of Appeals. I also promised to consult frequently with the student leadership and set up a student *ad hoc* committee to do exactly that. I then met with them several times and tried to straighten out some of the problems at Highlands. I also indicated that for the first time in years I was going to do some major construction at the university, which was badly needed. I accomplished that as well. It was the only construction to take place at Highlands for many years.

I should also point out that mock student elections were held in 1968, and out of all of the institutions of higher learning I carried all of them decisively with the exception of New Mexico State University. Bobby Mayfield prevailed in that mock election for governor, as he was a both a graduate and a resident of Las Cruces.

No violence took place at Highlands, and for that I was most grateful. The press was pretty much quiet about the success in connection with the situation at Highlands. But some of the press in Albuquerque and on the East Side said that I had pandered to the students at Highlands because they were mostly Hispanic. I said that wasn't the case, but that's the way they viewed it.

I am reminded of a saying that goes as follows:

Among Life's Dying Embers
These are my regrets:
When I'm right no one remembers.
When I'm wrong no one forgets.

No one forgot the situation at UNM. But everyone forgot what took place at Highlands University because there was no violence.

Through the years there's been a lot of discussion of injuries at UNM, but very few people ever comment on the fact that 33 people were killed in a riot at the penitentiary even though I had repeatedly warned that unless they straightened out the situation at the penitentiary that is what would result. In any event, we didn't have any difficulties at the other institutions of higher learning, and that pretty much ended it except for the situation at UNM, which was a continuing problem. I suppose in that sense I was lucky because those were indeed troubling times. I did my best, but that was all that I could do.

In the Aftermath of the University Riots

After I left office and during the administration of Governor Bruce King there continued to be a great deal of difficulty in connection with the University of New Mexico. For instance, a takeover group in Albuquerque had gathered at Roosevelt Park, which was midway between the University of New Mexico and downtown. They marched down to the park, destroying a good many buildings that were along their path. They trashed businesses, burned buildings and eventually Bruce King had to alert the National Guard. On

June 14th and 15th of 1971 they arrested 283 rioters and put them in jail. Likewise, there were several people injured, but oddly enough a lot of this really didn't work its way into the press, and to this day I continue to be blamed for what took place at the university, and many times they forget that the actual calendar of events actually came after I left office. It was not a very good situation and frankly I don't think that Governor Bruce King could have handled it very much differently than I did except that he did make considerably more arrests.

State Parks

During my terms in office I probably took more interest in state parks than had any governor in the history of New Mexico. I certainly created more parks than any other governor. The reason for my interest in state parks was a many-faceted thing, which I shall attempt to explain. I think that the best illustration comes in a conversation that I had with former secretary of state Henry Kissinger during a dinner at the White House shortly after President Nixon's first trip to China. I asked Kissinger what his impression was of the Chinese statesman Chou En-Lai and he recalled to me a conversation that he had with Chou during his visit to China. He said that he had asked what he thought the influence of the French Revolution would be on the world. Chou replied in a very succinct manner, stating "Well, that it is too early to tell." I think the same would apply to the long-term development of state parks in New Mexico.

I would point out that there is a great difference between the amounts of money allocated to the state parks and recreation areas in my terms in office and that of the current governor, Bill Richardson. During my term in office the budgets of the State Parks and Recreation Commission in 1970 was not overly generous. The general fund furnished $500,000, and other state funds furnished monies for 140 staff out of the 293 people that worked there. I financed the creation of additional state parks out of the Severance Tax and Governor Richardson has financed his on the basis of its being an enterprise agency. There is a vast difference between the two. By the time I left office we had 35 state parks. The 14 state parks that I created were: Brantley Lake, Heron Lake, Leasburg Dam, Manito, Manzano, Polona Creek, Perch Dam, Paseo Del Rio, Canyon Rest Area, Living Desert Park and Museum, Clayton Lake, Villanueva, Conchas Lake and Coyote Creek.

Plaques placed in the parks at the time of their creation have been removed and replaced by other plaques which give credit to individuals who had absolutely nothing to do with their creation. In Carlsbad, I created a state park in 1967 and the plaque was removed in 1971, promptly upon my departure from office. A couple of years later it was replaced by a plaque which indicated that the park was created by quite a different set of individuals. This bothered some people who were involved in the actual creation of the park, including Representative Bob Light and Senator Fincher Neal. The bill creating the park was originally sponsored by both Light and Neal, and Light had actually donated the land. He called me, understandably upset, when the plaque was replaced by another sign crediting an entirely different set of individuals. It was not until the year 2007 that the situation was rectified. In that year Carlsbad Mayor Bob Forrest declared me the man of the year and credited me with creating that particular state park. Mayor Forrest gave me a replica of the original plaque. More importantly, at the time of the ceremony the old plaque was placed under the new one. There was quite a contrast in the information contained on the two. It wasn't the only instance where creative work was done to shift the credit for the creation of state parks. I didn't really care, although I did think that plaques should tell the truth.

Another disturbing change in policy is found in statutes in the State of New Mexico. "All concession contracts shall be subject to the approval of the State Board of Finance. From moneys collected under the provisions of section 75 – 35 – 5 an amount of one hundred dollars shall be placed in a suspense fund for the purpose of making refunds. All other receipts under the provision of section 75 – 35 – 5 shall be deposited in the General Fund."

I continue to feel that funds should not be shifted from Game and Fish funds which are in effect trust funds so that they can be used for the purchase of park land. I think that the integrity of that fund should be preserved. Woody Guthrie put it best in his *Ode to Pretty Boy Floyd*: "It's through this world that I ramble, I have seen lots of funny men. Some rob with a six gun and some with a fountain pen."

Trust funds are supposed to be held in trust; they should be preserved intact and not be used for other purposes. This quote is noteworthy. It is especially noteworthy when you consider that today we have 35 state parks and have only 4 million visitors. This is the same number of park visitors that we had when I was in office, so the number of visitors has not grown. It illustrates that the center of emphasis that has been placed on state parks has shifted dramatically through the years.

I remember the old saying that "He reset his watch; it was set by every clock he passed." There were a number of reasons that I established so many state parks and, oddly enough, one of them was that land was cheap. That old sage of Taos, Dough Belly Price, used to say, "The good Lord ain't making any more land and you better value what you have." Land was cheap and we could obtain it from the federal government, and in many instances for a dollar and a half an acre.

There were other reasons for establishing parks and one was that it was good for the local residents. For instance, Villanueva State Park in San Miguel County was located several miles from the main highway and a passable road did not exist between the Village of Villanueva and the main highway. They generally had to go by horseback down the old gravel paths which connected the two.

During my campaign for governor I promised that I would create a road from Villanueva to the main highway and that I would also create a state park in Villanueva. Senator Ike Smalley, a powerful figure in the legislature, wanted a main highway built to Pancho Villa Park. He came in to talk to me about it and I said, "Why don't you include a piece of legislation that will require the state to build roads to state parks?" He did sponsor the legislation and I was able to use that state law to construct the highway between Villanueva and the main highway. Both the state park and the paved road as well would be a big advantage to the residents that lived there.

A good many of the state parks were valuable economic assets in that they brought people to the area. A good example of that was the park that I created in Carlsbad, as well as Coyote Creek State Park, which I established in Mora County. Coyote Creek State Park brings a good many people into Mora County that wouldn't go there otherwise. It greatly helps the economy of Mora.

It was also very interesting in that about two weeks after my first election I went to Villanueva to meet with the people there. They put on a reception for me and more than 1,500 people attended, a good many of them on horseback, to escort me up to the village of Villanueva by horseback. It was a wonderful sight to behold and they certainly appreciated that I was interested not only in the road, but also in the state park.

The governor at that time was also chairman of the Recreation Priority Board, which controlled all the funds that went into the various cities and towns for recreation. I used a lot of that money to establish parks. For instance, in Albuquerque, many of the city parks were established with funds from the state. On one occasion they brought in a list of their priorities for city parks. I took one look at it and noted that all the parks in the Northeast Heights area were given priority over those in the valley. The valley parks were last and the Heights parks were first on the list. I simply turned the request upside down and started building parks in the valley because I figured that parks in the Heights would take care of themselves. Indeed they did. Many of the parks in the Heights were created by developers or as a part of the development. The valley developers contributed almost nothing, but I contributed the money and the parks were built there.

I think that essentially the trouble with our people in New Mexico is their poverty of desire. They should push for the creation of parks and they should see to it that the existing parks are properly maintained and that they're provided free access without admission fees if they are residents of the community. Parks should be free. They shouldn't be simply a source of revenue.

I have long been an advocate for parks and I think that we should become aware of their importance. As Jonathan Swift once said, "Vision is the art of seeing the invisible." We should have been acquiring land for parks all through the years, but unfortunately we didn't, and now it has become prohibitively expensive. This is kind of a punt on first down mentality; it has certainly been costly not only when it comes to acquiring new parks, but also as to maintenance.

It's amazing what we could have purchased by way of raw land through the years compared to what the cost would be now. The legislature made a habit of turning down governors like Bruce King and myself when it came to the purchase of land; they weren't thinking of the future when they did it. It's my thought, now and then, that no one ever went broke underestimating the intelligence of the legislature. In any event, that's all in the past and we can only now hope that we do better in the future.

Eagle Nest Lake

Eagle Nest Lake is one of New Mexico's gems. I tried to get the state to buy it during the last year of my second term as governor.

I entered into negotiations to buy the lake and the adjoining land from Les and Linda Davis, the owners. They were close friends and have remained so during the subsequent years. They made me an offer which I didn't think the state could refuse. They wanted to sell the lake and 4,885 acres that were owned by the C and S Ranch. They also wanted to sell the water and fishing rights for a grand total of $2 million. I thought it was an incredibly good deal for the state. The problem was that the legislature, in its wisdom, didn't agree.

I commissioned a consultant's report by Lomax Appraisal and Consultation Services. They submitted a report on February 18, 1969. They appraised the land alone at $2.7 million. That included the lake, which was 905 acres, and its 18,500 acre feet of water. The dam that created the lake had been built in 1917 for a cost of $220,000. The report also said that the parcel of land that included 2,117 acres of subdividable land was worth $684,850. The lake itself was valued at $995,000. The fishing rights came in at $610,000. They set the recreational value at $835,000. It was clear that it was a great deal for the state.

State Parks Director Jim Dillard and I went to the legislature and made concerted efforts to get lawmakers to appropriate money to buy the lake. Les and Linda made it clear that the price could be negotiated downward. They were doing me a favor by offering to sell the lake and land to the state at an incredibly reasonable price.

The legislature, though, took a different view of things. They said I had already created and built 10 state parks and they saw no reason for another. And, they didn't think it was worth the $2 million. At that point in time, the legislature didn't put a high value on recreational land and additional state parks. I argued long and hard that the land alone was worth much more than the asking price and that the profits from fishing would more than make up for the cost.

At the time, the state was paying $22,000 a year for fishing rights at the lake because the ranch had leased the lake to the state. But there were many years when they didn't lease it out. They had a private fishing concession that was operated by Tal Neal. His associate was former state Senator Bill Gallagher, whom I had appointed to the State Fair Board. After talking with them I had a pretty good idea what the potential income from fishing would be.

I argued long and hard, but I lost.

Years later, during Governor Bill Richardson's administration, the state bought the lake and 851 acres of land. The cost: $20 million! Of that, $11 million came from the state's Game Protection Fund. So it seems that the property was worth considerably more than the legislature thought at the time.

On August 3, 1999, I got a letter from Les and Linda. She recalled our conversation at my second inaugural reception. She remembered that I had pulled her and Les out of the receiving line and reminded them of the fact that I wanted to buy Eagle Nest Lake. She knew of my affection for the lake and she said in the letter that she wished we could have completed the deal.

In the end, the legislature made them a great deal wealthier. I'm sure she thanked them for their generosity.

White Cane Law

New Mexico passed the first White Cane Law to be enacted in the United States. It would become the civil rights law for persons with visual disabilities. All of the states of the union now have a White Cane Law; it covered a broad spectrum of things that were important to the visually impaired. Anatole France once said, "The rarest courage is courage of thought." This law was passed during the great unrest in seeking civil rights laws. I felt that it was on the same level as protecting civil rights in instances involving racial discrimination. The law provides, among other things, for a jail term of 90 days and $100 fine for violation of the law. Subsequently it was implemented by Fred Schroeder, director of the New Mexico Commission for the Blind, and he deserves much of the credit for its effective implementation. Gregg Trapp was also instrumental in implementing the law after he came into office. It truly was, in effect, a race between education and ignorance.

Prior to the passage of the law the concept of "contributory negligence" was assumed as an absolute defense for any accident involving the blind. For instance, if they were walking on the sidewalk and a drunk drove up onto the sidewalk and hit them there was no liability because it was legally assumed that the visually impaired person was guilty of contributory negligence. The thinking was that it was partly the blind person's fault for being on the sidewalk without being able to see a drunk driver approaching and not being able to get out of the way. Likewise, before the passage of this law it was required by law that all visually impaired persons had to be accompanied during air travel by a sighted person or they couldn't board an airplane. The White Cane Law also gave the same rights to streets, highways and public buildings, sidewalks and public accommodations as applied to everyone else. Likewise, it covered guide dogs. It also covered employment and rehabilitation. That was particularly important because New Mexico has the highest average wage for the blind in the United States. Iowa is second. We do still have a long way to go on employment. I was also concerned about the fact that no sight impaired person had ever served on the commission. I had supported this provision of the law very strongly. Albert Gonzales, who was appointed to serve on the Board of Regents for the School for the Blind was an important supporter of the White Cane Law. I also pushed very hard to increase the appropriations under the bill. I wanted to increase the services for the blind and also allow special appropriations to cover the use of Braille. I was fortunate indeed to have Representative John Mershon, who supported the law and always liked to balance the budget. He also represented Otero County where the School for the Blind was located. He gave full support to my efforts and I always appreciated his efforts.

Senator Ike Smalley said he was going to oppose the law because he thought that it would cost too much money and that he didn't think he was in favor of it. I pointed out to him that he lived in an area of New Mexico where when your dog runs away that it was so desolate that you could watch it run away for three days after it began its journey. He said, "What's your point?" I replied that, "Well, my point is that you have a lot of area, and you have a lot of roads. If you want appropriations for roads I would strongly suggest that you support the White Cane Law." He said, "I can see your point, and it looks like a pretty good piece of legislation to me," and he supported it.

I should also mention that President Lyndon Johnson was most interested in it, and his heart was always in the right place. Johnson took a lot of criticism for acts that he undertook while he was president, and this is one place where I think that he behaved in a truly compassionate manner. Governments may err, presidents can make mistakes, but the immortal Dante tells us, "The divine justice weighs the sins of the warm hearted on a different set of scales." On this issue he was not only compassionate, he was right.

The National Federation of the Blind, which in effect is the voice of the nation's blind and visually impaired, was very supportive and they deserved much of the credit for creating a White Cane Law. They not only gave me a lot of support in connection with it, but they were able to persuade a number of legislators to go along with the project. They were particularly effective when they supported my idea of having a visually impaired member of the New Mexico Commission for the Blind. Fred Schroeder was the first director of that commission, and in 1986 we were ultimately successful in requiring that a sight-impaired individual be placed on the commission. He was certainly most instrumental in getting that done, as was Art Schreiber, who has always been a most valuable asset in promoting aims of the Federation of the Blind and in seeing to it that they get a fair shake. He is a very effective individual and a great friend of mine. We still have a long way to go.

The White Cane Law serves as a tangible reminder that persons who are blind or visually impaired are independent, self-reliant, mobile and capable, and it also meant that they had a variety of rights guaranteed to them, which was very, very important. The law also covered guide dogs and the right to a safe and functional use of public facilities and places of public accommodation and other places to which the public is invited. Without the law we would be in a different era altogether.

After much pushing for a successful agency for the blind, the New Mexico Commission for the Blind was created in 1986, and Fred Schroeder was hired as its first director.

I am extremely proud of the White Cane Law and I think again that New Mexico was able to accomplish a first and also to lead the nation in at least one area of endeavor.

The Cumbres Toltec Scenic Railroad

I became extremely interested in the preservation of the Cumbres Toltec Railroad early in my first administration. I had a number of discussions with people in the Los Alamos area and eventually was able to get together with Chama Mayor Eddie Vigil to discuss the preservation of the railroad and infusion of new industry in to the Chama area. Chama's main employers prior to the creation of the Cumbres Toltec Scenic Railroad were mercantile establishments and two sawmills. The sawmills began to go under and eventually closed and laid off all their employees.

Robert B. Turner wrote wonderful book called *The Thunder of Their Passing: A Tribute to the Denver, Rio Grande's, Narrow Gauge, Cumbres Toltec Scenic Railroad*. It is the definitive history of the railroad. By way of a little history, I would point out that the railroad runs between Chama, New Mexico, and Antonio, Colorado. It passes over a very rugged terrain, and at one place reaches an altitude of 10,050 feet. It runs for 64 miles from the Narrow Gauge Mainline, and is one of the most scenic Railroads in the country, and believe me, I have seen them all. I have ridden narrow gauge railroads in Germany, Wales, New Zealand, Oregon, New York State and many other places too numerous to mention, but this is truly an amazing railroad. It is set in some of the most spectacular scenery that you could find. It was originally owned by the Denver and Rio Grande Railroad. During the course of purchasing this railroad I conducted a number of negotiations with the Denver and Rio Grande. Fortunately, it eventually led to the purchase of the railroad.

The original railroad was put together by General William Jackson Palmer, an entrepreneur and railroad builder. He had moved to the West in the 1870s and he incorporated the Denver and Rio Grande Railroad on October 27th 1870. The capital stock of the company was $2.5 million. It wasn't an easy thing to build. It had a long and checkered career when it came to construction, but eventually was completed. The railroad functioned for many years as a fairly successful concern. Then, in the 1950s it began to decline rapidly. By 1963, the Alamosa Refinery finally closed and it brought an end to the shipment of oil from the Gramps near Chama to Alamosa. The Denver and Rio Grande's net losses became significant in that the losses for the Alamosa to Farmington narrow gauge were $513,924 in 1964. In 1965, in spite of reduced winter costs, they lost an even larger amount, $563,182. The total revenues for the narrow gauge traffic for the Rio Grande system in 1965 were reported at $614,716. Then on January 1, 1967, the Rio Grande announced that it would no longer run any more public excursions because of the deteriorating conditions of the tracks. This meant that the railroad was going to collapse in a very short time. The losses continued to escalate with no end in sight. Finally, on July 17, 1968, freight operations came to a complete halt.

In early 1968 I was becoming more and more concerned about the railroad and took a detour on a trip back from Farmington to Santa Fe by way of Chama. I noticed that the railroad was busily pulling up track in spite of the fact that they didn't have a required Order of Abandonment that had either been granted or applied for. I was chairman for four terms of the Federal Four Corners Commission and they pretty much gave directions for the work that they engaged in and I became an enthusiastic proponent of preservation and really worked diligently to develop a coalition of support. The commission funded a study which ultimately was presented to Colorado Governor John Love and me. Love favored the preservation at first, but he was very reluctant to have the State of Colorado involved.

Then I did something that was rather interesting. I called Governor Nelson Rockefeller of New York, knowing full well that

Love and Rockefeller were close. I asked Rockefeller if he could encourage Love to participate in the preservation. He called Love, and lo and behold, Love pretty much changed his mind and became a supporter.

There were other people who were working to preserve the railroad, including state Representative Clarence Quinlan, who represented Antonito in the legislature, as well as state Senator Hugh Fowler. They both sponsored state legislation with preservation in mind. Also, Bob Burgraff started a Colorado society for preservation of the narrow gauge. In New Mexico, Terrence W. Ross, an Albuquerque architect, became the chairman of the Denver and Rio Grande Western Narrow Gauge Railway Preservation Association. He then began to come into my office with great regularity and he circulated, along with others, a petition which received tens of thousands of signatures supporting a National Parks Service takeover of the railroad. He really was the driving force behind the effort. He was enthusiastically joined by John Prichard of Los Alamos, Hermann Barkman of Santa Fe, and Allen Stevenson and Ernie Rorbart of Albuquerque.

At the same time, Mark McMahon, who was the publisher and editor of the *Los Alamos Monitor*, began to try to gather support for the railroad. McMahon was the chairman of a committee that I set up to work towards the purchase of the railroad between Chama and Antonito. The major mover behind all of this was Eddie Vigil, who was Chama's mayor from 1960 to 1969. Terry Moynahan who was the manager of the Kit Carson Co-op in Taos, also helped. Moynahan was not only interested in the railroad, but also encouraged the project because of the potential for the sale of electricity, not only by co-op, but also by the Rio Arriba Electric Co-op which operated in Chama. We then established a steering committee and commenced to work on the project.

I later found out that Carl M. Turner was executive secretary of the New Mexico Rural Electrification Association that also worked on the project, although I was not aware of his efforts at the time. In July of the same year we held a meeting in the governor's office. One of the primary difficulties we had was the impression that the Railway Brotherhoods were not interested in the project and that they would oppose it on various grounds and didn't want their members working on it. This was incorrect. When 22 Railway Brotherhoods held their National Convention in Clovis, I was the keynote speaker and I pitched for the railroad and received an enthusiastic response and an offer from the brotherhoods to send their volunteers to Chama to work on the railroad.

At the same time I was busy trying to bring movies into New Mexico. One movie we landed was George Kennedy's *The Good Guys and Bad Guys*. Kennedy, Robert Mitchum, Marty Balsam and I were all in the cast and I persuaded Kennedy to film it in Chama. He was delighted to do so. However, when we bought the railroad we paid $547,000, which was split between Colorado and New Mexico. When Kennedy used the railroad in the film, he paid $50,000 that we were able to use for the purchase.

In early 1969, the New Mexico and Colorado legislatures authorized an eight-member Railroad Authority. I quote the Colorado bill, "to provide a method for the acquisition and operation of any railroad of historic and scenic importance in Colorado to promote the public welfare by encouraging facilities and use of recreational facilities in the remote areas of the state inaccessible by other routes and by preserving, as a living museum for future generations, a mode of travel which helped in the development and promotion of the territory state." New Mexico created a similar commission.

I appointed a number of people to the commission including Eddie Vigil, Franklin Jones, Jim Dillard, Ed Hartman and several others. The passage of the bill by the legislature did not mean that the railroad was safe because there were no funds allocated for its development and preservation. New Mexico and Colorado were very leery about large public investments in an old railroad.

On July 14, 1969, the Interstate Commerce Commission announced its decision in connection with the Rio Grande, and the abandonment was approved subject to appeals. Likewise, The Rio Grande had to continue supplying trucking services at rates that were equivalent to the railroad rates. The ICC also concluded that the Abandonment Hearings were inappropriate for determining rate changes and that the rate changes could result in a considerable competitive disadvantage for the railroad's former users. With all of the legal requirements completed, The Rio Grande abandoned its narrow gauge, with the exception of its Silverton branch, on the 29th day of December 1969. It delayed any scrapping while preservation was still likely. This caused me to really move into action and I invited Governor Love to meet in Chama on several occasions. He landed his state airplane at the airstrip at the Chama Land and Cattle Company just south of Chama. We spent a full day talking about the railroad. It seemed that we were gaining on the whole project in that the states of Colorado and New Mexico each appropriated $295,000 for the joint purchase. I signed the New Mexico appropriation bill on February 27, 1970, and Love signed the corresponding Colorado bill on March 6, 1970. At that point it looked like we were sailing towards a success. However, there were a few problems.

The Rio Grande agreed to sell 64 miles of track and nine locomotives, a caboose, 28 pieces of non-revenue rolling stock, a building and over a hundred freight cars and tools and other equipment for a total of $574,124. The Colorado Authority approved the purchase in May of that year, and on June 5, the New Mexico Railroad Authority held a meeting in my office.

Franklin Jones said that the value of scrap on the railroad far exceeded the purchase price. Jim Dillard said that he was going to back them up, and Eddie Vigil took a look around the room and came over and whispered into my ear that the deal was going to be defeated by a margin of one vote. I talked with Dillard and reminded him that he was the Parks Director at my pleasure and he changed his vote and voted "yes." It carried by one vote. The following month the railroad was purchased and the deal was completed. There were other legalities which required an Interstate Compact between the states, and that was finally approved by Congress on October 24, 1974.

The Cumbres and Toltec Scenic railroad was a reality.

Entertaining at the Mansion

As governor, it is an important but very pleasant duty to entertain in the governor's mansion. We would invite people from all over the state, not just the usual dignitaries, but some who would rarely expect to be invited to the governor's residence and entertained. We kept the place busy enough so that when Governor Bruce King moved in we had had worn out all the carpeting and it had to be replaced.

Every year we would host a fiesta at the mansion, or as I called it "the Cargos' Fiestcita," and we would get together a variety of people, a real mixture. I will never forget the year when I went out to the plaza in Santa Fe with Mayor George Gonzalez and we invited the people there to come to the mansion the next day. Mayor Gonzalez, whom I had supported in his election, joined me in issuing the invitation. "Come to the governor's mansion: bring along some food, bring along a little beer, and bring along your families," we told them all. We promised some special guests, and we'd provide entertainment. Among the special guests, local celebrities were Cleo Fernandez, widow of the late congressman from New Mexico, Antonio M. Fernandez; as well as Mrs. Ruben Rodriguez of Santa Fe; and Imelda Espinosa Chavez, widow of Dennis Chavez, the long-time senior senator from New Mexico.

Mrs. Chavez would always stay at the mansion whenever she came to Santa Fe, as she and the senator had not maintained a residence in Santa Fe, and well, she had to stay somewhere. In fact, when we would take her to an event or out to eat she was among those who referred to me as "My governor." She enjoyed that a great deal and we certainly enjoyed having her. In addition to that, she had been a strong supporter of mine, as had Mrs. Fernandez. They were staunch supporters, and it was only natural to honor them and have them visit.

The day after our plaza invitation, we had over 5,000 people at the mansion. The famed Aztec Dancers appeared, as did the Lopez Brothers, and of course, Mayor Gonzalez. Cars were parked stretching all the way from the mansion to the Masonic Temple, which was a considerable distance from the mansion. It was the only place many of the guests that day could find to park, and they had to hoof it up to the mansion from there on foot. That day will always be important to me. It was a pleasure for us to open our house to our fellow New Mexicans.

Hispanics and the Governorship of New Mexico

From 1928 until 1935 there were large numbers of Hispanic Republicans in New Mexico. Many people realized that I was without a doubt the most successful politician when it came to cultivating Hispano support. Republican Bronson Cutting was a wealthy man who owned the *Santa Fe New Mexican* newspaper. However, he ultimately defeated Democratic Congressman Dennis Chavez in the Senate election in 1934. However, this was also during the Great Depression, and I think he got lucky.

If you consider all of the other factors that go into the equation undoubtedly conducted the most successful campaign when it came to gathering Hispanic voters. We had had only three Hispanic governors. Jerry Apodoca, the 23rd governor, was elected in 1974.

An observation on the history in the United States: at the time of the American occupation and conquest of Mexico there were approximately 60,000 Hispanos in New Mexico, approximately 70,500 in California, 5,000 in Texas and maybe a thousand in Arizona. Thus, there was a large population of Hispanos in New Mexico, especially in the northern part of the state. And they had been there for many, many years. Likewise, they had been very active in state politics. In addition to that, New Mexico had a strong Democratic organization that had been well established by the time I ran for governor. Every Hispanic-dominated county had a strong Hispanic Democratic politician who dominated their respective counties. Likewise, 40.1 percent of the state's population in 1966 was Hispanic. You also had to factor in both the eastern and southern parts of the state, which were overwhelmingly Democratic. You can get from the voter registration figures that it gave a decided advantage to Democratic candidates. Mr. Fred Buckles once observed in his column "Inside the Capital," that in order to elect a Republican governor such as Ed Mechem, a Republican had to secure a normal 10,000 vote Republican majority in Bernalillo County. Jerry Apodoca won the 1974 governor's race by cutting the vote of Republican Joe Skeen from the normal 10,000 vote majority to a plurality of 7,443. Skeen won Bernalillo County by 56,819 votes to 49,276 for Apodoca. In my quest for re-election I defeated Fabian Chavez by a slim margin of 1,231 votes in Bernalillo County. The margin of victory that I had received had to be explained by the votes cast in the Hispanic counties in New Mexico.

In 1948 Manuel Lujan Sr. ran against Thomas J. Mabry and had received 24.2 percent of the vote in Little Texas on the East Side, and had run quite strongly in the Hispanic counties in that he was mayor of Santa Fe. Another fact was that after the Democratic primary election a very powerful Hispano politico Eugene Gallegos openly supported Lujan. But Lujan did not receive a majority that was sufficient in the Hispano counties to prevail in the race for governor. His opponent, Thomas J. Mabry, got 75.8 percent of the votes in Little Texas and was able to prevail.

Professor Maurilio Vigil observed in connection with the 1968 election: "However, the most crucial consideration in 1968 was Cargo's strong support in the Northern Hispano Counties. Lonesome Dave, known for going contrary to the convention in his campaign techniques of campaigning independently of the Republican organization, built a strong northern constituency by his program initiatives, which included in construction of Villanueva Park and other recreational parks in Northern New Mexico, and the completion of the Rio Grande Gorge Bridge designed to connect the northern part of the state in his first administration. Cargo ingeniously got maximum mileage out of the important political asset that he had in his wife, who was a Hispana, and quite often delighted political rally audiences by referring to his children as my little coyotitos."

He also said, "Another possible flaw which may have operated against Chavez in the North was his low profile to northern Hispanos. It was ironic that in his campaign the Hispano politico was more at home delivering fiery oratory to Anglo audiences than he was in mingling with Hispano crowds and trading pleasantries and the native dialect as it is the Hispano political custom. This kind of campaigning Cargo was most adept at."

Another observation that he made was that "the election returns for 1968 tell clearly the story of the 1968 election. Chavez was still able to cultivate enough support—45.7 percent in Little Texas to prevent a Cargo landslide. Cargo received 53.8 percent. Chavez was not able to generate enough support in the Northern Counties to prevail."

As I have said, the support of the Democratic Party organization gave me and the leadership of the Democratic Party in the Hispanic counties obviously had to be reckoned into the result.

It should also be noted that Jerry Apodoca drew 67.8 percent in the northern Hispanic counties, which was 13.3 percent more than

Fabian Chavez got in 1968. Apodoca prevailed in the election by approximately 4,000 votes but it's very clear that the votes came from outside of Bernalillo County. I was able to put together a victory that Mauricio Miera was unable to do in 1940 against John E. Miles, and Manuel Lujan was unable to do in 1948 against Thomas J. Mabry. Literally, the election was won in the Hispanic counties.

There were a number of events that occurred that were important in the election. One was the type of campaigning that I did. I spent an enormous amount of time in the northern counties going literally door-to-door and hand-to-hand looking for votes. I would go to Las Vegas for instance and start in the business area. Then I'd go up and down the street and hit every store and every restaurant and every business. If I went to Mora I would literally knock on the door of every house and then I would go and have lunch, usually with senior citizens, and then visit places where people congregated, such as the post office.

Another thing that I think got me votes in the Hispanic counties is that we had huge, huge political rallies. We had one rally in Mora in 1966 that drew 10,000 people. In Tierra Amarilla we had close to 15,000 people. In Espanola we had 11,000. We had a rally in Las Vegas with 8,500. The rallies were all well orchestrated in that Steve Quintana and others would go with sound trucks throughout the area advertising the rally, and then they would organize them meticulously. If we went to Questa, for instance, we would have the high school band leading a parade. We would have horses by the score, and we had high school cheerleaders carrying banners in front of the parade. In Mora we turned out 10,000 people. An important part of it was that Fermin Pacheco was the Democratic chairman and I would urge him to contact all the Democrats in the area and have them attend the rally. Then Mary Pacheco would organize the Democratic women and they would cook beans and chile and all kinds of other food for the rally. All of these rallies were well organized and they were dramatic.

This happened in both elections, and oddly enough, the press did not report many of these activities, and the net result was that my election came as a huge surprise. For instance, the press in Albuquerque had no idea of what was going on in the rest of the state. It was an interesting way of campaigning and it was colorful indeed. In Mora we had the entire football team leading the parade along with the cheerleaders, and we also had a high school band, and most people couldn't tell whether they were going to a football game or a political rally. It was very effective and huge crowds played a part in the election. I will never forget a day in Espanola when we had a turnout of over 11,000 people. At the rally was no less than the Democratic County Chair Emilio Naranjo. In addition to that we would invite Democratic candidates to appear if they were not opposed by a Republican. This all made it very interesting because it appeared that they were in support of my candidacy. In most instances they were. I likewise had a lot of support from Democratic legislators. I think there were only two out of the northern counties that didn't support me openly. In any event, I think that the type of campaign I waged had a lot to do with my victories.

STATUS OF WOMEN

In October of 1968, I requested a report from the Governor's Commission on the Status of Women and asked that they prepare to have legislation introduced to make the committee a statutory committee. I wanted to do it before the election in 1968. I appointed Louise Bundy as the one responsible for the report and she did put it together. Eventually there would be such a statutory committee. I did start one of the first committees on the status of women in the nation, and it has been very successful.

Prisons

I had appointed a Prison Board which included Victor Salazar and Paul Robinson, who was a former district attorney in Albuquerque. We had done our best to try and turn the state's prison system into a prototype of the federal prison system. However, when the board chose J. E. Baker to be the warden of the Santa Fe Penitentiary, there was some resistance.

Baker came from the federal system and closely followed my directions in trying to modernize the State Penitentiary. He brought in people from the College of Santa Fe to teach extension classes, and at one time had almost a third of the prisoners enrolled in some kind of college course. He set up a good many work and forestry programs. He was an outstanding warden and would have fully modernized the system if he had been given the chance. However, the state Senate refused to confirm him, and I had to appoint another individual both as warden and as corrections secretary. Of course, some legislators and some of my political opponents immediately criticized me for having a "troublesome turnover" of wardens and corrections secretaries.

Eventually I brought in a highly professional individual who was very well qualified to hold the positions, Howard Leach, and I made him Corrections Secretary. It was impossible to go ahead with many of the reforms that the Prison Board and various administrators thought were necessary in order to modernize the penal system.

A grand jury was then impaneled, and by law they had to report on the conditions at the penitentiary. They reported that both Leach and Warden Felix Rodriguez were doing a good job and that they were highly competent. Leach and Rodriguez were in office when Bruce King became governor and they served capably in those positions after I left office. Unfortunately, not much more was done as a way of reform. I repeatedly warned Governor King that there would be a riot if they didn't continue with reforms.

My Going Away Party

On December 6, 1970, a number of friends and supporters held a banquet in my honor as the outgoing governor. More than 500 people attended the event that was held at the New Mexico Film Center in Santa Fe. It was hosted by Mr. and Mrs. Willie Ortiz and Mr. and Mrs. Bob Ortega, and it attracted not only many of my supporters, but also Governor-elect Bruce King, outgoing Lieutenant Governor Lee Francis, and folk singer Burl Ives, who canceled an appearance on the Tom Jones national television show to attend. He entertained with his guitar and sang several ballads that he'd recorded. Cecilia Webb also sang at the event. She worked in the governor's office as the first African-American to be employed in the executive branch of government. It was a festive occasion, and the music and entertainment were outstanding.

In addition to that, 26 governors throughout the country and Senator Clinton P. Anderson sent telegrams with best wishes. I was also presented with a mission bell that was 125 years old, and a road runner plaque.

I told everyone, "I hope we have left New Mexico in better condition after four years, and I hope we have done a lot to improve relations between various groups and that we have relegated racial prejudices to the dustbin of history." Bruce King gave a nice speech about me and Ida Jo, and he wished us well in the future. He was very gracious to appear and, of course, did so as a good friend.

Andy Carter

In 1970, as my second term was coming to an end, I decided to run for the U.S. Senate. I thought it was the logical next step after being governor. I also thought I had a good shot at going to the Senate because I had been governor for four years and—at least I thought—had quite a following.

Along the way, though, a man by the name of Andy Carter got in my way. He beat me in the Republican Senate primary that year, and my dreams of going to the U.S. Senate were dashed.

Carter had been a prominent Democratic legislator from Roosevelt County, and he had been very active on the House's Appropriations Committee. He was a real powerhouse with the Democrats, and, he was very conservative.

But he had switched parties, and in 1964 he headed the Barry Goldwater for President campaign in New Mexico. A lot of established Republicans didn't like Andy because he had been a very active Democrat. In fact, they didn't like him because he had been convincing conservative Democrats to switch parties and join the Republicans.

Andy had been a supporter of mine. In 1968 when I was opposed in the primary, Andy got out and supported me. I didn't know how much until I was at the Hilton Hotel in downtown Albuquerque one night when the manager came up and asked me if I was going to go down and visit my campaign headquarters. I had no idea what he was talking about, and he walked me down to the basement.

It was a little campaign war room. Andy was there and he had maybe 20 people on the telephones and they were making phone calls around the state for me. I was surprised to say the least.

But by 1970, things had changed. Andy was a staunch conservative who thought he had a chance against me, a moderate Republican. He also wanted to take over the Republican Party in the state. I announced for the primary, and then later, he did. I had the support of the Old Guard like Ed Mechem and Tom Bolack. Andy had the support of what was becoming the ultraconservative wing of the state's Republican Party.

I had announced reasonably early and had the support of the national Republican Party, including President Richard Nixon. I remember we were at the Kentucky Derby that year in a box. Nixon was there, and so was Republican Senator Everett Dirksen from Illinois.

Nixon turned to me and said:

"I'm going to support you in the primary. You're the only one who can get elected, the only one who can win."

"Well, what about Andy Carter?" I asked.

"Oh, the hell with him," Nixon said.

Incidentally, a reporter for the *Albuquerque Journal* overheard the conversation. But, he never reported it.

I was attacked repeatedly during the primary by the party's ultraconservatives, particularly in connection with the appointment of Steve Torres, a former state legislator whom I had appointed to the New Mexico Tech Board of Regents. The substance of the attack was meaningless since it was mentioned only on the east side of the state. As a matter of fact, Torres was reappointed five times by four successive governors. He had the longest tenure as a regent in the history of New Mexico. Carter didn't do much good to attack me on that appointment. In 1995, Torres was declared to be a New Mexico distinguished public service award recipient in state government in the university category.

It is also worthy of note that in the last 77 years New Mexico has had only one Republican attorney general, two Republican auditors and treasurers and not a single secretary of state from the Republican Party. The GOP has truly been a minority party, so I had to attract Democrats in order to win the race. Unfortunately, I was attracting Democrats and not Republicans.

The Native Americans tried to give me some help, but few of them were registered as Republicans, and I was the only Republican that they supported with any regularity. In early February, Joe H. Herrera, executive director of the Commission on Indian Affairs, wrote to me expressing the commission's deep appreciation for what he described as excellent cooperation and coordination during my terms as governor. He indicated also that many of them would be supporting me for senator if I got the nomination. Also, Domingo Montoya, the governor of Sandia Pueblo, wrote an impassioned letter to me in late January of 1970. He was quarreling with Congressman Manuel Lujan Jr. about the registration of Indians to vote. Lujan had gotten after Montoya very strongly, saying that men had been complaining that somebody from the Bureau of Indian Affairs was telling the members of the Sandia Pueblo how to register in a town vote. Montoya wrote a letter to Lujan disagreeing with him and saying that they were not being told how to register or how to vote, and then he said, "Governor Cargo realized that Indians would register and vote as they pleased, and that they certainly knew how to split their tickets and that they voted for him unanimously." I didn't want to get into the fight, but I did defend him. I appreciated his endorsement.

Victor Sarracino and Benny Atencio also joined in and endorsed me, as did Ramos Sanchez. Virtually every pueblo had endorsed me in the primary, as well as Peter McDonald, chairman of the Navajo Nation.

On April 3, 1970, Andy Carter's campaign put out a nationwide letter appealing to "Conservatives for Carter." The letter was written by Robert G. Hanagan, who was chairman of Carter's campaign committee. It went out to voters all over and contributors scattered throughout the nation. Tens of thousands of these letters were sent out, and they were sent essentially to people who had appeared on Barry Goldwater's and Ronald Reagan's contribution list. Oddly enough, Goldwater apologized to me personally for some of the contents of the plea for money.

The letter said that I was an ultra-liberal governor and that I was friendly with New York Governor Nelson Rockefeller. I was indeed friendly with Rockefeller, so that part was correct. He went on to emphasize that even as a Democrat that he had headed the Draft Goldwater movement in New Mexico and was one of the principal organizers of the national Draft Goldwater movement. He also asserted that in polls conducted a week prior to in the primary I had a lead of about 2,600 votes, which I think may have been correct.

The letter also said that Carter's budget was a modest one, and it was certainly far from it. It also asserted that he was "not a wealthy man." This was not true in that he was a millionaire. They also claimed that there were too many liberal Republicans in the Senate and the party did not want to add one more. He then went on to add that if I were nominated in the primary I would add to the number of liberal Republicans in the Senate and that this would be bad for the Republican Party. He didn't make any claim that he could win the election, but said that it was absolutely necessary that I be defeated.

An interesting claim that they made was that the NAACP had me in their pocket, as evidenced by the fact that on March 20, 1970, I had addressed a regional NAACP meeting in Albuquerque. The opposing campaign faulted me as being a staunch supporter of civil rights, and this charge was certainly true. Then it was noted that as a conservative Democrat in the legislature, and a powerful one to boot, Carter had consistently opposed all civil rights legislation that came before the House of Representatives in Santa Fe. That was true, but it was an effort to show that I would probably get all of the African-American votes. On that he was again correct, as I had gotten 90 percent of the African-American vote in all of my other election endeavors, and the support that I had received from them was expected to be just as high in the next general election.

I was also faulted for having hired African-Americans to state government and really opening up to the hiring of even more. Their campaign especially referred to the fact that I had hired Don Perkins, who had been a running back for the Dallas Cowboys and also an African-American, but clearly they were playing the race card. The pamphlet didn't end there. They also charged that I had once refused to cross a picket line and that therefore labor had me in their hip pocket. The first part was true. I did refuse to cross the picket line, but labor was hardly secure in my hip pocket because Senator Joe Montoya had considerable support among labor. It was very likely that he was going to be endorsed, not only in the primary, but in the general election.

Carter also claimed that I built a political machine which consisted of Republicans and Hispanics and—horror of horrors!—that I had great support among Democrats who lived in the northern part of the state.

He also claimed that I had hired Hispanics into state government in high positions and that that likewise was a dangerous thing. Lastly, he said that I depended on mass rallies and that I would have huge numbers of people in attendance and that that was not good either. That charge was probably partially true in that we did have huge political rallies. He raised a lot of money nationally for his campaign by making an appeal along these lines, but one of the people he sent the letter to happened to be my own brother. My brother Jerry was a professor at that time at the University of Syracuse and he didn't respond with a donation but wrote a letter in protest saying that the appeals were all wrong and he resented it.

Around that same time Earl Perry mentioned me in a column. Later to work for the New Mexico AFL-CIO, Perry had been extremely active in the Democratic Party, and particularly in the campaign of Governor John Burroughs, and was highly respected. Perry wrote that "The intent of Republican Governor David Cargo to run against U.S. Senator Joseph M. Montoya is clear for 1970. Cargo cut into the strong Democratic vote on the east side of the state where it has taken Montoya years to build up a substantial following. Montoya is confronted with a great deal of unrest among the native people of the state, and a block vote usually enjoyed by him over the years he has spent in the light of office. Cargo has proved to be an effective campaigner with guts to burn when it comes to infighting and slugging it out with his opponent on any grounds. His mistakes seem to have cost them very little in the eyes of New Mexico voters."

Andy Carter's voting record in the House of Representatives was really fairly interesting. For example, when he was in the House in 1957 his voting record was decidedly conservative. The only person who was more conservative during that session was, oddly enough, future governor Jack Campbell. On issues regarding working people, Campbell cast eleven votes against, and not a single one in favor of working people or organized labor. Campbell voted against eliminating attacks on the benefits of injured workers and against increasing the minimum wage. He voted against public employee unions. He voted against protection of sawmill workers, he voted against prohibiting racial or ancestral discrimination in public housing. He voted against repealing the old-age lien law on welfare recipients and he voted against lowering the school tax for manufacturers. In other matters he consistently voted no on most everything.

Carter in his other legislative endeavors voted in a similar manner almost every time. He voted totally against civil rights bills and increasing the minimum wage and anything that had to do with civil rights. It was a totally negative legislative record, and I'm afraid that it all mitigated against him in general elections, except when he ran as a Democrat on the east side of the state.

When we had a large rally in Tierra Amarilla, people showed up to support me, including future Congressman Joe Skeen and Cliff Hawley, who ran against me on two separate occasions for governor.

Senator-to-be Pete Domenici showed up at other rallies, although it was not clear whether he was supporting me or not, although it was rumored that he was in support.

Another person who got into the campaign on the side of Andy Carter was future governor Gary Johnson. He contributed to Carter's campaign and appeared in an ad in the *Albuquerque Journal* with Carter. He was unknown at the time, but be that as it may, he did make his first appearance in politics, even though I had no idea who he was. He was never politically active again until he successfully ran for governor in 1994.

On March 26, we had a fundraiser that was held in Albuquerque. Tom Bolack sat at the head table. My finance co-chairman, Phillip Hubbel, and longtime Republican national committeemen Albert Mitchell, Holm Bursum, Manuel Lujan Sr. were there as well. So were a number of others such as Sonny Johns, Willie Ortiz and other Republican leaders.

The most important, of course, was Archdiocese of Santa Fe Archbishop James Peter Davis, who took care of the spiritual matters at the dinner. Davis stayed at the mansion whenever he was in Santa Fe. We visited regularly.

The archbishop supported me, as did Manuel Lujan Sr., the all-time moderate liberal Republican, who was elected mayor repeatedly in Santa Fe. He also happened to be the father of future Congressman Manuel Lujan Jr.

Lujan Sr. had supported me at the pre-primary convention in 1966, and actually wanted to be the one to have placed me in nomination at the convention. He barely missed out doing that, and I felt badly for him.

There were nearly 400 people at the dinner, which I thought had given me a good start in the campaign. But I knew it was going to be a very difficult battle against the old Goldwater supporters and the party's ultraconservatives. Strange thing about that was that Goldwater and I were actually good friends. He used to have me fill in for him in Arizona when he was tied up on business in Washington, DC. He would regularly get me to appear, and indicated he would support me.

One reason Goldwater supported me was that he was at odds with Ronald Reagan, who would later go to be a two-term Republican president. The two didn't get along particularly well. Goldwater never did give me a formal endorsement, and that might have been just as well.

During the dinner I raised the issue of Senator Montoya's so-called ship-jumping bill, which gave U.S. citizenship to Chinese mariners who jumped ship in New York City. There were a good many of these bills, and it was alleged that money had exchanged hands in return for citizenship papers. I don't know if Montoya was directly involved in the money portion of this, but in any event, the Senate's Ethics Committee took up the matter was sharply critical of a couple of Montoya's staffers.

I also read a letter from President Nixon, and from the Republican Governors' Conference. There was an indication that 30 of the 32 Republican governors would attend the conference, which was scheduled to be held in Albuquerque in May of that year. I expected that most of those governors were going to support me for the Senate race. I had also hoped to get endorsements from Nixon and Agnew.

Forty-four months before the Senate primary election, Carter came within 16,217 votes of upsetting Senator Clinton P. Anderson. Under the circumstances he did fairly well, although he ran 21,000 votes behind me in Bernalillo County. Carter carried 11 of New Mexico's 32 counties, and had a 848-vote-margin in Anderson's own Bernalillo County. He also carried Catron, Chaves, DeBaca, Harding, Lincoln, Roosevelt, San Juan and Sierra counties.

Newspaper columnist Eric McCrossen thought I might run extremely well in the northern counties. One of his columns said, "Montoya, incidentally, was showing increasing signs of political panic."

I don't know whether he panicked or not, but apparently he

felt that I would be a threat in the primary because he called me and tried to persuade me to wait and run for the vacant seat that would be created two years later when Senator Anderson retired.

There was a sidelight to the whole matter that created some levity. Senator Montoya received a letter at his Santa Fe office asking him to serve on Carter's State Advisory Board. An aide to Carter apologized, saying, "it must have been a mistake unless Senator Montoya has changed his registration from Democrat to Republican." He went on to say, "the letters were to have been sent to Republicans only."

Carter also started attacking former governor Bolack and former Republican National Committeeman Albert Mitchell. He said they weren't effective in the Republican Party anymore because a new conservative group had moved in and taken over the party.

A number of the party's leaders, including Mechem, held grudges against Carter because he had joined the party after being an active Democrat for a long time. Mechem, Bolack and Mitchell were especially critical of him.

Carter had also been active on Reagan's behalf at the 1968 Republican National Convention. He deeply resented the fact that Agnew had initially supported Nelson Rockefeller rather than Nixon as the Republican presidential nominee. He kept referring to Agnew as a "wolf," and at the Republican convention in Miami, as a "dangerous left-winger." He tried to persuade the New Mexico delegation to vote against Agnew for vice president.

Rick Edwards had entered the primary against Montoya on the Democratic side, but didn't pose too much of a threat to the longtime senator. Montoya was easily renominated. However, gubernatorial candidate Jack Daniels joined Carter in attacking me over the situation at the University of New Mexico. Daniels was more moderate than some of the people who opposed him in the primary. Former District Attorney Alexander Seresse attacked the students as all being campus radicals and said he "would fire most of the university's administration if elected governor."

Tom Clear had gotten into the Republican gubernatorial primary, and was running against Pete Domenici. He charged that, "I'm happy that finally Governor Cargo and Mr. Domenici have let it be known that they are running together." He also said that he had "commissioned a poll that showed he was leading Domenici for the gubernatorial nomination." Carter also resumed his attack against Montoya, saying that "he should be honest with the Senate Ethics Committee to justify his conduct in submitting 702 pilot relief bills," which were designed to keep illegal aliens from being deported. He also claimed that each bill had a $2,000 price tag. I didn't think the facts justified such an attack, but that was what Carter did.

Carter also attacked me by saying that in 1966 I had no vote-getting power and that I was elected governor by a mere 10,000 votes. Of course, he lost the election by considerably more that year when he ran for the U.S. Senate. He also went after me for supporting a move to lower the voting age to 18. He thought that was ridiculous and that 18-year-olds were juveniles and that they didn't have the necessary sense of responsibility to vote. In addition to that, he said they had never held jobs.

Carter also criticized me for not calling out the National Guard during the strike in New Mexico, and said, "but when New Mexico public school teachers walked out on strike two years ago Governor Cargo displayed ineptness, whereas President Nixon had called out federal troops during an illegal postal walkout." He said "Cargo should have done the same." He also criticized my refusal to cross a picket line that January at the Santa Fe La Fonda Hotel to attend a prayer breakfast.

I took exception to that because I came from an area of the country where people didn't cross picket lines just for the sake of obtaining some kind of political advantage. But Carter was insistent and said that "New Mexico would make a tragic mistake and that they are sending another Senator Jacob J. Javits to the Senate" and that I was closely aligned with the left wing of the Democratic Party and they had supported me for governor.

Carter also attacked me by saying that in Hispanic counties like Valencia County, I hadn't been very strong. He said that in 1966 I carried the county by only 326 votes over the late Gene Lusk. Of course, he didn't say that he had lost that same county that same year to Senator Anderson by 1,628 votes.

Carter was particularly strong in Chaves County. One of his strongest supporters was state Representative Max Coll of Roswell, one of the most conservative members of the legislature. He had been the most conservative member of the Constitutional Convention. He was teamed up at the time with Carter in Chaves County and supported him strongly. Later, of course, Coll moved to Santa Fe, became a Democrat, and became one of the most liberal members of the legislature.

State Auditor Harold Thompson also entered the Senate primary. He got little support and was a distraction in that he probably hurt me somewhat in the race.

Ultraconservative Wing of the Republican Party

The displeasure of the ultraconservative wing of the Republican Party of New Mexico was long lasting indeed. There are many examples, running from well before my tenure as governor and running just about into the present day. In 1996, Representative Jose Abeyta sponsored an appropriation in the 42nd New Mexico state legislature to provide funds for a David Cargo Library in Mora. As a result of the split, there were 43 votes in favor of the appropriation and just nine opposed. Every single Democrat in the legislature voted for the appropriation, while just nine Republicans voted no. This was their way of making their views about me known. They were all ultraconservatives, including Jerry Alwin, Frank Bird, C. Christensen, T. Dolliver, A.C. Hawkins, T.E. Macko, D.M. Parsons and R.P. Wallach.

Probably the most prominent member of the legislature to cast this symbolic vote against me was Minority Leader Ted Hobbs. It was clear that the appropriation was going to pass the legislature but even then they wanted to take one last swing at me, and they did. They well knew that House Bill 501 was going to pass, and they also knew that virtually every Democrat was going to vote for it.

I have been building libraries and in northern New Mexico for many years now. At this time there are around fourteen library projects either under construction or construction is planned in the near future. I did all of the legal work to set them up and raised all the money to build the libraries; I even obtained all of the computers and books to be placed in the libraries. It has taken a tremendous effort on my part. I might add that almost all of the libraries bear my name and they are almost all in heavily in Democratic areas with the exception of the library in Corona, which is in heavily Republican Lincoln County.

It was obvious in the case of the Mora library that certain Republicans were trying to embarrass me. Still, I appreciated the fact that the legislators in the benefited areas and others from throughout the state who knew enough to value my efforts in that area had supported me in connection with the construction of libraries. I will never understand why that particular group of legislators thought it was necessary to vote against me so many years after the race against Andy Carter. They did cast the vote and they did their best to embarrass me and to prevent the libraries from being built. The libraries went up without them.

Contemporary History

You actually invite trouble when you attempt to write contemporary history. The contemporary historian is subject to a number of criticisms including the fact that he is beset by his own prejudice and his own need to justify or excuse all of his mistakes or to amplify or enlarge his virtues and especially if he is prominent in the events that he describes.

Certainly one of the greatest historians of all time was Thucydides and he wrote about the Peloponnesian war and he figured in that war as a general but was finally able to rise above partisanship and narrow concerns to take a rather eclectic view of the war. He was convinced that the war between Spartacus and Athens was one of the most momentous events of his or any other time and he tried to report it truly and to leave the truth as a permanent possession to posterity and those that read of history. I will attempt to emulate Thucydides and hope that I can emulate his genius and perspective in connection with these events. I know that I have humble virtues and I will attempt to be honest but I think that you should understand the limitations I am laboring under. I will try to record this as fairly and honestly as I can and if I make mistakes they are certainly not intended.

I was born on the 13th day of January 1929 in Dowagiac, Michigan and my parents were schoolteachers in Dowagiac and my father was Frank Cargo and my mother was Mary Cargo. In the event that you were wondering where Dowagiac is located, it is located equal distance between Pokagon and Cassopolis in Cass County Michigan. I hope this gives you a better idea exactly where Dowagiac is.

My grandfather George Cargo's forbears came from Ireland and his forebear was James Cargo born in County Antrim/Down, Ireland on the 14th day of September in 1817. He married Jane Rusk who was born in the same village. Their son William Cargo was born in Ireland and died on October 4th 1878 in Artemisia Township, Gray County, Ontario, Canada. Their descendent George Albert Cargo married Emily McGuire (actually Maguire). George and Emily had nine children, four of whom were born in Caldwell, Simcoe, Ontario, Canada and the rest of their children were born in Bangor, Michigan. My grandfather William George Cargo was born on March 23rd 1878 in Caldwell Ontario. He subsequently married Patti Ruth Martin. My grandfather William George Cargo moved to the United States at a very early age. He may well have been an illegal immigrant, I don't know whether or not if he ever actually legally became a citizen of the United States of America but in any event, he did what many good Democrats do, he voted anyway.

The Cargos interestingly enough were only listed in the census in Ireland during the 19th century as living in specific areas in three Ulster Counties, Dewitt Antrim, Barony Belfast (lower), County Down in the adjacent Baronies of Castlereagh (lower), Ards (lower), Tyrone County Barony of Omagh and in County Monahan in Ireland. This was corroborated by several of my contemporary relatives including the late William Cargo who was Ambassador to Nepal during his career in the State Department. I also discussed it with my grandfather William George Cargo before he died in Bangor, Michigan on the 21st day of April 1948. I also knew his father and he had an Irish burr, to say the least. My grandfather likewise, on occasion, would speak with a bit of an accent. My aunt Velma was married to Thomas Earl Stafford and he was a printer by trade and worked for the *Bangor Advance* which was a newspaper located in Bangor, Michigan. He subsequently worked for the *Kalamazoo Gazette* and was active in the typographical Union. My great grandmother Emily McGuire was apparently born in Ireland or at least the records indicate that she was although it is possible that she actually was born in Canada shortly after the arrival of her parents from Ireland.

My grandmother Hattie Martin was born in Arlington Township Van Buren County, Michigan and her parents apparently came from Ohio by way of upstate New York and her father was a veteran of the Civil War. He joined the Union Army as a drummer boy and participated in the war including fighting in the battle of Lookout Mountain and fought in a number of battles in Georgia. He lived to be well over a hundred and I used to visit with them frequently when I was a small child and discuss the Civil War with him. He voted as he shot and therefore was a Republican. His wife lived to be 101 and I clearly knew her as well.

Likewise, on the Martin side of the family one of their forbears was Henry De Long who was born in Detroit, Michigan in 1797. He died in Arlington, Michigan in 1863 and his first wife was a woman named Mary who was an Ojibwa Indian. His grandfather was Francis De Long who was born in 1760. He enlisted in the American Army on September 13, 1777. He was ultimately taken prisoner by the English forces in Charleston, South Carolina and was taken to the island of Jamaica where he was held for six years. He was then transferred to Halifax for a year and then sent to Montréal and ultimately he was sent to the West Indies. In 1862 at the age of 102 years eight months the old Veteran was laid to rest in Hartford, Michigan and prior to his death he stated that he fought in the Revolutionary War and he was ready to fight again in the Civil War but unfortunately he was unable to undertake that project.

Some 15 years ago I made a trip to county Down and more particularly the town of Crawfordsburn and sure enough there were Cargos in the area and they said that in recent years that some of the Cargos had moved to the United States but had lost track of them. He said it seemed like only yesterday. But unfortunately I think they're off by a hundred years. Likewise, I would note that the Chief Librarian for the Belfast Library system is a relative by the name of David Cargo.

My maternal grandfather was John Fay Harton and he was

born in Van Buren County, Michigan and his parents were Benjamin and Mary Hart and they were both born in Ireland. Unfortunately there are very few records of my grandfather's parents because he was orphaned at the age of one or two and moved to Kansas from Michigan and all records have either been destroyed or lost. He apparently was conceived in Ireland and born in Michigan but the records are sparse.

I didn't want to engage in genealogical buccaneering but I would point out that my paternal Grandmother's ancestor John Kinnersley Hooper who was a wine merchant and political figure in London in 1820–1830s served several terms as Lord Mayor of London. He served with some distinction and was remembered fondly by all.

My uncle Marion Cargo was a bricklayer by trade and he also was a business agent at one time for the brick layers union. Interestingly enough there was a trade union tradition with my family. Oddly enough my Cousin Ambassador William Cargo presented a lunar rock to his Majesty King Birendra at his coronation in Katmandu, Nepal in 1973.

Chronology
David Francis Cargo

January 23, 1929: Born to Francis and Mary Cargo in Dowagiac, Michigan

Lived in Dowagiac until 1945 when my parents took teaching jobs in Jackson, Michigan

1947: Graduated from Jackson High

1951: Obtain undergraduate degree from the University of Michigan

1953: Got my Master's Degree in Public Administration from the University of Michigan

1953–1955: Served with the U.S. Army in Germany during the Korean War

1955: Entered the University of Michigan Law School

1957: Obtained my law degree; and passed both the Michigan and New Mexico Bar exams

1957: Moved to New Mexico and went into private law practice

1958–1960: Worked as an assistant district attorney

1958: Elected president of the New Mexico Young Republicans

1962: Elected to the New Mexico State Legislature from Bernalillo County; filed a lawsuit to reapportion the state legislature

1964: Re-elected to the state legislature

1966: Elected governor for a two-year term

1968: Re-elected governor

1970: Defeated in the Republican primary for the U.S. Senate

Index

A

Abalos, Alfredo, 150
Abeyta, Jose, 326
absentee voting, 155
academic freedom, 281, 283–284, 289–290
Acoya, Clarence, 150
Adler, Jerry, 139, 144
Administrative Procedures Act, 99
AFL-CIO, 91–95, 101, 240–243
African-Ameicans, 40, 45
   in Michigan, 20
   in New Mexico, 20, 118, 221, 315, 320
Agnew, Kimberly, *161*, 255
Agnew, Spiro, 256, 258, 261–262, 323–324
Agricultural Labor Act, 93, 245
Aguilar, Antonio, *172*
Aguilar, Pepe, *172*
Alarid, Michael, 225, 239
Albuquerque, NM, 50, 52, 80–81, 84, 92, 236–237, 287–290, 296–297
Albuquerque Bernalillo County Water Authority Board, 101
Albuquerque City Labor Board, 101
Alianza Federal de Mercedes, 143, 192–203, 217
Alwin, Jerry, 327
Amador, Albert, 105, 108
Amaya, George, 117
Anaya, Santiago, 193
Anaya, Toney, 195, 249
Anaya, Trinidad, 110, 179
Anderson, Clinton P., 52, 108, 151, 174–175, 323–324
   and Blue Lake, 253, 256, 259, 263
   and Congressional districts, 82–83
   and potash severance tax, 270, 272
   support for Cargo, 225–226, 239
Anderson, Robert O., 113–115
Apodaca, Eddie, 86
Apodaca, Jerry, 195, 310, 311–312
Apprenticeship Council, 99, 149
Aragon y Garcia, Ignacio, 207
Archuleta, Alex, 150
Armijo, Roberto, 149, 291
Aston, Reginaldo Rodgers, 149
Atchison, Ray, 75
Atcitty, James, 81
Atencio, Benny, 318
Avalos, Alfredo, 236
Aztec Dancers, 309

B

Baca, George, 116, 156, 226
Baker, J.E., 314
Baldwin, George, 179–180
Balsam, Marty, 141, *160*, 306
Barber, Jim, 150
Barkman, Hermann, 305
Bayard, New Mexico, 128–130, 233–235
Beck, Stewart, 149
Begay, Wilburt, 251, 254
Beier, Bob, 88–89, 288
Beimer, Rodger, 265, 273
Belin, David, 33
Benites, Joe, 154
Bennett, Kay, 151
Bennett, Wallace, 270
Bernal, Paul J., 257, 259–260, 261

333

Best, Hannah, 154
Bird, Frank, 327
Bishop, Robin, 154
Black, Kenneth, 75
Blackman, Roy H., 268
Blakeny, Alan, 277
Blocker, Dan, 139, *163*
Blue Lake, *161*, 250–264
Boards of Regents, 149, 277–292, 317
Bolack, Tom, 19, 65, 86, 250–251, 324
    support for Cargo, 113–114, 317, 322
Boone, Fred, 75
Boucher, Mayo T. (Terry), 75, 77
Boyd, Robert J., 268, 269
Bradbury, Norris, 149, 279, 280
Bradford, Richard, 140
Bradley, William T., 150
Branch, David, 226
Brasher, Jerry, 76
Bratton, Howard, 279
Brooks, R.C., 96, 244
Brusseau, Ramona, 154
Budke, Maralyn, 131, 269, 272
Bundy, Louise, 154, 313
Burgraff, Bob, 305
Burguete, Dan, 150
Burroughs, John, 54, 94, 110–112, 116, 225
Bursey, Joseph A., 116
Bursum, Holm, 322
Bursum Bill, 252, 255
Bustamante, Simon, 73–74, 75
Busto, Rudy, 203

C

Calloway, Larry, 199, 201, 204
Cameron, A.C., 274, 276
Campbell, Charles, 153
Campbell, Jack, 60, 64–65, 67–69, 73, 79–80, 82, 94–95, 108, *160*, 180, 186–188, 321
    and Alianza Federal de Mercedes, 193
    and Constitutional Convention, 189
Canones, New Mexico, 103–109, 203, 209

capital punishment, 155
Capitol Building Commission, 97–98, 229
Cargo, David, 109–110, *171*
Cargo, David Francis, *159–165, 167, 169–173*
    and African-American community, 20, 118, 221, 319–320
    and Alianza Federal de Mercedes, 193, 197–203
    attorney for Carnuel Land Grant, 85
    and Blue Lake, 250, 251, 253–255, 257–262
    campaign for constable for Manchester Township, 42–45
    campaign for governor in 1966, 110–127, 177–178, 222–223
    campaign for governor in 1968, 98, 176, 179–180, 223–224, 226–244
    campaign for NM State Legislature in 1962, 53, 55–62, 91–92
    campaign for NM State Legislature in 1964, 84–91
    campaign for senate 1970, 316–326
    campaigns for governor, 176–178, 186–188
    campaigns for office, 230
    childhood and education, 25–32
    chronology, 332
    and Congressional districts, 82–83
    Congressional hearing testimony, 207–219, 220–221
    early interest in politics, 27, 28–29, 33–38, 39–45, 45–47
    early years in New Mexico, 50–52
    efforts in NM State Legislature, 82–83
    employment, 28, 30–32
    family, 25, 28, 32, 109–110, *171*, 328–331
    as governor, 96–100, 108, 128–155, 188–221, 228–230, 244–247, 257–259, 269–292, 293–309, 313–315
    Hispanic support, 89, 92, 112, 179–180, 310–311, 320
    honored in Michigan, 198–199
    and labor movement, 25–26, 60, 85,

89, 91–101, 153, 233–234, 240–247
law practice, 52–53
law school and bar exams, 49–50
and libraries, 134, 326–327
military service, 47–49
Native American support, 318
in NM State Legislature, 66–81,
  92–93, 102–103
and potash severance tax, 264–276
and reapportionment, 54–55, 66–81,
  113
and state parks, 107, 133–134, 216,
  293–297, 298–299
support for Eisenhower, 33, 35, 42
support for Ford, 36
University of Michigan, 32–33, 46,
  47–49
Vietnam War opposition, 279, 281,
  285–290
work in District Attorney's office,
  51, 53–55
and Young Republicans, 33, 34,
  36–38, 45–46, 51
Cargo, Emily McGuire, 329–330
Cargo, Francis (Frank), 25, 28, 32, 328,
  332
Cargo, George Albert, 329
Cargo, Ida Jo, 109–110, 137–138, 140,
  159–160, 165, 166, 171, 172
  and Alianza Federal de Mercedes,
    197–198, 201
  family, 179, 207
  and Hispanic support for Cargo, 88,
    179, 207, 311
Cargo, Jerry, 320
Cargo, Mary, 328, 332
Cargo, Patrick, *171*
Cargo, Patti Ruth Martin, 329
Cargo, Veronica, 109–110, *171*
Cargo, William George, 329
Cargo vs. Campbell, 67–81
Carlsbad, NM, 266–272, 274–277, 294,
  296
Carmack, George, 237–238
Carnuel Land Grant, 85, 88
Carr, Pim, 75–76
Carr, Tom, 153, 241

Carrillo, John, 96, 245
Carter, Anderson, 84, 241, 316–326
Casaus, F.M., 196, 197
Case, Paul, 225
Castillo, Mark, 106
Castle, Bill, 139, 146, *167*
Chacon, Juan, 235–236
Chacon, Matias, 75
Chama, NM, 142–143, 303–308
Chavez, Dennis, Jr., 206–207
Chavez, Dennis, Sr., 41, 51, 64–65
  political advice, 52, 156
  support for Cargo, 56–58, 61, 180
Chavez, Eduardo, 193
Chavez, Fabian, 65, 153–154, 235–238
  and Alianza Federal de Mercedes,
    203
  campaign for governor in 1968,
    226–227, 240–241, 310–312
  campaign for lieutenant governor in
    1966, 224
  election results, 180, 186–188
  and potash severance tax, 265
  and reapportionment, 69, 73
Chavez, Imelda Espinosa, 206–207,
  308–309
Chavez, Lorenzo, 278
Chavez, Tibo, 76
Chee, Jake, 251, 254
Chino, Wendell, 144
Christensen, C., 327
civil rights legislation, 151–152, 319–
  320
Clark, Houston, 268
clean air and water, 151
Clear, Tom, 51, 325
Cleary, Pat, 34, 35
Clements, Geneva, 154
Coll, Max, 326
Congress of Industrial Unions (CIO),
  26, 27
Congressional districts, 82–83
Constitutional Convention, 188–190
copper strike, 128–130, 233–234
Cordova, Vivian, 17–18
Cornett, Hollan, 268
Corona, Bert, 206

Courthouse Raid, 191–203, 204–205
  Congressional hearing, 206–221
Coyote Creek State Park, 296
Cruz, Paul J., 94, 95–96, 153, 242, 244
Cullen, Charles, 137, 146, 271, 273
Cumbres Toltec Scenic Railroad, 303–308
Cutting, Bronson, 51, 261, 309

D

Daniels, Jack, 324
Danziger, Jerry, 135
Darmitzel, Bill, 268
Davis, Charlie, 57, 111, 116, 225
Davis, James Peter, 152, 155, 258, 322
Davis, Les, 298–299
Davis, Linda, 298–299
Davis, Thomas E., 85, 87–90
de Cola, Tony, 58–60
De Long, Henry, 330
De Luna, German, 236
de Valera, Eamon, 48–49, *169*
Deer Bird, 257, 260
Delayo, Leonard, 222
Delgado, Edmundo, 191
Democratic Party in New Mexico, 11–14, 19–22, 52–57
  party registration and election results, 180–188
Department of Education, 104–108
Dillard, Jim, 298, 306, 307
Dillon, Richard, 52
Dirksen, Everett, 40, 248, 317
Discrimination in Employment Act, 246
Dobson, Leon, 96, 242, 244
Dolliver, T., 327
Domenici, Pete, 287, 322, 325
Dortort, David, 137, 139, 146, *163*
Dowagiac, Michigan, 25–28, 123–124, 199, 328, 332
Dunagan, Ed, 268

E

Eagle Nest Lake, NM, 298–299
Easley, Mack, 65, 118, 225

Eastham, John, 152, 228
Eaves, J.W., 142
Eaves, Mel, 287
Echo Amphitheater occupation by Tijerina, 194, 201
education issues, 104–108, 154, 236–238
Educational Commission, 149
Edwards, James, 81
Edwards, Rick, 324
Ehrlichman, John D., 256
Eisenhower, Dwight D., 33, 35, 40–42, 168
Employment Security Commission, 99
Equal Employment Opportunity Act, 241, 246
Espinosa, Reynaldo, 222
Espinoza, Gilberto, 52, 55–56
Evans, Dan, 223
Evans, Ernestine, 98
Evans, Max, 135, 136, 137, 138–140
Executive Orders, 98, 148–149

F

Fair Employment Practices Commission, 99, 150
Fair Housing Act, 93, 246
Fair Trade for liquor, 92
Fanning, James J., 241–242
Feather, Bill, 126, 265, 273
Felter, Edwin, 105
Ferguson, Robert E., 238
Ferguson, Tom, 268
Fernandez, Cleo, 149, 308–309
Fiorina, Mrs. L.G., 154
Fogelson, Buddy, 142
Fonda, Jane, 142, 284, 285
Fonda, Peter, 142, 284
Ford, Gerald, 34, 35, 36, *164*, 199
Foreman, Ed, 154, 272, 282
Forrest, Bob, 294
Fowler, Hugh, 305
Francis, E. Lee, 199–200, 315
Frankenstein, Richard, 27
Frumpkin, Gene, 283

G

Gabaldon, Henry, 57–58
Gallagher, Bill, 299
Gallegos, Eugene, 310
Gallegos, Orlinda, 108
Gallegos, Tony, 108
Gant, Joe, 266, 270–271
Garcia, Cecil, 57
Garcia, Elipio, 108
Garcia, Ernie, 117
Garcia, Margaret, 154
Garcia, Raymond, 150
Garcia, Robert G., 206
Gardner, Richard, 202
Garson, Greer, 142
Gasparini, Lou, 135, 137
Goldwater, Barry, 41, 66, 84–92, 319, 322–323
Gonzales, Albert, 301
Gonzalez, Alonzo, 57, 111, 225–226
Gonzalez, Anselmo, 85, 90
Gonzalez, Arsenio A., 93
Gonzalez, George, 98, 226, 308–309
Gonzalez, Neal, 96, 245, 268
Good, Jeff, 75
Good Guys and the Bad Guys, 139, 141–143, *160*, 306
Gordon-McCutchan, R.C., 258–259
Government Committee on Reorganization of State Government, 152–154
Governor's Commission on the Status of Women, 154, 313
Governor's Mansion, 309
Grass Root Democrats, 60
Green, Jim, 94
Greer, Nathan, 150
Griffin, Robert, 256, 260
Gutierrez, Avelino, 149, 278–279

H

Haley, James A., 252, 254, 263
Hall, Jimmy, 268
Hamilton, Don, 135
Hanagan, Robert G., 318–319
Hanna, Mark, 139
Hannett, A.T., 52
Harman, Fred, 135, 136
Harris, Fred, 255, 256, 260
Harris, Gail, 269
Harris, LaDonna, 255
Harrison, Will, 63–64, 82–83
Hart, Benjamin, 331
Hart, Mary, 331
Hartman, Ed, 131, 272, 306
Harton, John Fay, 27, 330–331
Harvey, H.C., 268
Harvey, Paul, *165*
Hatfield, Mark, 281
Hauser, Ted, 268
Hawkins, A.C., 327
Hawley, Cliff, 110, 116, 197, 321
Hayes, William, 273
Heady, Ferrell, 46–47, 152–154, 280, 283, 285–287, 289–290
Heidel, F.L. Finis, 76, 152
Hennessee, G.T., Jr., 150
Herald, D.B., 274
Hermann, John, 268
Herrera, Joe H., 251, 318
Highlands University, 290–292
Highlands University Board of Regents, 149
Hill, Spencer, 80
Hinshaw, Gil, 265, 268
Hipsky, Elmore, 242
Hispanic voting, 20, 66, 74, 155–156, 309–313
  and reapportionment, 83–84, 90
  support for Cargo, 89, 92, 112, 179–180, 320
Hispanics in state government, 278, 291, 320
Hobbs, Ted, 327
Hodge, Ernestine, 221
Hoffa, James R., 45
Holand, Tom, 116
Hoover, Tom, 140
Horn, Calvin, 225, 280, 282
Horton, J.H., 150
Hubbel, Phillip, 322
Hudson, Henry, 268

Human Rights Commission, 150, 190, 236, 246
Hurley, Patrick J., 41, 52, 57
Hyman, Kenneth, 139

I

Ignacio, Helen, 106
Ignacio, Rose, 106
Inman, Thelma, 107
Irion, Frederick C., 79, 80
Ives, Burl, 138, 145, 146, 315

J

Jackson, MI, 28, 42, 199
Jaramillo, Henry, Jr., 281
Jenkins, Myra Ellen, 259
John Birch Society, 201–202
Johns, Sonny, 113–114, 322
Johnson, Albert N., 150
Johnson, Gary, 100, 322
Johnson, Lyndon, 65, 84, 88–89, *173*, 247–248, 281, 301
    and copper mining strike, 128–130, 234
Jolly, John P., 200, 285, 287–288
Jones, Franklin, 131–132, 272–273, 274, 306, 307
Jones, Jack, 224
Jymm, Monroe, 81

K

Kandel, Lenore, 281–282
Kelsey, David, 225
Kennedy, Burt, 137–139, 141–143, 145, 146
Kennedy, George, *160*, 306
Kerr, Walter, 132, 271
Kiker, Henry, 52, 56–57, 87–88
King, Bruce, 73, 75, 77–78, 83, 109, 148, 157, 280, 315
    and Alianza Federal de Mercedes, 203
    and Constitutional Convention, 189
    primary campaign in 1968, 225
    and State Penitentiary, 315

UNM student protests, 290, 292–293
Knowlton, Clark, 206, 219–220
Koch, Jamie, 140
Kopac, Steve, 137
Kutsche, Paul, 108–109

L

Labor and Industrial Commission, 99
labor movement, 25, 26–27
labor support and endorsements, 60, 85, 91, 94–96, 101, 228–230, 240–247, 320
land grants in New Mexico, 192, 217–218
Landon, Michael, 139, *166*
Larrazolo, Paul, 278
Lawrence, Bill, 288–289
Leach, Howard, 314–315
Lee, Tom, 251, 254
LeMaire, Charles, 135, 136, 137
Leonard, Harold "Fats", 225
Lewis, John L., 26–27
Lewis, Robert, 250–251
libraries, 134, 326–327
Light, Bob, 294
Longacre, Henry, 96
Looney, Ralph, 135–136, 137, 147
Lopez, Junio, 22, 233
Lopez Brothers, 309
Lovato, Medaro, 108
Love, John, 133, 304–305, 307
Lujan, Duven, 96
Lujan, Manuel, Jr., 83, 253, 258–260, 318
Lujan, Manuel, Sr., 52–53, 310, 312, 322
Lusk, Gene, 103–109, 110–112, 115–117
    and Alianza Federal de Mercedes, 193
    campaign for governor in 1966, 94, 118–127, 139, 156, 225, 233
    election results, 180, 186–188
    and potash severance tax, 266

M

Mabry, Thomas J., 310–311, 312
Macko, T.E., 327
Madrid, Luis, 57

Magoosh, Winona, 154
Maldonado, José, 149
Manchester Township, MI, 42
Maple, Cyrene, 279
Marlow, Frank, 85, 90
Martel, Frank X., 45–46
Martin, Hattie, 330
Martin, Homer, 27
Martin, John, 36
Martinez, Alex, 75, 83
Martinez, José Maria, 196–197
Martinez, Lecho, 57
Martinez, Manuel, 192
Martinez, Tiny, 156, 234
Martinez, Walter, 67–68
Mayfield, Bobby, 75, 131, 198, 225, 291
McAtee, Toulouse and Marchiondo, 50–51
McCall, Tom, 223
McCarthy, Eugene, 38
McCarthy, Joseph R., 34, 37
McCrossen, Eric, 323
McDermitt, Jim, 33
McDonald, Peter, 318
McGinnis, Mac, 176–178
McKinney, Robert, 115–117, 150, 224
McMahon, Mark, 305
McMillion, John, 119–122, 124, 133–134, 135
Mead, Ed V., 69, 70
Mechem, Edwin, 19, 51, 63, 126, 153, 324
  as governor, 58–60, 64–65, 86, 128
  support for Cargo, 113, 317, 324
Melody, Gordon, 75–76
Mercure, Alex, 206, 213
Merino, S.Q. Chano, 95, 96, 188, 232–233, 235, 245
Mershon, John, 67, 131, 301
Metcalf, Lee, 259
Middlestadt, Chuck, 135–137, 140
Miera, Mauricio, 312
Miksovic, John, 96
Miles, John E., 312
Miller, Alberta, 154
Milliken, Bill, 199
Minimum Wage Act, 97, 99, 242, 246

Minimum Wage for State Employees, 246
Mining Safety Advisory Board, 97
Mirabel, James, 257
Mitchell, Albert, 113, 115, 322, 324
Mitchell, J.S., 268
Mitchum, Robert, 141, *160*, 306
Mix, Tom, 136, 137
Mondragon, Roberto, 67, 155
Montoya, Domingo, 256, 318
Montoya, Joseph M., 108, 130, 224–226, 234
  and Blue Lake, 256
  campaigns for office, 65, 86, 321, 323–325
  and Congressional districts, 82–83
  and Indian voting, 250–251
  and labor support, 320
  and potash severance tax, 265, 270, 271–272, 274–275
  support for Cargo, 111, 239
Montoya, Ricardo M., 95, 150, 242, 244
Montoya, Samuel Z., 117
Montoya, Tom, 116, 225
Moore, Irving, 52, 55–56
Mora, Ben, 87
Mora County, NM, 157, 296, 312–313, 326
Morales, Nacho, 96, 233–235
Morgan, Frank, 80
Morgan, Ike, 116, 238–239
Morgan, R.C., 69, 77, 152
Morris, Tom, 83
Moynahan, Terry, 305
Moynihan, Daniel Patrick, 248
Municipal Employees Collective Bargaining, 93, 245

N

NAACP, 33, 221, 319–320
Nabokov, Peter, 202–203
Napolitano, Leonard, 279
Naranjo, Emilio, 105, 116, 155, 157–158, 226, 313
National Federation of the Blind, 302
National Governors Conference, 285, 288

National Guard
   and Courthouse Raid, 199, 200, 203, 219
   UNM student protests, 286–287, 289, 292–293
Native American Graves Protection and Repatriation Act, 261
Native American support for Cargo, 318
Native Americans, 248–264
Navajo Nation, 249–250
Neal, Caswell, 67, 70–73, 78, 81, 266
Neal, Fincher, 67, 294
Neal, Tal, 299
Neal, T.D., 150
Neel, Norman, 204
New Mexico Act Against Discrimination, 246
New Mexico Advisory Council on Human Rights and Employment, 150
New Mexico Cattle Growers Association, 81–82
New Mexico Commission for the Blind, 300, 302
New Mexico Federation of Labor, 60
New Mexico Film Commission, 135–148
New Mexico Legislative Council Service, 67
New Mexico State Citizens Committee on Human Rights, 150–151
New Mexico State Hospital, 59, 148
New Mexico State Penitentiary, 99, 143, 292, 313
New Mexico State University Board of Regents, 149, 278–279
New Mexico Taxpayer's Association, 59
New Mexico Technical University Board of Regents, 317
Newton, Jim, 141
Nixon, Richard, 248, 284–285, 288, 325
   and Blue Lake, 254, 256–259, 263–264
   support for Cargo, 317, 323
Norvell, David, 67

O

Occupational Disease Benefits Increase, 93
Occupational Disease Disablement Act, 93, 247
Old Age Lien, 62–63
Ortega, Arturo G., 149, 279, 280
Ortega, Bob, 315
Ortiz, Arthur, 266
Ortiz, Willie, 113, 315, 322
Ortiz y Pino, Jose, 222

P

Pacheco, Fermin, 156, 157, 312
Pacheco, Mary, 312
Parker, Mrs. John T., 154
Parsons, D.M., 327
Parsons, Joe, 76–77
Pate, Ted H., 268
Patton, James, 102–103
Peck, Gregory, 146
Perkins, Don, 132–133, 278–279, 320
Perry, Earl, 320–321
Pickens, William, 287
Pickett, Seven-Foot, 52
Pollack, Kenneth, 283
Popejoy, Tom, 280
port of entry, 151
Porter, Fern, 154
potash severance tax, 264–277
Prentice, Lawrence, 60–62, 75, 92, 202
Pressnell, Gene, 268
Previtti, Bill, 135, 137
Price, James A., 91, 94, 96, 241–243, 245
Prichard, John, 305
Prince, Bert, 196
Prince, Brad, 282
Public Works Minimum Wage, 247

Q

Quinlan, Clarence, 305
Quinn, Anthony, 141, 145, *162*
Quintana, Steve, 57–58

R

Railway Brotherhoods, 60, 179, 306
Rainer, John C., Sr., *161*, 250, 255–256, 257–258, 262
Rand, Frank, 150
Raymond, August, 96, 245
Reagan, Ronald, 38, 140, 147, *165*, 248, 319, 323, 324
reapportionment and Constitutional Convention, 189
reapportionment lawsuit, 54–55, 66–81, 84, 113
Reck, Frank, 42–43
Red Sky at Morning, 140, 143–144
Redding, Jack, 92
Relative Responsibility, 62–63
Republican National Convention, 39–42
Republican Party, 21, 26–27, 28, 33–46, 51
Republican Party in New Mexico, 55–56, 66, 85–86, 117, 317–319, 326–327
    party registration and election results, 180–188
    Young Republicans, 51
Resnick, Joseph, 206–221
Reuther, Walter, 27
Rhodes, James A., 200, 223
Ricer, Newell, 268
Richardson, Bill, 100, 137, 293–294, 299
Riders Association, 151
Right to Work, 93, 97, 240, 242, 245
Rio Arriba County Courthouse raid, 194, 199–203
Rio Grande Gorge Bridge, 227, 311
roads and highways, 227
Robb, John D. Sr., 149
Robbin, Tim, 96
Roberts, Austin, 75, 83, 280
Roberts, Thomas R., 149, 279
Robertson, Jim, 269, 272
Robins, Harry, 51
Robinson, James, 273
Robinson, Paul, 51, 314
Robles, Tom, 91, 94
Roca, Casimiro, 190–191

Rockefeller, Nelson, 133, 223, 232, 269, 304–305, 319, 324
Rockefeller, Winthrop, 133, 223, 232
Rodriguez, Al, 95
Rodriguez, Felix, 314–315
Rodriguez, Henry, 55, 57, 91–92, 96
Rodriguez, Mrs. Ruben, 308
Rodriguez, Ruben, 236
Rogers, Ted, 264–265
Romero, Ed, 225–226
Romero, Juan de Jesus, 257, 260
Romero, Quirino, *161*, 257, 262
Romney, George, 199, 223
Rorbart, Ernie, 305
Rose, Joe, 268
Rosenberg, Mike, 270

Ross, Terrence W., 305

Rubin, Leon, 151
Runnels, Harold, 131, 281–282
Russell, James, 268
Rutherford, Jim, 55
Ryan, Murray, 233

S

Saiz, Nick, 194, 200–201, 204–205
Salazar, Casilda, 195, 205
Salazar, Eulogio, 194–195, 200, 205
Salazar, Jacob, 108
Salazar, Preciliana, 108
Salazar, Roberto, 193
Salazar, Victor, 111, 116, 225, 226, 314
Salman, David, 68
San Ysidro, New Mexico, 120–122
Sanchez, Alfonso, 191, 198, 204
Sanchez, Jesus, 86
Sanchez, Manuel, 57
Sanchez, Ramos, 318
Sanchez, Raymond, 189
Sanders, F.W., 96
Sando, Joe, 261–262
Sarracino, Victor, 318
Sawyer, Fern, 150
Scarborough, James, 204
Schaefer, Jack, 135, 136

Scherer, Stretch, 135
Schneider, Albert, 149
Schreiber, Art, 302
Schroeder, Fred, 300, 302
Sedillo, Filo, 111, 117, 156, 179–180, 226
   and Constitutional Convention, 189
segregation in public schools, 44,
   189–190
Sena, Gordo, 17–18
Seresse, Alexander, 324
Simms, John, 52, 62–63, 153
Sitton, Jack, 268
Sizemore, Luther, 96, 245
Skeen, Joe, 310, 321
Sklower, Max, 135
Skrondahl, Dick, 135, 136, 140, 147
Smalley, Ike, 77, 296, 301
Smith, Haskell, 273
Smith, Leo, 150
Smith, Willis A., 77
Spanish Heritage Day program, 155
Stamm, Jack, 135
Stanley, Fred, 117
State Collective Bargaining Act, 100
state employees, 97–98, 228–230, 246
State Fair Commission, 150
State Investment Council, 150
State Labor Department, 99
state parks, 293–297
Stevenson, Adlai, 38, 43–44
Stevenson, Allen, 305
Stewart, Byron L., 151
Stowers, Harry, Jr., 225
Summerfield, Arthur, 34–36
Sutin, Jonathan B., 150
Sutton, Michael, 151
Sylvestre, Flor, 172

T

Taft, Robert A., 33, 37–38, 46
Taos Pueblo, 250, 251–264
Tapia, Larry, 56
Teachers' Activities, 93, 245
Thatcher, Ross, 269, 272–273, 274–275,
   276–277
Thurmond, Strom, 281
Tierra Amarilla Land Grant, 192

Tierra Amarilla, NM, 194, 199–203,
   204–205, 321
Tijerina, Cristobal, 197
Tijerina, Reies Lopez, 191–197, 201–
   203, 205, 208
Toles, Penrod, 74, 94, 234, 240–241
Tondre, Joe, 53
Torres, Steve, 317
Toulouse, Jim, 51, 230
Trantham, Bert, 96
Trapp, Gregg, 300
Trotter, W.C., 150–151
Truchas, New Mexico, 143–144
Trujillo, Miguel H., 249
Tucker, Merle, 186–188
Turner, Carl M., 305–306
Turner, Robert B., 303

U

Udall, Stewart L., 260
Unemployment Benefits, 246–247
union support, 85, 91, 94–96, 101, 188,
   228–230, 240–247
United Auto Workers-Congress of
   Industrial Unions, 27
United Steel Workers of America,
   233–236
University of Michigan
   Cargo as student, 32–33
   Young Republicans Club, 33
University of New Mexico, 277–292
   academic freedom, 281, 283–284,
     289–290
   Board of Regents, 149, 278, 279–281
   demonstrations and riots, 285–290,
     292–293
   president, 152, 280
uranium industry, 54
U.S. Forest Service, 208–210, 216–217
   and Blue Lake, 251–253, 261–262
   Cargo worked for, 31
   and land grants, 192, 194

V

Vietnam War opposition, 279, 281,
   285–290
Vigil, Andy, 226

Vigil, Charlie, 150
Vigil, Eddie, 303, 305, 306, 307
Vigil, Johnny, 98, 155, 226
Vigil, Martin, 285, 287, 288–289
Vigil, Maurilio, 311
Villanueva, NM, 133–134, 216, 295–296, 311
vocational education, 151

W

Walker, E.S. Johnny, 83, 206
Wallace, George, 224
Wallace, Mike, 288
Wallach, R.P., 327
Wallis, Hal, 140
Ward, J.D., 258
Watkins, Lon, 116
Watson, Marvin, 108
Wayne, John, 146, *163*
Webb, Cecilia, 315
Wells, Frank, 118
White, Sherman A., 270, 271
White Cane Law, 300–302
Whitlock, Lewis, 268
Wildlife Society, 151
Wilkins, Roger, 32–33
Wilkinson, Borens W., 244
Wilkinson, Lawrence, 96, 279, 280
Williams, Lionel, 282, 283
Wimberley, Hoover, 197, 286
Witt, Boston, 67, 73, 79, 81, 98, 102–103, 229
Wolf, Walter, 279
Workers Compensation Act, 93, 97, 99–100, 241, 242, 247
Wright, J.S., 269–270

Y

Young Republicans Club, 45–46
Young Republicans in New Mexico, 51

Z

Zinn, Frank, 117

www.ingramcontent.com/pod-product-compliance
Lightning Source LLC
Chambersburg PA
CBHW022103150426
43195CB00008B/240